Anna Maria Cirincione – Corrado Izzo – Rosa Olimpo

I care English

ISBN 978-88-6432-141-7

Medusa Editrice

Anna Maria Cirincione – Corrado Izzo – Rosa Olimpo
I care English

ISBN 978-88-6432-141-7

Coordinamento didattico ed editoriale
Matteo Speraddio

Revisione linguistica
Luisa Grosso - Edward J. Roberts

Disegni originali
Maria Porro

Progettazione e realizzazione grafica
Francesco Visicchio (Lopez)
Per **www.unanet.net**

I documenti riprodotti potrebbero contenere degli errori presenti negli originali.

Medusa Editrice sas di Sabato Del Sorbo & C
Via Picenna, 17
80046 San Giorgio a Cremano (NA)
Telefono e fax 081.47.42.30
www.medusaeditrice.com
medusaeditrice@libero.it

Stampa
Alfa Grafica
Viale delle Industrie, 40
80040 San Sebastiano al Vesuvio (NA)
Tel. 081.596.44.79 - Fax 081.596.90.52

Anna Maria Cirincione – Corrado Izzo – Rosa Olimpo

I CARE ENGLISH

Medusa Editrice

PRESENTAZIONE

Il titolo

Il titolo *I care English* vuole sottolineare l'interesse e l'attenzione per l'inglese, lingua internazionale indispensabile per accedere alla cultura globale veicolata dai nuovi media.

Questo orizzonte culturale planetario costituisce già – e costituirà ancora di più per le donne e gli uomini di domani – una dimensione quotidiana dell'esistenza, in cui la conoscenza delle lingue e la confidenza con le altre culture saranno indispensabili sia nella vita lavorativa che nelle relazioni interpersonali.

Un ruolo importante gioca in questo la scuola, in tutte le sue componenti e in tutti i suoi aspetti, tra cui i libri di testo. Tra questi, un ruolo specifico lo giocano i libri di "civiltà", funzionali allo studio delle lingue straniere.

La proposta didattica

I testi di civiltà inglese hanno rappresentato a lungo il primo approccio alla cultura anglofona per gli alunni della scuola secondaria di primo grado. Oggi non è più così, perché gli alunni che arrivano dalla scuola primaria conoscono i primi rudimenti della lingua inglese e utilizzano modi di dire e di fare tipici della cultura inglese veicolati dalle canzoni, dal cinema, dai fumetti e dai video che pullulano su *Youtube* e sulle altre piattaforme di socializzazione virtuale.

Abbiamo pensato, per questo, a un libro di civiltà che proponesse un approccio più sistematico alla cultura anglofona, valorizzando le conoscenze e le competenze già in possesso degli alunni, per concorrere a sistematizzarle, potenziarle e ampliarle.

Si è puntato per questo decisamente sul-

le capacità operative degli alunni, assunte come punto di forza nell'avvio del processo di apprendimento, per stimolare e raggiungere – è il vero obiettivo di ogni pratica didattica – la loro autonomia operativa.

È questa la motivazione profonda della molteplicità delle attività proposte – alcune anche molto semplici come il colorare, completare, rintracciare, sistemare... – che tendono a coinvolgere, a incuriosire, a interessare tutti gli alunni, anche quelli meno motivati o che si stancano più facilmente.

I care English è infatti un libro nato dalla viva pratica didattica e si propone come uno strumento flessibile per operare al meglio nelle condizioni concrete in cui docenti e alunni si trovano a lavorare nelle aule delle nostre scuole.

Per questo, l'attenzione alle competenze linguistiche – *listening*, *speaking*, *reading*, *writing* – accompagna continuamente lo svolgimento dei contenuti, perché nelle poche ore riservate all'insegnamento e apprendimento della seconda lingua non ci si può concedere il lusso di trascurare neppure per un momento l'esercizio e l'uso della lingua. Per lo stesso motivo, si è riservata molta attenzione agli esercizi lessicali, perché lo studio dei vari aspetti della cultura anglofona significhi anche un continuo e spontaneo arricchimento lessicale e linguistico.

Una delle idee forza intorno alla quale si articola la struttura dell'opera è di dare l'opportunità ai docenti di poter modulare le proprie lezioni secondo il livello della classe e dei singoli alunni, usufruendo di una molteplicità di spunti originali quali canzoni, disegni, scrittura di testi liberi e guidati. Le attività contenute nel testo sono state concepite per essere utilizzate da alunni diversi per capacità e competenze, pertanto il docente potrà selezionare i contenuti che ritiene più adeguati e testare tutte le competenze linguistiche con lo svolgimento delle differenti attività proposte.

PRESENTAZIONE

L'ARTICOLAZIONE DEL TESTO

Il testo è organizzato in undici capitoli, che presentano i vari aspetti della vita e della cultura anglofone, a partire dal più semplice (realtà vicine al quotidiano dei ragazzi come la famiglia e la scuola) al più complesso (la storia, le istituzioni politiche, la letteratura...).

I primi nove capitoli hanno una struttura fissa, sottolineata dai colori rosso, blu, verde e giallo.

I capitoli si aprono in genere con un dialogo tra due adolescenti. Serve a introdurre il tema e a far prendere confidenza con le principali funzioni comunicative. I dialoghi sono registrati con la voce di *native speakers*, per favorire l'apprendimento della giusta intonazione, in situazioni comunicative della vita quotidiana.

Segue la sezione contrassegnata dal rosso solitamente dedicata agli aspetti culturali del Regno Unito; contiene molteplici attività tese a suscitare nei ragazzi interesse per la lingua inglese e per la cultura e la mentalità del popolo britannico, fornendo anche stimoli di carattere comparativo per un confronto con la nostra cultura.

La sezione contrassegnata dal blu è in genere dedicata agli USA; è organizzata in esercizi e attività pratiche tesi a sviluppare negli alunni curiosità, interesse, disposizione alla ricerca e abitudine all'approfondimento.

La sezione contrassegnata dal verde è dedicata alla preparazione degli esami di Stato conclusivi del primo ciclo di istruzione. È significativamente intitolata *Exam trainer*, perché è una vera e propria palestra per preparare gli alunni ad affrontare le varie tipologie di prove scritte. In questa sezione, molto operativa, sono sempre presenti anche attività di *listening* per rinforzare le capacità di ascolto.

La sezione contrassegnata dal giallo è, infine, dedicata agli esami dei *Grade* 3 e 4 proposti dal *Trinity College* di Londra per gli alunni della scuola secondaria di primo grado. Il testo fornisce alcuni strumenti pratici per la preparazione a sostenere gli

PRESENTAZIONE

esami orali: istruzioni sulle modalità di svolgimento dell'esame; domande guida per la conversazione con l'esaminatore; illustrazione per esercitarsi alla descrizione orale.

L'unità di questi capitoli è assicurata dall'argomento, che si articola nelle varie sezioni, proponendo aspetti conoscitivi diversi e attività coerenti con i diversi obiettivi didattici da raggiungere.

La rubrica *Did you know?* – riproposta continuamente – ha la funzione di sollecitare e rafforzare la curiosità e l'interesse degli alunni.

Gli ultimi due capitoli hanno una struttura meno articolata. Il decimo si sofferma sugli altri Paesi di cultura anglofona; l'undicesimo affronta due problemi di grande attualità: l'*Unione Europea* e la *Brexit*; l'impatto dei nuovi mezzi e delle nuove modalità di comunicazione sugli adolescenti.

L'apparato iconografico – foto, cartine, disegni – è particolarmente abbondante perché il libro di *civilization* sia anche un viaggio visivo nei Paesi di cui si studia la lingua e la cultura.

GUIDA E BES

Il testo è accompagnato da un'agile guida che fornisce ai docenti elementi di programmazione, prove di verifica, correzione degli esercizi.

Viene inoltre fornito materiale specifico per gli alunni con BES, stampato con accorgimenti tipografici che tendono ad alleviare le tipiche difficoltà di questi alunni. Tutti gli argomenti sono stati rimodulati per renderli realmente fruibili agli alunni con BES e le attività proposte tengono conto delle varie esigenze compensative.

I care English è un libro misto ed è completato da materiale aggiuntivo e da esercizi interattivi accessibili on line sul sito

<u>www.medusaeditrice.it</u>

Il libro è acquistabile anche in versione digitale scaricabile dal sito della Medusa Editrice.

INDEX

INDEX

CHAPTER 04: The Political System

CHAPTER 05: British and American History

INDEX

CHAPTER 06: Festivals

CHAPTER 07: Life in Britain and the USA

INDEX

SPEAK ENGLISH?
YOU'RE WELCOME
HELLO!
SEE YOU SOON!
GOOD MORNING!
HAVE A NICE DAY!
DO YOU SPEAK ENGLISH?

CHAPTER 01

THE FAMILY

DIALOGUE

My family

John: Hello! What's your name?

Luca: My name's Luca.

John: How old are you, Luca?

Luca: I'm 14 years old.

John: Where are you from?

Luca: I'm from Rome. I'm Italian but I live in London with my family. My dad's an insurer. He works for an important insurance company.

John: My dad's an engineer in London. Your English is quite good.

Luca: Thank you. I love English.

John: Very good. Have you got any brothers and sisters?

Luca: Yes. I've got one brother and one sister. My brother Mario's 17. My sister Anna's 10.

John: I've got only one brother. His name's Tom.

Luca: How old is Tom?

John: He's 9. He's at Primary school.

Luca: I've got a big family in Italy. My grandparents on my mum's side live in Rome. My grandparents on my dad's side live in Milan.

John: I haven't got any grandparents but I've got lots of relatives: two uncles, two aunts, three cousins.

EXERCISE

1 Answer the following questions.

1. Is Luca English?
2. Does he live in Rome?
3. Where does his dad work?
4. What does John's dad do?
5. Has Luca got two brothers?
6. Has Luca got a sister?
7. How old is she?
8. How many brothers has John got?
9. Is Tom at Secondary school?
10. Has Luca got a big family?

THE BRITISH ROYAL FAMILY

Queen Elizabeth II and her husband, Prince Philip, have got four children: Princess Anne, Prince Charles, Prince Andrew and Prince Edward. The Queen has eight grandchildren. William and Harry, the sons of Prince Charles and Princess Diana Spencer, are her most famous grandchildren.
Queen Elizabeth lives in *Buckingham Palace* in London.

Hello! I'm Prince Charles, the Prince of Wales, the heir to the throne of England. I'm 68. I took a degree in History. I've got two children, William and Harry. Their mum is Princess Diana, my first wife who died in a car crash in 1997. My present wife is Camilla Parker Bowles.

Hello everyone! I'm Kate, Duchess of Cambridge. I'm 35. I became a Princess on 29th April 2011 when I married William. I live with my family in Kensington Palace in London.

Hi! Nice to meet everyone! I'm William. I'm a Prince and Duke of Cambridge. I'm 35. I took my degree in Geography. On 29th April 2011 I married Kate Middleton. Our children are George and Charlotte.

Hi ! I'm Henry, William's brother. I'm a Prince and my nickname is Harry. I'm 33. Clarence House in London is my residence.

ACTIVITIES

1 Complete with the words in the box.

sceptre	queen	prince	king
princess	castle	throne	crown

____

____

____

____

____

____

____

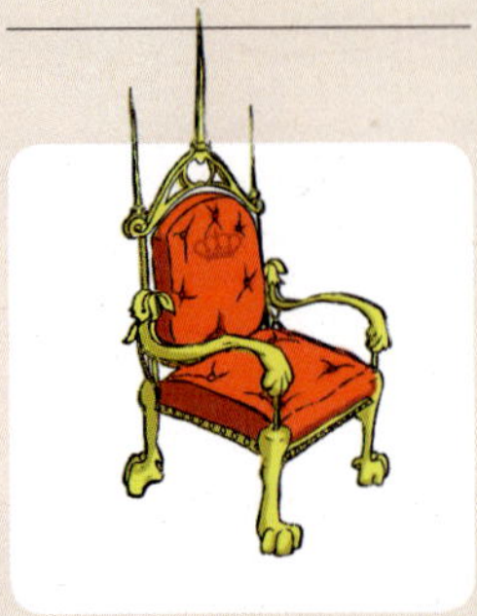

____

2 Match the words.

a. Relatives	**1.** Zio
b. Parents	**2.** Papà
c. Grandparents	**3.** Sorella
d. Mum	**4.** Fratello
e. Dad	**5.** Genitori
f. Brother	**6.** Famiglia
g. Sister	**7.** Zia
h. Aunt	**8.** Parenti
i. Uncle	**9.** Nonni
j. Family	**10.** Mamma

ACTIVITIES

3 Complete the family tree.

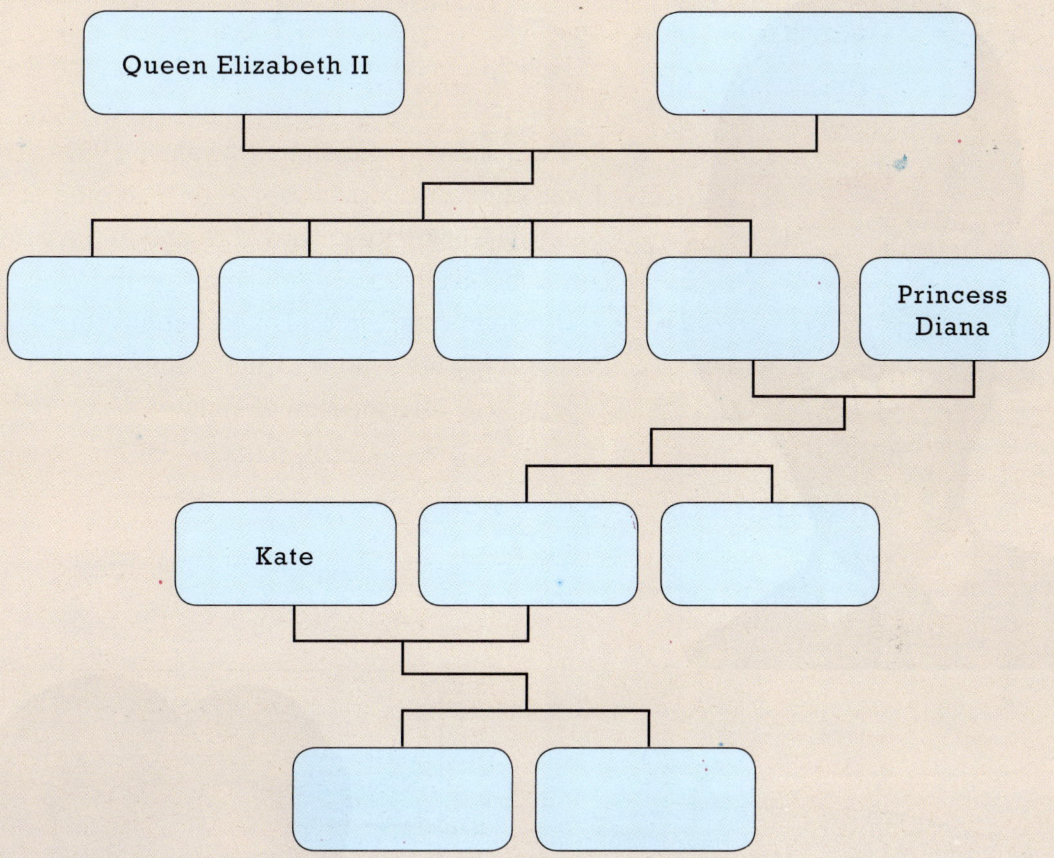

4 **Answer the following questions.**

1. Who is the Queen of the UK?
2. How old is she?
3. When did she become Queen?
4. Who is Prince Charles?
5. How old is he?
6. Who are Prince Charles's brothers and sister?
7. Where does the Royal family live?
8. Where do they go on holiday?
9. Who is the Queen's husband?
10. Who are William and Harry?
11. How old are they?
12. When did William and Kate marry?
13. How many children have they got?
14. What happened to Lady Diana in 1997?

OBAMA'S AND TRUMP'S FAMILIES

Hello! I am Barack Obama and I was the 44th President of the United States of America. I was born in Honolulu, Hawaii, in 1961. I was elected in November 2008. I studied at Columbia University in New York and at Harvard Law School. I lived with my family in the White House in Washington DC for eight years. My life's story is interesting, let's meet my family!

Hello! I am Michelle La Vaughn Robinson and I am Barack's wife. I was born in Chicago, in 1964, I am an American lawyer. I met Barack in 1989. I became his wife in 1992. As First Lady, I was close to the political issues of my husband and supported them with many initiatives.

DID YOU KNOW?

- In 2009 Barack Obama received the Nobel Prize for Peace.
- Barack Obama published an autobiography in 1995: *Dreams from My Father: a Story of Race and Inheritance*.
- He was the first African-American President in the history of the USA.
- Marian Robinson is Barack Obama's mother-in-law. She lived at the White House with her daughter, her son-in-law and her granddaughters. Marian helped the family and looked after Sasha and Malia.

ACTIVITIES

1 Translate each word into Italian.

a. Wife
b. Stepfather
c. Husband
d. Granddaughter
e. Half-sister
f. Mother-in-law
g. Son-in-law
h. Widow

ESERCIZI ON LINE www.medusaeditrice.it

2 Say if the following sentences are True (T) or False (F). Correct the false ones.

a. Barack Obama was the 44th President of the USA. T F
b. The President was elected in 2006. T F
c. Michelle is a lawyer. T F
d. Marian isn't Michelle's mother. T F
e. Barack and Michelle got married in 1990. T F
f. The couple has got one daughter. T F
g. Obama's family lives in New York. T F

Hello!
I am Donald John Trump.
I was born in New York City in 1946 and I am the 45th President of the USA.
I won the elections in November 2016. I'm a manager.
My wife is Melania Knauss.
I've got three sons and two daughters. I love my two grandchildren.

ACTIVITIES

3 Answer the following questions.

1. Who was Barack Obama?
2. When was Obama born? Where?
3. Where did Obama's family live?
4. Who is Michelle Robinson?
5. When did Barack and Michelle marry?
6. Where did Barack's mother -in- law live?
7. When were Natasha and Malia Ann born?
8. When was Trump elected?
9. Who is Trump's wife?
10. How many sons and daughters has Trump got?

4 Read the text and translate into Italian.

Obama's family

Obama's parents met at the University of Hawaii. His father, Obama Senior, grew up in a small Kenyan village. In 1959, Obama Senior won a scholarship and He went to the University of Hawaii. It was there that the University's first black student met Ann Dunham, a girl from Kansas. They got married but when Barack was only two years old his father left him and his mother for a new scholarship at Harvard where he became an economist. Obama Senior and Ann separated in 1964. He died in 1982.

After the divorce, Ann Dunham met an Indonesian student, Lolo Soetoro and she married him. In 1967 they moved to Indonesia and in 1970 Ann had a daughter, Maya, who is Barack's half-sister. Barack didn't stay long with his stepfather because he returned to Hawaii for a scholarship and he lived at his grandparents' house. Ann went back to Indonesia but some years later and divorced Soetoro. Ann was an anthropologist who worked in the Anthropology Department at the University of Hawaii.

In 1994, she became ill and moved back to Hawaii to live near Obama's widowed grandmother. She died in 1995. Ann's difficulty in paying for her medical bills encouraged and influenced her son to reform the American Health Care System.

5 Answer the following questions.

1. What was Obama's father's job?
2. Who was Ann Dunham?
3. Where did Barack's parents meet?
4. Who was Lolo Soetoro?
5. What is the name of Barack's half-sister?

ESERCIZI ON LINE www.medusaeditrice.it

6 Say if the following sentences are True (T) or False (F). Correct the false ones.

a. Barack Obama's father was American. T F
b. Ann Dunham was Barack's mother. T F
c. Obama's parents met at University. T F
d. The President lived with his grandparents. T F

EXAM TRAINER

STEP BY STEP

How to do a reading comprehension exercise

La lettura e la comprensione di un brano potrebbe essere la prova scritta di lingua inglese all'Esame di Stato.

Ecco le regole da seguire che ti aiutano a svolgerla.

- Osserva il titolo e il brano prima della lettura.
- Leggi le domande e cerca di capirne il significato.
- In genere il questionario contiene due tipi di domande: le *Comprehension questions* che riguardano la comprensione del brano e le *Personal questions* che ti sono rivolte per conoscere la tua opinione sul brano.
- Leggi il brano e sottolinea i vocaboli che non conosci. Usa il dizionario per scoprirne il significato.
- Rileggi il brano sottolineando le parti che riguardano le risposte alle domande.
- Nelle risposte stai attento agli errori di grammatica e di ortografia. Fai attenzione all'uso dei tempi verbali: normalmente nelle risposte occorre utilizzare lo stesso tempo delle domande.
- Ricordati di rispondere in terza persona alle *Comprehension questions*.
  Si risponde in prima persona alle *Personal questions*.
- Quando hai terminato, controlla le risposte prima di consegnare l'elaborato.

READING COMPREHENSION

Diana, Princess of Wales

Lady Diana Spencer, well-known as Lady D, was Prince Charles's first wife. She died in a car crash in Paris in 1997 when she was 36. She and her family lived in Althorp, a country house five miles from London. The Princess is buried in this estate on the island called "Round Oval" that is in the middle of a little lake.

Her interests and jobs

Diana loved music so she learnt to play the piano, she was a good swimmer and studied ballet, too. But children were her passion. In fact in London she worked as a dance instructor for young people, then as a playgroup pre-school assistant, as a nanny for an American family and finally as a nursery teacher.

It was at this time, aged twenty, she met and fell in love with Charles, Prince of Wales and heir to the throne of England. They got married in 1981 in St. Paul's Cathedral in London and had two sons, Prince William and Prince Harry.

Diana was a sensitive woman: she was very interested in a lot of charities and important causes such as the suffering of the homeless, lepers and AIDS victims. She also campaigned for the abolition of landmines.

An unlucky marriage

Her marriage wasn't very happy: Princess Diana and Prince Charles separated in 1992 and divorced in 1996. There was an age difference of 13 years between them.

Moreover he was unfaithful to Lady Diana with Camilla Parker Bowles, his present wife. In fact because of this Diana suffered from depression and eating disorders. Some months later her life changed after she met an Egyptian film producer, Dodi Al-Fayed, who became her lover.

But in 1997 their love story ended in tragedy when they died in a fatal car crash in the Pont de l'Alma road tunnel in Paris. Millions of people around the world watched the funeral in Westminster Abbey in London on 6th September 1997. The famous singer and friend of the Princess, Elton John, wrote and sang the popular song *Candle in the wind 1997* for the occasion. For many months after her death people brought flowers, candles, cards and personal messages to the gates of Kensington Palace.

EXERCISE

1 Answer the following questions.

1. Who was Lady Diana?
2. Where did she live?
3. What is there in Althorp?
4. What do you think of her?
5. What was her main job?
6. Who did Diana fall in love with?
7. Where did they get married?
8. Who are Princess Diana's children?
9. What were Diana's interests?
10. Why did Princess Diana and Prince Charles divorce?
11. What did Princess Diana suffer from after the divorce?
12. Who was Diana's lover?
13. Where did Diana and her companion die?
14. Would you like to be a Prince / Princess? Why / why not?

LISTENING ACTIVITY

Listen to Elton John's *Candle in the Wind 1997* song and complete the text.

Link: http://bit.ly/2fCjF8W

fall country life hearts miss nation
legend try name lived rain rose

Candle in the Wind 1997

Goodbye England's ....
May you ever grow in our hearts
You were the grace that placed itself
Where lives were torn apart
You called out to our ....
And you whispered to those in pain
Now you belong to heaven
And the stars spell out your ....
And it seems to me you lived your
....
Like a candle in the wind
Never fading with the sunset
When the ....set in
And your footsteps will always fall here
Along England's greenest hills
Your candle's burned out long before
Your ....ever will
Loveliness we've lost
These empty days without your smile
This torch we'll always carry
For our ....'s golden child
And even though we ....
The truth brings us to tears
All our words cannot express
The joy you brought us through the years
And it seems to me you .... your life
Like a candle in the wind
Never fading with the sunset
When the rain set in
And your footsteps will always
.... here
Along England's greenest hills
Your candle's burned out long before
Your legend ever will
Goodbye England's rose
May you ever grow in our ....
You were the grace that placed itself
Where lives were torn apart
Goodbye England's rose
From a country lost without your soul
Who'll .... the wings of your
compassion
More than you'll ever know
And it seems to me you lived your life
Like a candle in the wind
Never fading with the sunset
When the rain set in
And your footsteps will always fall here
Along England's greenest hills
Your candle's burned out long before
Your legend ever will

Elton John

Trinity College London
Graded Examinations in Spoken English (GESE)

TRINITY GESE GRADE 3
CEFR level A2.1

L'esame del Grade 3 ha la durata di 7 minuti. Consiste in una conversazione nella quale l'esaminatore dopo un saluto iniziale rivolgerà al candidato alcune domande personali e generiche molto spesso legate anche all'osservazione di un'immagine: *Look at the picture!*
Il candidato dovrà dimostrare di comprendere, rispondendo adeguatamente con appropriato lessico, utilizzando corrette strutture grammaticali e buona pronuncia.

TRINITY GESE GRADE 4
CEFR level A2.2

L'esame del Grade 4 ha la durata di 10 minuti. Si divide in due fasi. Nella prima fase (5 minuti), il candidato presenterà il Topic Form preparato. Nella seconda fase (5 minuti), l'esaminatore sceglierà uno o due punti del Topic Form e rivolgerà domande relative.
Il candidato dovrà fare, alla fine dell'esame, una domanda all'esaminatore aderente al Topic Form presentato e mostrerà, durante la conversazione, di possedere le competenze linguistiche richieste per il livello di certificazione.

Nella scuola secondaria di primo grado gli studenti generalmente raggiungono il Grade 3 e il Grade 4 del Trinity Graded Examinations in Spoken English (GESE). I gradi delle certificazioni sono legati al Common European Framework of Reference (CEFR).

Per saper parlare di argomenti diversi e avere conoscenze linguistiche adeguate, saranno utili le esercitazioni di Speaking che seguiranno.

Improve your English fluency by speaking as much as you can!

TRINITY GESE GRADE 3

CEFR level A2.1
Total exam time: 7 minutes.

Conversation:
- Good morning
- What's your name?
- What's your surname?
- Can you spell it, please?
- What's the date today?
- How old are you?
- When's your birthday?
- Where were you on your last birthday?
- Who was with you?
- How old are the people in your family?
- Do you have to do any housework?
- Do you tidy your room?
- How often do you make your bed?

Look at this picture!

Examiner:
- Where is the family?
- What are the people doing?
- How many sofas are there?
- Where are they?
- What is on the wall?
- What colour is it?
- What is the time in the picture?
- What is the mum wearing?
- Ok, Thanks a lot. Bye!

You: Thank you. Goodbye.

CHAPTER 02

THE SCHOOL

DIALOGUE

At school

Lucia: Hello Andrew!

Andrew: Hi, Lucia!

Lucia: Where are you going, Andrew?

Andrew: I'm going to school. I have my Maths test, today.

Lucia: I'm going to school, too. But I have no tests, today.

Andrew: I love Maths but I'm a little worried about my test.

Lucia: I don't like Maths very much. I prefer studying English. Why are you worried?

Andrew: I didn't study yesterday so I didn't revise my lessons.

Lucia: Don't worry! You are so good at Maths. I'm sure your test will be fine.

Andrew: I hope so, Lucia! What are you doing in the afternoon?

Lucia: I'm going to the tennis club. Are you going there, too?

Andrew: Yes, I am. What's the time, Lucia?

Lucia: It's half past eight. It's time to go to school. Let's go, now!

Andrew: Alright. See you in the afternoon at the tennis club, Lucia.

Lucia: See you, Andrew.

EXERCISE

1 Answer the following questions.

1. Are Andrew and Lucia going to school?
2. Has Lucia got a Maths test?
3. What is Lucia's favourite subject?
4. What is Andrew's favourite subject?
5. Why is Andrew worried about his Maths test?
6. Is Lucia good at Maths?
7. What does Lucia think about Andrew?
8. What time is it?
9. When will Andrew and Lucia meet?
10. Where will they meet?

BRITISH EDUCATION

In Great Britain Education is compulsory from five to sixteen years of age and it's free.

Nursery school

From two to five years of age children go to nursery school where they do activities such as playing, singing and listening to stories in order to improve their language.

The British school system is divided into:

Primary school	Secondary school	Higher education

Primary school

When they are five, children go to *Primary school* that lasts 6 years and is divided into Infant School from 5 to 7 where they learn to read, write and the basics of Arithmetics. They then go to Junior School from 7 to 11 where they study History, Geography, Maths, Science, English, P.E. (twice a week) and a foreign Language, usually French or German. They take tests called SAT (Standard Assessment Tasks) when they finish *Infant School* and at the end of *Junior School.*

Secondary school

After Primary school from 11 to 16 years of age students go to *Secondary school* that starts with Year 7 and finishes with Year 11. At Secondary School they study the three basic subjects that are English, Maths and Science plus History, Geography, I.T. (Information Technology), Music, Art, P.E. (Physical education), R.E. (Religious education) and a foreign Language. They can study French, German or Spanish but in some schools Italian, too. When the students are 16 they take an examination called GCSE (*General Certificate of Secondary Education*).

This exam marks the end of compulsory education. After the GCSE they can choose to go to work or they can stay at school until 18 and attend Year 12 and Year 13. At the end of the last year they take another examination called A-level (*Advanced level exams*). This certification is important for the students who want to go to university.

Higher education

At 18, after secondary school, students can go to universities, colleges or polytechnics and study for a degree.

ACTIVITIES

ESERCIZI ON LINE www.medusaeditrice.it

1 Look at the picture and complete with the words in the box.

classroom science lab canteen music room sports hall
IT room art room school office toilet

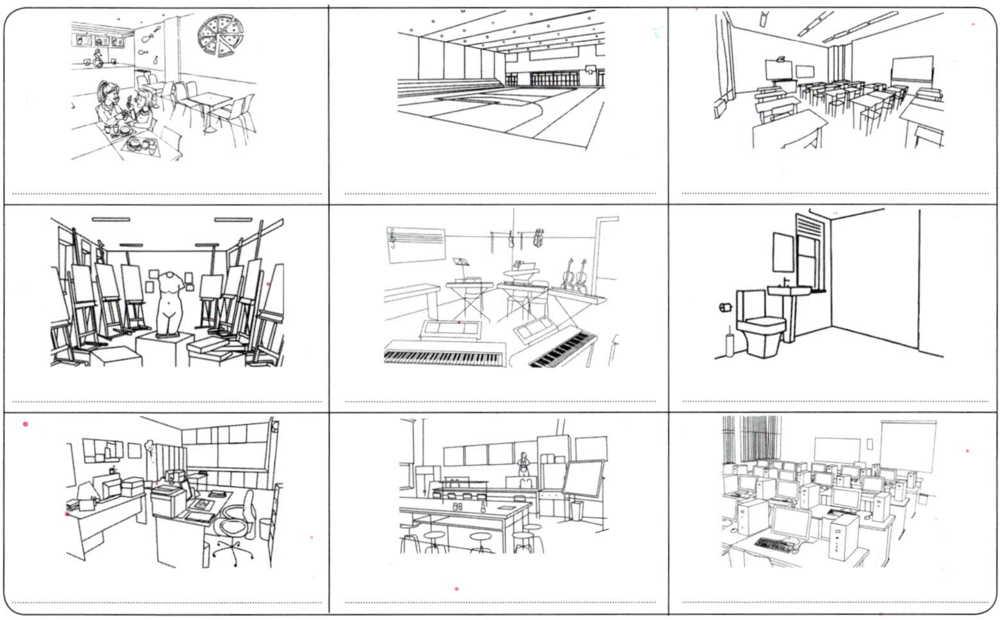

2 **Read the text "British Education" and answer the following questions.**

1. What school do British children go to from the ages of two to five?
2. How many years does Primary School last?
3. How is Primary School divided?
4. What do British children study at Primary School?
5. When do they go to Secondary School?
6. At what age does compulsory education finish?
7. What's the CGSE?
8. What subjects do students study at Secondary School?
9. Can students stay at school after taking the GCSE?
10. What's an A-level? Why is it important?
11. What foreign languages do British students learn?

Life in a college: Eton

Eton College is the most famous boys' public school in the world. It is situated in Eton, in the south-east county of Berkshire, in England. The County is also called the Royal County of Berkshire because of the presence on its territory of the royal palace of Windsor.

Eton College was founded by King Henry VI of England, in 1440, as a charity school to provide free education to 70 poor boys. The original name of the school is *King's College of Our Lady of Eton besides Wyndsor.*

Who attended Eton in the Past...

It is considered the most famous and prestigious boarding school in the UK.

It is an exclusively male school and both Prince William and Prince Henry, Prince Charles's sons, studied at Eton.

Important people such as the Duke of Wellington, the writers Horace Walpole and George Orwell, the romantic poet Percy Bysshe Shelley and the ex Prime Minister David Cameron attended the College, too. The school has got 25 boys' houses, each headed by a House Master.

...and Nowadays

Almost all of the boys who attend Eton go on to Oxford or Cambridge University.

Students here are called Etonians and over 1300 pupils are educated in the College. They can study Maths, Biology, Chemistry, Physics, Computer Science, Latin, Greek, History, Geography, Art History, Economy and Modern Foreign Languages.

They can also practice extracurricular activities such as Drama, Music, Literature and Sport (cricket, horseback riding, soccer, rugby, tennis, volleyball).

At Eton College the school year is divided into three academic terms called *halves*: the *Michaelmas Half*, from early September to mid December. New students are admitted only at the start of this half. The *Lent Half,* from mid-January to late March. and the *Summer Half,* from late April to late June or early July.

DID YOU KNOW?

- When it was founded, only 70 students could attend *Eton College*. They lived in the Royal dormitory of the College.
- In the little town built around the school there is still one of the dormitories of the College whose members are called *King's Scholars*.
- King's Scholars use the letters "KS" after their name. They enter the school by means of annual scholarships. Their uniform is different from the uniform of the ordinary students who are called Oppidans from the Latin word *Oppidum* that is town in English.

ACTIVITIES

1 Translate each word into Italian.

a. Boarding school
b. College
c. County
d. Dormitory
e. Extracurricular activities
f. Royal Palace
g. Scholarship
h. School Year
i. School subject
j. Uniform

2 Say if the following sentences are True (T) or False (F). Correct the false ones.

a. Eton College is situated in the County of Berkshire. T F
b. The school was founded by Henry VIII of England. T F
c. It was a charity school founded to provide free education to 70 poor students. T F
d. The school has got 35 houses. T F
e. Each house is headed by a headmaster. T F
f. Over 1500 students are educated at Eton College. T F
g. Prince Charles studied at Eton. T F
h. At Eton the school year is divided into two halves. T F
i. New students are admitted at the Lent Half. T F
j. The Summer Half is from March to June. T F

3 Answer the following questions.

1. Where is Eton College situated?
2. Why is the County of Berkshire called Royal?
3. Who founded the College?
4. How is the College considered?
5. What is the original name of the school?
6. Who studied at Eton?
7. How many boys' houses are there in the College?
8. How many students are educated at Eton?
9. What are Eton students called?
10. How many halves are there in a school year? What are they?

ESERCIZI ON LINE www.medusaeditrice.it

4 Fill in each blank using the following words: Royal County - was founded - free education - 25 houses - 1300 students - is divided - are admitted - dormitory - KS - Oppidans.

Eton College is situated in the __________ of Berkshire. It ____________________ by King Henry VI. It was a charity school to provide ______________ to poor students. There are ______________________ in the school. At Eton over ___________________ are educated. The school year ________ _________ into three terms. New students ______________________________ only at the start of the *Michaelmas Half.*
When the College was founded, the students lived in the Royal _____________.
King's Scholars enter the school by means of annual scholarships. They use the letters __________ after their name. The ordinary students are called the _____________________.

RISORSE ON-LINE
www.medusaeditrice.it

AMERICAN EDUCATION

Education System in the USA

The United States has a decentralized Education System based upon its Federal Constitution which reserves power over education to the states and local authorities, as well as to individual schools and higher education institutions. The law requires children to attend school from ages 5 to 18 and the standard school system is from Kindergarten to 12th grade.

There are *public schools* which are free, paid for by the state and federal taxes and *private schools* which parents pay for out of their own pocket.

The benefits of public schools

The benefits of public schools are:

- *teachers are better qualified;*
- *students spend more time studying core subjects;*
- *public schools can sponsor more activities;*
- *the student population tends to be more diverse.*

The Advantages of Private Schools

The advantages of private schools are:

- *schools and classes tend to be much smaller. On average, private schools have a student-teacher ratio of 9:1 as opposed to about 17:1 in public schools;*
- *there is often less bureaucracy. Teachers have more creative control over teaching;*
- *parent involvement is strong.*

American students have to attend school until they are 18 years of age but if they prefer to have a job they can leave, with parental consent, at 16. School generally begins the first week of September and finishes the third week of July. Schools are closed on: *Labor Day, Thanksgiving Day, Martin Luther King's Day* and *Memorial Day*. Students also have a winter and a spring break.
The school day usually starts at 8.30am and finishes at 3.30pm, students have an hour break for lunch at 12.00am and they usually eat at school. All school districts establish their own times but they all schools are closed on Saturdays.

Different levels of Education

Each of the 50 American states has its own educational programs. Generally at *Kindergarten* children have one teacher. They play and learn the best way to stay together and also begin to develop their skills like reading, matching words and images and start writing.

At *Elementary school* pupils are taught by one or two teachers, they learn different subjects like History, Geography, Art and Arithmetic.

At *Middle School* students have many teachers who teach them Science, a foreign Language and IT (Information Technology).

When they start *High School* they have compulsory subjects but they can also choose something close to their interests. Students usually select about 4-5 classes and move from class to class during the day. There are After School activities or clubs like Music, Drama and many others until 5.00 pm. Sport is really important in American schools, each school has its own sport team that competes in different tournaments.

At the end of High School, students receive a certification during the "*Graduation*" ceremony. This level of education is called *Higher Education* and they receive it without doing exams but if they want to study at university or go to a college they'll have to pass the *Scholastic Aptitude Test* or SAT.

Students receive a *Bachelor's degree* at the end of their university studies.

DID YOU KNOW?

- *Cheerleading* was introduced in the late 1800s, cheerleaders support school sport teams.

- In the USA there is a formal party called the *School Prom*. It is an important event that celebrates the end of exams and takes place at High School. It is a formal ball, boys wear a suit and girls a ballgown.
- Each student has the *Year Book* which is a photo album of the most important events at school. Teachers and schoolmates sign it.
- Students have letter grade assignments: A, B, C, D are passing grades, E and F are non passing grades.

ACTIVITIES

1 Translate each word into Italian.

a. Federal Constitution
b. Law
c. School system
d. Public school
e. Private school
f. Kindergarten
g. Elementary school
h. Middle school
i. High school
j. University

ESERCIZI ON LINE www.medusaeditrice.it

2 Say if the following sentences are True (T) or False (F). Correct the false ones.

a. The United States has a decentralized Education System. T F
b. The law requires children to attend school from the ages of 3 to 18. T F
c. The standard school system is from Kindergarten to 12th grade. T F
d. Public schools aren't free. T F
e. School generally begins the second week of September. T F
f. School finishes the third week of June. T F
g. At Kindergarten children have one teacher. T F
h. In American schools there aren't any After School activities. T F
i. At the end of High School, students receive a certificate. T F

3 Answer the following questions.

1. From what age is education in the USA compulsory?
2. Are public schools free?
3. Is the student population of a public school more diverse?
4. Are classes smaller in private schools?
5. When are schools closed?
6. What time does the school day usually start?
7. How many break times are there?
8. What are the most popular after school activities?
9. Are sports important in American schools?
10. Do the sport teams compete in different tournaments?
11. What do the students receive at the end of High School?
12. What does SAT stand for?
13. What is the Bachelor's degree?

4 Fill in each blank using the following words: *schoolmates – Elementary School – children – Education System – High School – Graduation – prom – USA – Kindergarten.*

In the USA .... attend school from ages of 5 to 18.

The breakdown of the............................ is ....to ....,

Middle School to................................. During the..........................

ceremony students receive a certificate and usually have a .... with their

.... The most famous University in the..................is Harvard.

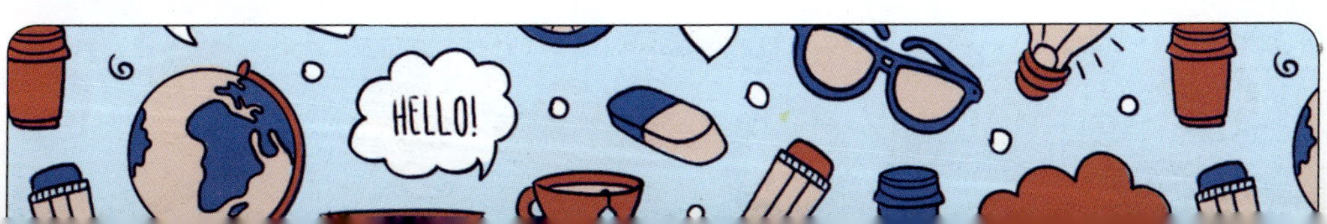

5 Read the text *American Education* and the information below. Complete the grid.

Pre-Kindergarten: ages 3-5 not compulsory.

Kindergarten: ages 5-6.

Elementary school: ages 6-11 (1st grade, 2nd grade, 3rd grade, 4th grade, 5th grade).

Middle school: ages 11-14 (6th grade, 7th grade, 8th grade).

High School: ages 14-18 (9th grade, 10th grade, 11th grade, 12th grade).

COMPULSORY LEVELS

SCHOOL	AGE	GRADE	ACTIVITIES or SUBJECTS	OPTIONAL AND AFTER SCHOOL ACTIVITIES
Kindergarten				
Elementary School				
Middle School				
High School				

6 Draw and complete a grid using your knowledge about how Italian schools are organized.

EXAM TRAINER

READING COMPREHENSION

My school day

Hello, I'm John! I'm a student at secondary school. My school is a state school, so it's free.

Most of British schools are state schools, but there are independent schools, too. In the latter parents pay fees for their children's education. Boys and girls in both types of school have to wear a uniform.

In the UK schools are open from September to the middle of July. I start school at about 8.45 a.m. that's the time of registration when the teacher calls students' names. At 9 all students meet in the main hall where there is an Assembly. After listening to the headmaster teachers eithertells us a story with a moral or talks about important events. Lessons start at about 9.25. They finish at 1 o' clock and then there's a break of an hour for lunch. Some pupils go home to eat, some take a packed lunch (usually sandwiches and a drink) with them or eat in the school canteen. In the afternoon there are classes from two p.m. to four p.m.

Clubs and school preferences

After school there are clubs, that's to say students do other activities such as sport, music, singing in a choir or drama. British children do a lot of sport at school such as football, that is very popular or netball, rugby, tennis, cricket and badminton. I've joined a choir club and I'm learning a funny song "Happy Days". It's fantastic!

My favourite school subject is Art and I love my Art teacher, Mrs Smith. She is very nice. I have my Art class on Tuesdays and Fridays. I don't like Geography. My Geography teacher is Mr Jones. He's very strict. In Secondary school we call teachers 'Miss' or 'Sir' or by their surname Mrs Smith or Mr Jones.

Now it's late and I have the first class of the day. Today is Monday. It's Maths, that's a bit difficult. Bye.

1 Read the text and answer the following questions.

1. Are state schools free?
2. What are independent schools?
3. When does school start in Britain?
4. What do students do in the morning?
5. Do students have lunch at school?
6. How many lessons are there in the afternoon?
7. What do British students do after school?
8. What sports do they do?
9. What's your favourite school subject?
10. Who's your favourite teacher?
11. Which lessons do you have on Monday?
12. Do you like homework?

LISTENING ACTIVITY

Listen to "Happy Days" a song by Pratt & McClain and complete the text with the words in the box.

Link: http://bit.ly/1RsafZk

comes - long - free - feels ready - week - cycle - share

Sunday, Monday, Happy Days.
Tuesday, Wednesday, Happy Days.
Thursday, Friday, Happy Days.
The weekend ....,
My................ hums,
................to race to you.

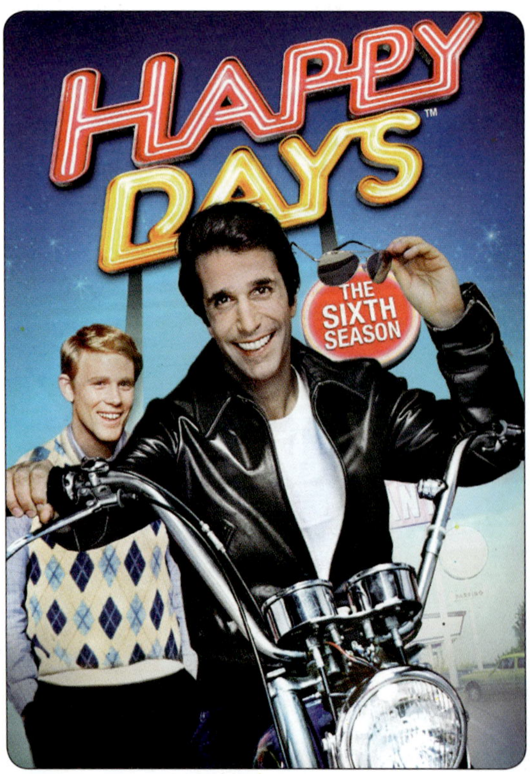

These days are all,
Happy and .... (Those Happy Days)
These days are all,
.... them with me. (oh baby)
Goodbye grey sky, hello blue.
There's nothing can hold me when
I hold you.
.... so right, it can't be wrong.
Rockin' and rollin' all week ....

Sunday, Monday, Happy Days.
Tuesday, Wednesday, Happy Days.
Thursday, Friday, Happy Days.
Saturday, What a day,
Groovin' all .... with you.

These days are all,
Share them with me. (Those Happy Days)
These days are all,
Happy and Free. (oh baby)
These Happy Days are yours and mine.
These Happy Days are yours and mine,
Happy Days.

STEP BY STEP

How to complete an open dialogue

Il completamento di un *Open-dialogue* potrebbe essere la prova scritta di lingua inglese all'Esame di Stato.

Ecco le regole da seguire che ti aiutano a svolgerla.

- Osserva il dialogo, leggi le battute e cerca di comprendere la situazione.
- Sottolinea i vocaboli che non conosci. Usa il dizionario per scoprirne il significato.
- Nelle risposte stai attento agli errori di grammatica e di ortografia. Fai attenzione all'uso dei tempi verbali: normalmente nelle risposte occorre utilizzare lo stesso tempo delle domande.
- Fai attenzione alle parole interrogative perché le risposte devono essere corrispondenti alle *Wh-questions* usate.
- Cerca di capire chi parla e quali funzioni comunicative comuni potresti usare.
- Quando hai terminato, ricontrolla le risposte prima di consegnare l'elaborato.

OPEN-DIALOGUE

Complete the following open-dialogue. A foreign student will come to your school for a week. You'll meet him at the station tomorrow. On the phone he's asking you for some information.

You: Hello Mark! How are you?
S: . . . .
You: Fine, thanks a lot. How old are you?
S: . . . .
You: Me too! What time does your train arrive? . . . .
S: . . . .
You: What do you want to know?
S: . . . .
Well, I'd like to know some information about your school. What school subjects will we study? And what time does school start and finish?
You: . . . .
S: I see. How will we get to school?
You: . . . .
S: How long does it take to go to school?
You: . . . .
S: What's the weather like in Italy? Here in Nottingham it's rainy and cold. I'm bored.
You: . . . .
S: What do you usually do after school?
You: . . . .
S: Let's visit Naples at the weekend. I'd like to see its monuments and eat your pizza.
You: . . . .
S: Oh fantastic! I look forward to meeting you. Thank you very much. Bye bye.
You: . . . .

TRINITY GESE GRADE 3

CEFR level A2.1
Total exam time: 7 minutes.

Conversation

Examiner:

- Good morning!
- What's your name?
- Where do you live?
- Are your parents Italian?
- Have you got any brothers or sisters?
- Have you got many friends?
- Do you meet them at the weekend?
- Do you usually go to pubs?
- Do you like beer?
- What's your favourite food?
- Does your dad like cooking?
- Can you cook?

Look at this picture!

Examiner:

- Where are these boys and girls?
- How many people are there?
- Are they playing cards?
- How many people are eating?
- What are they drinking?
- Is there a waitress?
- What does she look like?
- Are there children?
- What are they doing?
- What is on the wall?

Examiner:

OK. Thanks a lot. Bye

You: Thanks. Goodbye.

CHAPTER 03

GEOGRAPHY

DIALOGUE

London

Marco: London is a very beautiful city!

Colin: Yes, it's really ancient, too. It was founded by the Romans in the first century B.C.

Marco: There are a lot of interesting monuments in London.

Colin: And a lot of parks.

Marco: I visited *Buckingham Palace* last year. I know it's the home of the Queen when she's in London. I saw the changing of the guards, too.

Colin: I prefer going to the park in the afternoon. I love going jogging in *Hyde Park*. Hyde Park is one of the largest parks in London and it's one of the Royal Parks.

Marco: I went into Hyde Park last week with a friend of mine. I saw that the park is divided into two parts by the artificial Serpentine Lake. I saw Speakers' Corner, the traditional site for public speeches and debates. I saw the *'Diana, Princess of Wales, Memorial Fountain'*, too. It is located in the southwest corner of Hyde Park.

Colin: What are we doing, now?

Marco: Shall we go to *Piccadilly Circus*?

Colin: Let's go.

EXERCISE

1 Answer the following questions.

1. When did the Romans found London?
2. When did Marco visit Buckingham Palace?
3. When does the Queen live in Buckingham Palace?
4. Who prefers going to the park?
5. What is Hyde Park?
6. Who did Marco go to Hyde Park with?
7. What does the artificial Serpentine Lake divide?
8. What is *Speakers' Corner*?
9. Where is the Diana Memorial Fountain located?
10. What are Colin and Marco doing now?

THE BRITISH ISLES

The British Isles are *Great Britain*, the largest island, *Ireland* and other smaller islands such as the *Shetlands*, the *Orkneys* and the *Hebrides* in the north, the *Isle of Man* between Great Britain and Ireland and the *Isle of Wight* in the English Channel.

They are in the north-west of Europe and are surrounded by the *Atlantic Ocean*, the *North Sea* and the *English Channel*. The *Irish Sea* separates Great Britain and Ireland.

The climate is neither very hot nor very cold, but it often rains and it's quite windy: this is why the weather is so changeable. This aspect of the weather depends on the influence of the Gulf Stream from Mexico.

Great Britain is divided into three countries: *England* with London as its capital, *Scotland* with Edinburgh and *Wales* with Cardiff as its capital city.

Ireland is divided into two countries: the *Republic of Ireland* with Dublin as capital and *Northern Ireland* whose capital city is Belfast.

The political union between Great Britain and Northern Ireland is called the *United Kingdom* or *UK*. The capital city of the UK is London.

Ben Nevis is the highest mountain in the UK. It is in Scotland. The longest river is the *Severn* between Wales and England, but the most famous is the *Thames*, the river that flows through London. The largest lake is *Lough Neagh* in Northern Ireland.

The population of the UK is about 64 and a half million (64,500,000).

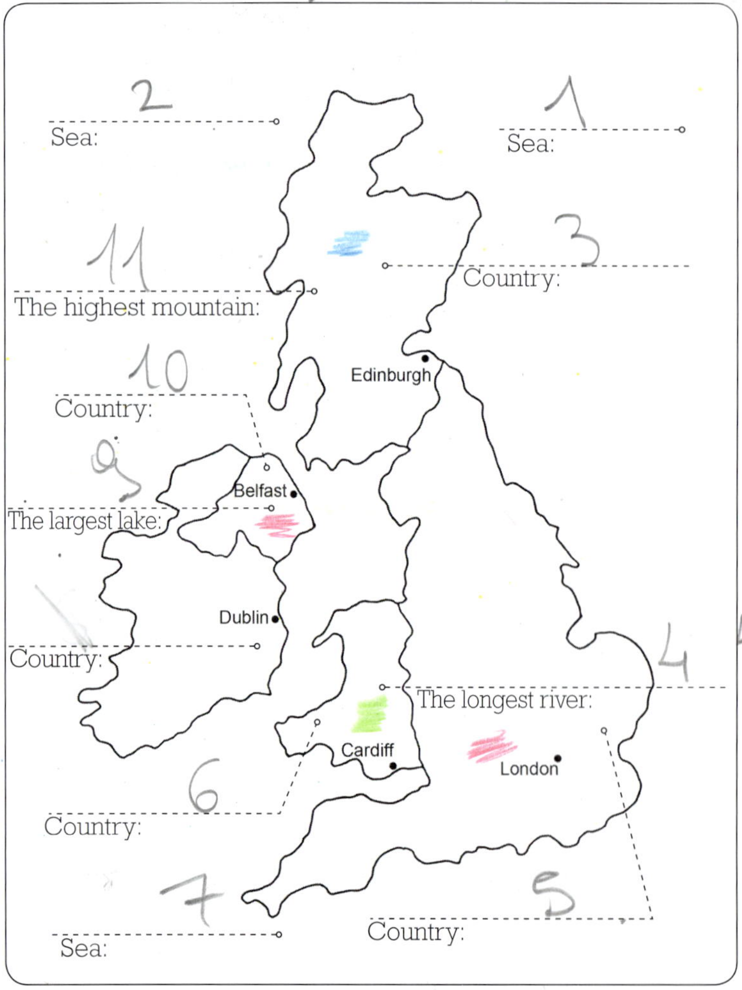

GOOD MORNING!
HAVE A NICE DAY!

ACTITIVIES

1 Read the text, look at the map and complete it with the main geographical characteristics. Colour England and Northern Ireland red, Scotland blue and Wales green.

ESERCIZI ON LINE www.medusaeditrice.it

2 Complete with the words in the box.

lake mountain river island city town village
nation/country sea/ocean hill plain volcano

NATION/COUNTRY

NATION

TOWN

VILLAGE

ISLAND

RIVER

LAKE

SEA/OCEAN

MOUNTAIN

VOLCANO

PLAIN

PLAIN

3 Read the text "The British Isles" again and answer the following questions.

1. Where are the British Isles?
2. Write down the seas that surround the British Isles.
3. Which sea is between Great Britain and Ireland?
4. What's the weather like in Britain? Why?
5. How many countries are there in Great Britain?
6. What's the UK?
7. What's the capital city of the United Kingdom?
8. How many countries are there in Ireland?
9. What's the capital city of the Republic of Ireland?
10. Where is Ben Nevis?
11. What's the longest river in the UK?
12. What's the largest lake?
13. What's the capital city of Northern Ireland?

2nd LESSON

WELCOME TO ENGLAND

1 Colour the map of England red and complete it with the following words.

Pennine chain Lake District Stonehenge Thames Oxford
Stratford-upon-Avon London York Liverpool Cambridge

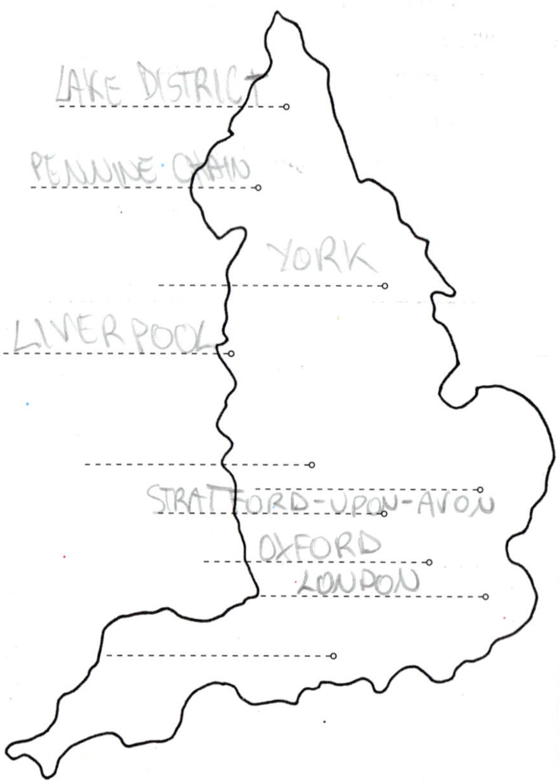

England is in the south-east of Great Britain.

2 Colour the English symbols.

The English flag is the St. George Cross. The cross is red on a white background.

The symbol of England is the red rose.

The Patron Saint of England is St. George. St. George's Day is on 23rd April. There are Scouts' parades with the Cross of St George in some churches on this feast day.

In England you can visit *Stonehenge*, the famous prehistoric monument; *Stratford-upon-Avon* where William Shakespeare's House is located; *Liverpool*, the Beatles' home town, *Cambridge* and *Oxford* with their Universities and finally *York* with its wonderful Cathedral.

The population of England is about 51 million.

Its currency is the pound sterling.

The national sport is cricket.

The capital of England is London.

3 **Complete the following grid.**

England	
1. Position	
2. Mountains	
3. Rivers	
4. Lakes	
5. Symbol	
6. Flag	
7. Patron Saint	
8. Capital City	
9. Important cities	
10. Population	
11. Currency	
12. Sport	

4 **SPEAKING. Speak about England using the various themes in the chart.**

LET'S VISIT LONDON

1 Look at the map and circle the main monuments in London.

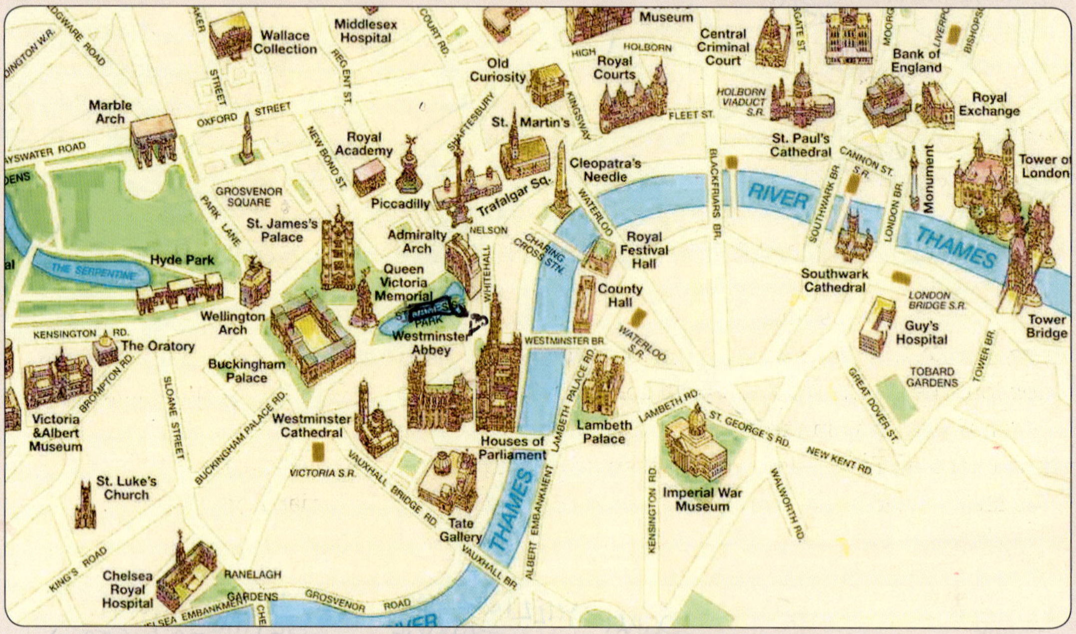

London is a large city. It has 7 million inhabitants. Its original name was Londinium, an important port founded by the Romans on the river Thames in 43 A.D.
In London there are a lot of monuments.

2 Read and complete the sentences.

Buckingham Palace is in London. The ..QUEEN.. lives here.

Big Ben is the famous ..CLOCK.. Tower. It's the symbol of ..LONDON.. .

The *Tower of London* is an ..OLD.. Norman fortress. The Crown Jewels are in it.

Trafalgar Square is the largest .... in London. The .... of Admiral Nelson is in the middle of it. There are two fountains, too.

Piccadilly Circus is the famous circular .... in London. It's called the .... of the world for the presence of young people of various nationalities.

Tower Bridge is the gate of London.
It opens and .... when a ship passes.
It dates back to the Victorian Age.

The *Houses of Parliament* are in the Palace of Westminster. This is the seat of the British ....

Westminster Abbey is an ancient and very large ....where there are the tombs of ...., queens and ....

St. Paul's Cathedral is the .... of London. Christopher Wren built it after the Great Fire destroyed London in 1666.

The best attractions in London for boys and girls are:

The London Eye, a huge wheel on the river Thames.

The *Changing of the Guard* at the gates of Buckingham Palace which takes place every day at 11.30 a.m.
The Royal Guards wear the famous red uniform and the black bearskin* on their heads.

* bearskin: colbacco.

The *Natural History Museum* where you can see dinosaurs, too. It's free.

London zoo which has about 650 species of animals.

The *British Museum* with its rich collection of international art and fascinating exhibits. It's free.

The popular wax museum *Madame Tussauds.*

3 SPEAKING

Speak about London and say:

- where London is located;
- who founded it and when;
- the number of inhabitants;
- some important monuments;
- the best attractions for boys and girls;
- what you'd like to visit.

DID YOU KNOW?

Cockney is an old English dialect. It is spoken in London in the area around the church of *St Mary-le-Bow*, between *St Paul's Cathedral* and the *Bank of England*. People who live in London use the word *cockney* to refer to a real Londoner. According to tradition real cockney is a person who can hear the bells of *St Mary-le-Bow Church* from his/her home.

Cockney is very difficult and uses rhyming words. The word means *cock's eggs* (a rooster's egg – which means an egg which is not well formed) and is usually used when referring to people's foolish behavior. It dates back to the 14th century when rural people used the term in a disparaging way to refer to Londoners as weak townsmen in contrast to the the strong and tough men of the countryside.

WELCOME TO SCOTLAND

1 Colour the map of Scotland blue and complete it with the following words.

Highlands Edinburgh Glasgow Loch Ness Tay Inverness

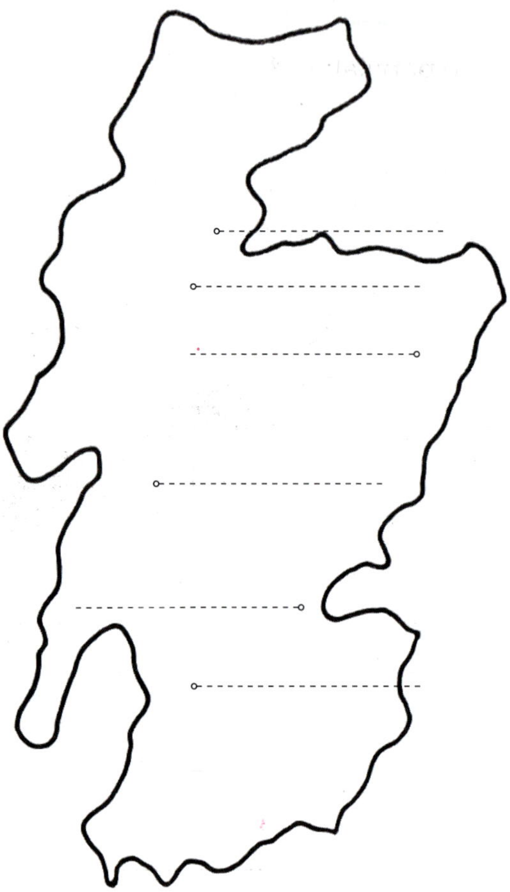

Scotland is in the north of Great Britain.

2 Colour the Scottish symbols.

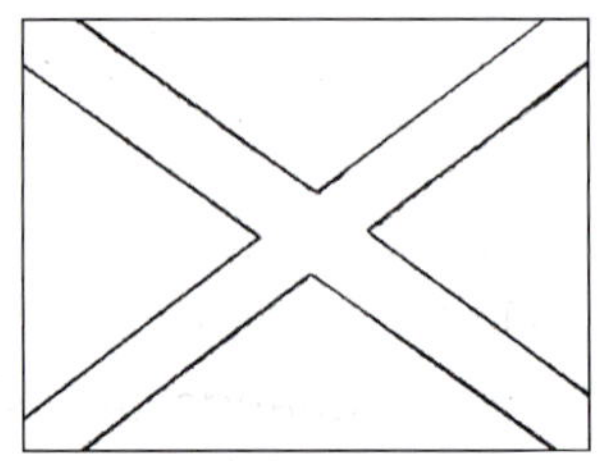

The Scottish flag is the *Cross of St. Andrew*. The cross is white and the background is blue.

The symbol of Scotland is the thistle. It's violet.

The Patron Saint of Scotland is St. Andrew. St. Andrew's Day is on 30th November. On his feast day there are parties with traditional music played on bagpipes.

DIVISO IN 3 PARTI

ISLAND — NORD
CENTRAL LOWLANDS — CENTRO
APPLANDS — SUD

In Scotland you can visit *Glasgow,* the industrial capital of Scotland; *Inverness*, the capital of the Highlands and *Loch Ness*, the popular lake with its legendary monster.

The population of Scotland is about 5.2 million.
Its currency is the pound sterling.
The national sport is golf.
The capital of Scotland is Edinburgh.

3 Complete the following grid.

Scotland	
1. Position	IS IN THE NORTH OF GREAT BRITAIN
2. Mountains	HIGHT LAND
3. Rivers	TAY
4. Lakes	~~LOKNESS~~ LOCH NESS
5. Symbol	IS THE THISTLE. IT'S A VIOLET
6. Flag	A CROSS OF SAINT ANDREW WHITE AND BLUE BACKGROUND
7. Patron Saint	IS ST. ANDREW
8. Capital City	IS EDINBURGH
9. Important cities	IS ABOUT 5.2 MILLION
10. Population	GLASGOW, INVERNESS
11. Currency	IS THE POUND STERLING
12. Sport	~~NATIONAL SPORT IS~~ GOLF

4 Speak about Scotland using the various themes in the chart.

LET'S VISIT EDINBURGH

1 Look at the map and circle the main monuments of Edinburgh.

Holyrood Palace — Edinburgh Castle — Princes Street — Scott Monument — St Giles's Cathedral — National Gallery of Scotland — Scottish Parliament — Royal Mile — Calton Hill

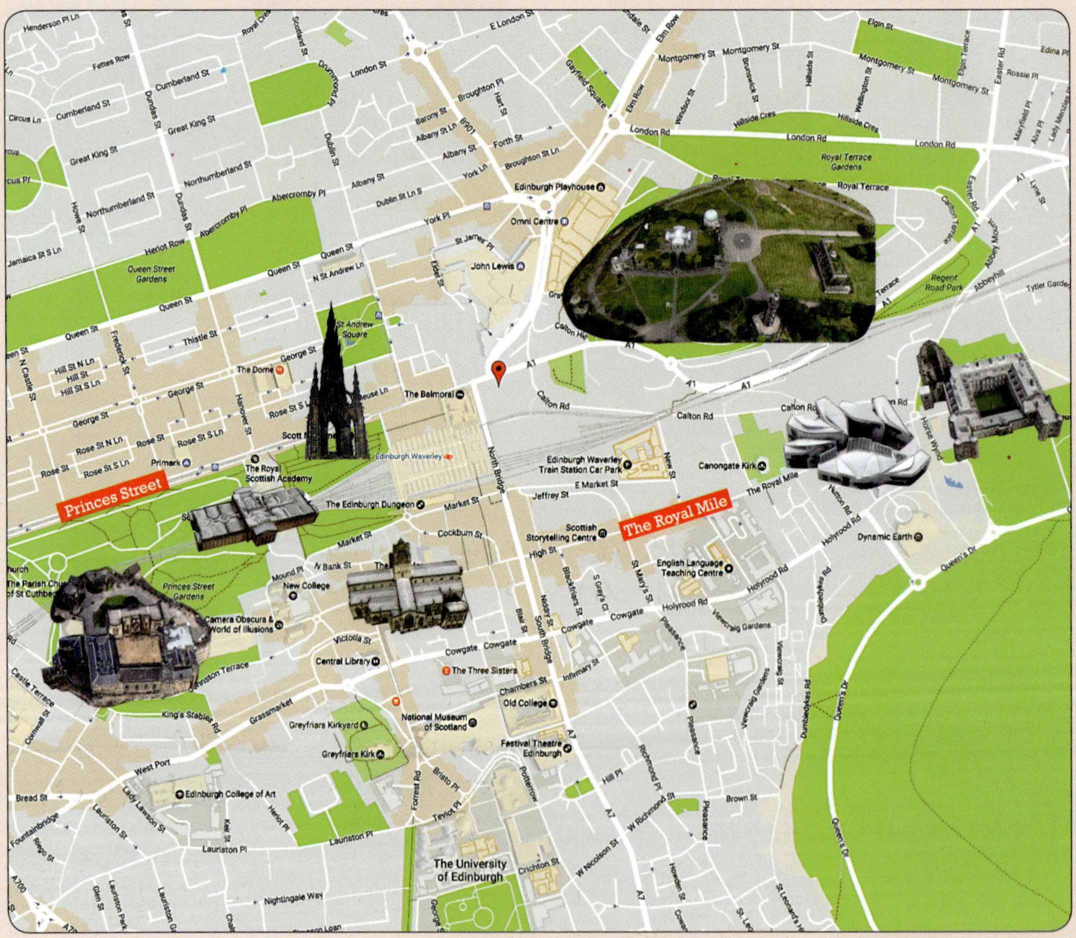

Edinburgh has a population of 472,000 inhabitants. It's a historic city with a beautiful castle. It's also the location of *Holyrood Palace*, where the Queen lives when she's in Edinburgh. The road between the *Castle* and *Holyrood House* is called the *Royal Mile*. Its main street is *Princes Street*.

Every August in Edinburgh there's a famous festival of music, theatre and dance and the *Royal Edinburgh Military Tattoo* which takes place in *Edinburgh Castle*.

2 Read the following words and then place them under the correct pictures.

bagpipes kilt castle golf whisky Holyrood House
Nessie, the Monster of Loch Ness Royal Edinburgh Military Tattoo

DID YOU KNOW?

In Scotland there are a lot of castles. Some of them are haunted by ghosts such as *Glamis Castle* which has nine ghosts.

Scottish men and boys wear a *kilt* that is a short skirt made of a woollen cloth with square patterns called *tartan*. The *bagpipes* is the traditional musical instrument of Scotland and is played by pipers.

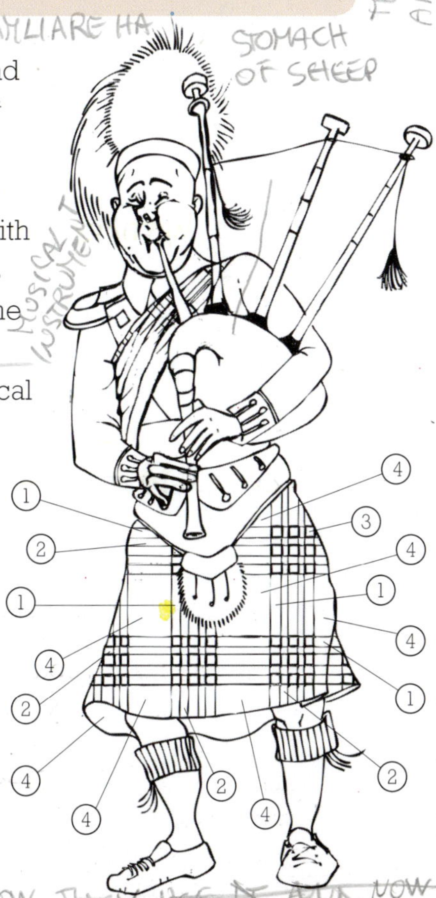

Color code:
1 - blue
2 - yellow
3 - green
4 - red
5 - white

4th LESSON

WELCOME TO WALES

1 Colour the map of Wales green and complete it with the following words.

Snowdon Cardiff Swansea Llangors Lake River Dee Cambrian Mountains

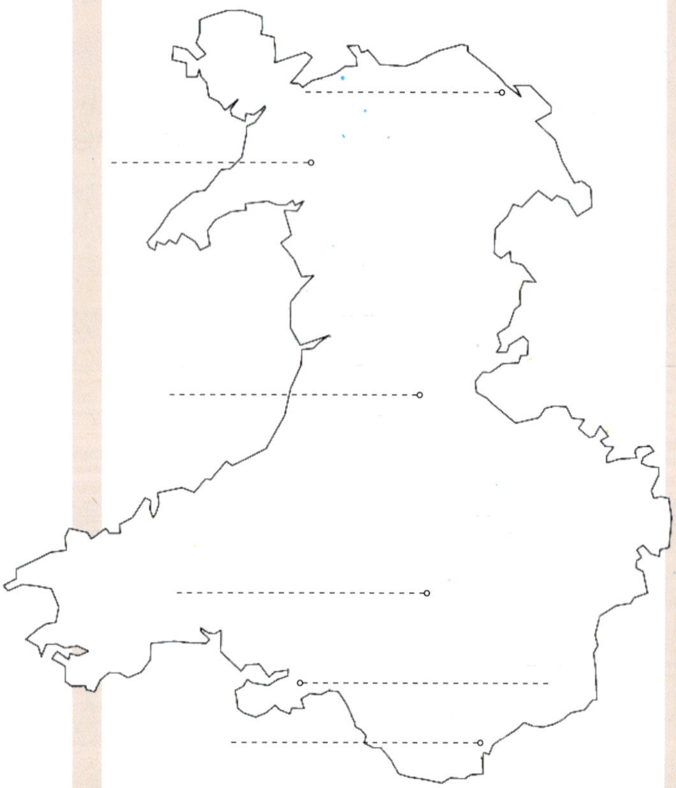

Wales is in the south-west of Great Britain.

2 Colour the Welsh symbols.

The Welsh flag is the Red Dragon. The dragon is red and has got wings. The top half of the background is white and the bottom half green.

The symbol of Wales is the daffodil. It's yellow.

The Patron Saint of Wales is St. David. St. David's Day is on 1st March. On his feast day people wear traditional costumes and there are parties with traditional Welsh songs.

The capital of Wales is Cardiff. It is an important port.
In Cardiff you can visit the *Millennium Stadium*. Concerts, football and rugby matches take place here.

The population of Wales is about 3 million.
Its currency is the pound sterling.
The national sport is rugby.

3 **Complete the following grid.**

Wales	
1. Position	
2. Mountains	
3. Rivers	
4. Lakes	
5. Symbol	
6. Flag	
7. Patron Saint	
8. Capital City	
9. Important cities	
10. Population	
11. Currency	
12. Sport	

4 **Speak about Wales using the themes in the chart.**

LET'S VISIT CARDIFF

1 Look at the map and circle the main monuments of Cardiff.

Castle Welsh Government Millenium Stadium Central Library
New Theatre Motorpoint Arena National museum

Cardiff has a population of 321,000 inhabitants. The *Welsh Assembly* is the Parliament. It's in Cardiff. Prince Charles, Queen Elizabeth's son, is called the Prince of Wales because he's the future King of England.

DID YOU KNOW?

The Welsh language

In Wales people speak English and *Welsh*, which is quite a difficult language. Here are some words in English and in Welsh:

English	Welsh
Wales	Cymru
Man	Dyn
Father	Tad
Mother	Mam
Sky	Nef
Sun	Haul
Moon	Lloer
Dog	Cri
Cat	Cath

Welsh or *cymraeg* was the language spoken by the Celts between the 8th and 6th centuries B. C.

King Arthur in Wales

A legend says that the tomb of King Arthur is in *Glastonbury Abbey* and that his knights lived under the ground at *Glastonbury Tor*, a large hill.

2 Complete the postcard.

A postcard from

Dear ....,
I'm in .... with my ....
The weather is .... It is .... and .... Every day I go visiting a .... Bye for now!

Name and surname ....
Address ....
Town/country ....

3 Speak about Cardiff and say: where Cardiff is located; how many inhabitants it has; mention some important monuments; a curiosity; what you'd like to visit.

WELCOME TO ULSTER

1 Colour the Republic of Ireland orange and Northern Ireland red then write the capital cities: *Belfast* and *Dublin*.

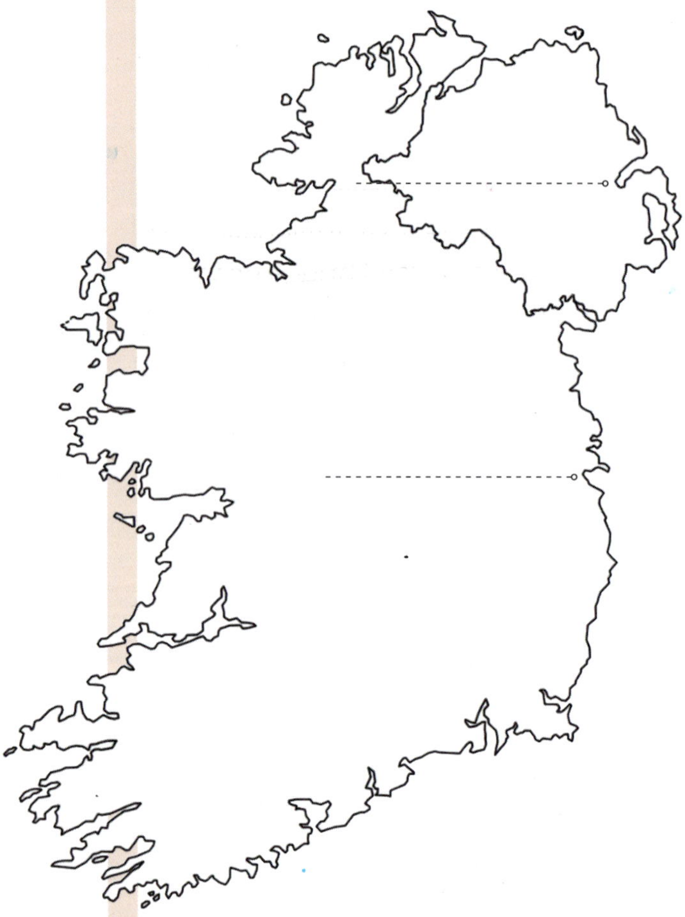

Ireland is divided into two countries: *Northern Ireland* or Ulster that is a part of the UK and the *Republic of Ireland*.

2 Colour the Irish symbols.

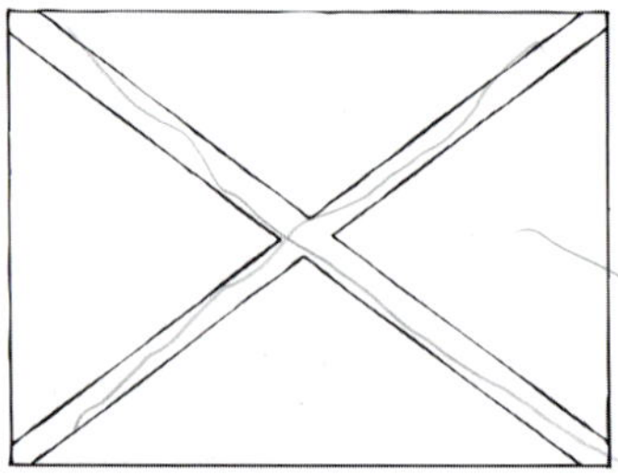

The Northern Irish flag is the Cross of St. Patrick. The cross is red and the background is white.

The symbol of Northern Ireland is the shamrock, it's green.

The Patron Saint of Ireland is St. Patrick. St. Patrick's Day is on 17th March. On his feast day there are parades and dances with traditional Irish songs and people wear green clothes.

LA STRADA DEL GIGANTE

MADE OF BASALT

The capital of Northern Ireland is *Belfast*, an important commercial and economic centre.

In Northern Ireland you can visit the *Giant's Causeway* that is made up of 40,000 stone columns. They're made of basalt and the tallest are 12 metres high. According to a legend the giant Finn McCool, an Ulster warrior and commander of the Irish army built them in order to create a land bridge on which he could bring his beloved lady-giant from the Hebrides to Ulster.

The population of Northern Ireland is about 1.7 million. Its currency is the pound sterling. The national sport is hurling.

7 HOUNDRED THOUSAND

3 **Complete the following grid.**

Northern Ireland	
1. Position	
2. Symbol	
3. Flag	
4. Patron Saint	
5. Capital City	
6. Places to visit	
7. Population	
8. Currency	
9. Sport	

4 **Speak about Ulster using the themes in the chart.**

LET'S VISIT BELFAST

1 Look at the map and circle the main monuments of Belfast.

Botanic Gardens | Grand Opera House | SSE Odissey Arena | Belfast City Hall | St Anne's Cathedral | Titanic Museum | Ulster Museum

Belfast has a population of 276,500 inhabitants. It's the capital of *Ulster*, a region of Northern Ireland, a part of the UK that was established in 1921. *Belfast* comes from the Gaelic words "Béal Feirste" that is to say "rivermouth[1] of the sandbank[2]"[3]. In fact it's on the sandbank, an area created by the confluence of two rivers: the *Lagan* and the *Farset*. In XX century Belfast became popular because the famous ship, the *Titanic*, was built here.

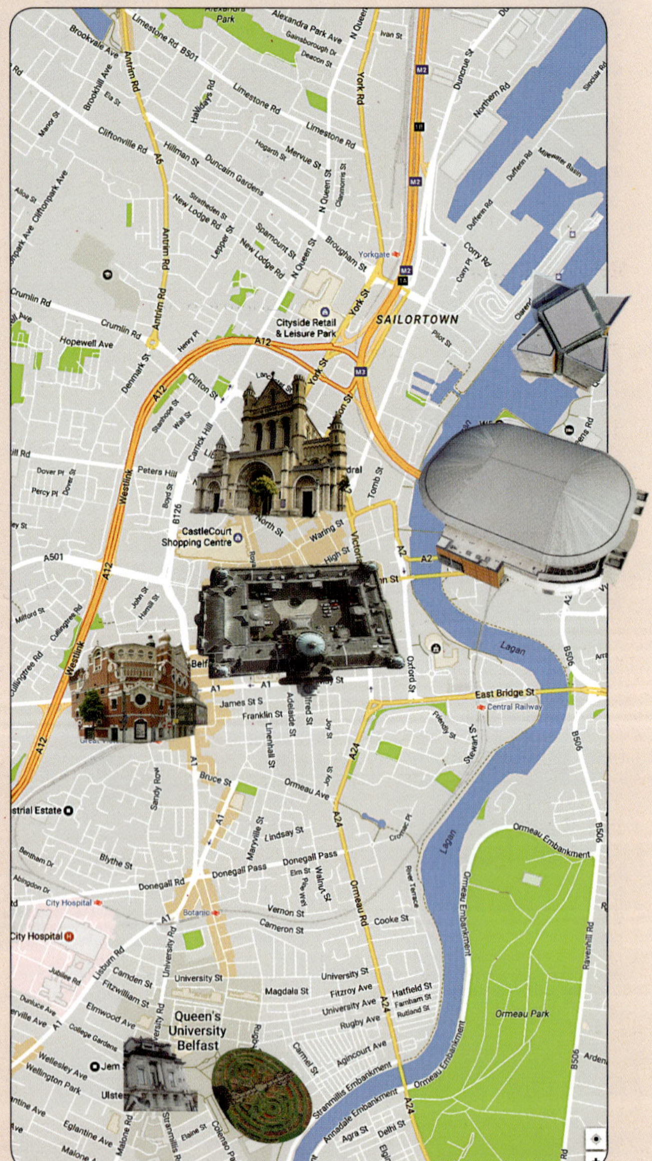

[1]**rivermouth**: bocca del fiume, foce;

[2]**sandbank**: banchina, guado sabbioso;

[3]**rivermouth of the sandbank**: guado sabbioso alla foce del fiume

2 Speak about Belfast and say:

- where Belfast is located;
- how many inhabitants it has;
- some important monuments;
- what you'd like to visit.

Belfast is the city where the *Titanic* was built by 15,000 workers from 1909 to 1912. It was the biggest ship in the world: it was 46,328 tons heavy, 269,90 metres long, a width of 28 metres, 58,5 metres high and could carry 1,343 passengers. The crew members were 885. Moreover it was one of the fastest ships in the world, provided with three big engines, which gave it a speed of 46 kilometres per hour.

On 31st March 1912 the Titanic left Belfast and sailed to Southampton in the South of England from where, on 10th April, it started its first cruise. From England the ship went to *Cherbourg* in France, then to *Queenstown* in Ireland and finally towards its final destination, *New York*. On the night of 14th April the Titanic hit an iceberg in the Atlantic Ocean and sank. Most of the people onboard died.

On 1st September 1985 the ship was discovered at the bottom of the sea at a depth of 3,810 metres by some sailors.

There are a lot of films about the story of the Titanic. One of the most interesting is Titanic Blood and Steel, which is about its construction.

On 1st September 1985 the ship was discovered at 3,810 metres under the sea by some sailors.

There are a lot of films about the story of the Titanic. One of the most interesting is *Titanic blood and steel*, which is about its construction.

ACTIVITY

3 Complete the fact file about the Titanic.

Fact file:

Ship: ....

Length: ....

Width: ....

Height: ....

Weight: ....

Speed: ....

Number of passengers: ....

6th LESSON

RISORSE ON-LINE

WELCOME TO EIRE

1 **The Republic of Ireland or Eire.**

Read and colour the drawings: Ireland, whose Gaelic name is *Eire*, is a part of the British Isles. The Irish Sea and St. George's Channel separate it from Britain. The highest mountain is *Carrantuohill* and the longest river is the *Shannon*. *Lough Corrib* is the largest lake.

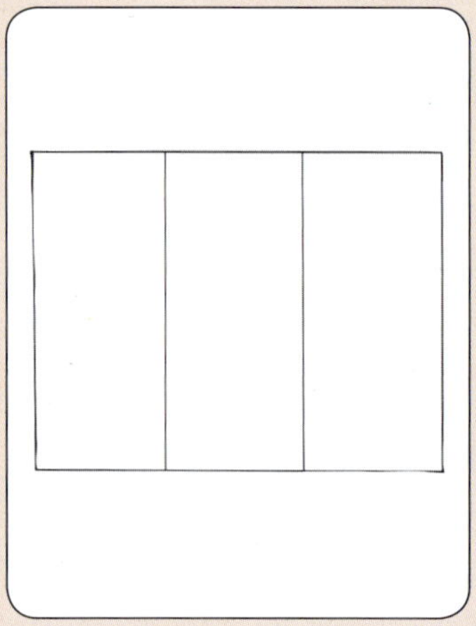

The Irish flag is green, white and orange.

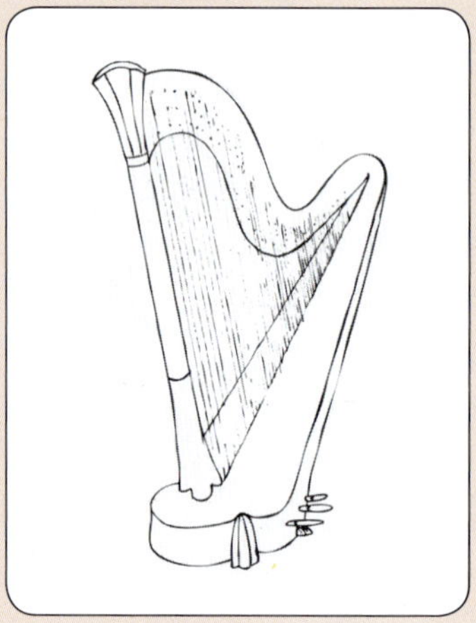

The symbol of the Republic of Ireland is the harp.

The capital of the Republic of Ireland is Dublin.

DID YOU KNOW?

Gaelic

Gaelic is a Celtic language which is still spoken by part of the population. English and Gaelic are the two official languages.

Hurling

The national sport of Ireland is *hurling*. This sport is played by two teams of 15 players each. They have to strike a leather ball over the goal posts with a hurley, which is a wooden bat.

Ireland is called the *Green Island*. The population of the Republic of Ireland is 3,500,000. Its currency is the Euro.

2 **Complete the following grid.**

The Republic of Ireland	
1. Position	
2. Mountains	
3. Rivers	
4. Lakes	
5. Symbol	
6. Flag	
7. Patron Saint	
8. Capital City	
9. Important cities	
10. Population	
11. Currency	
12. Sport	

3 **Speak about Eire using the themes in the chart.**

LET'S VISIT DUBLIN

1 Look at the map and circle the main monuments of Dublin.

Dublin Castle St. Patrick's Cathedral Mansion House Trinity College
National Museum Christ Church Cathedral Custom House

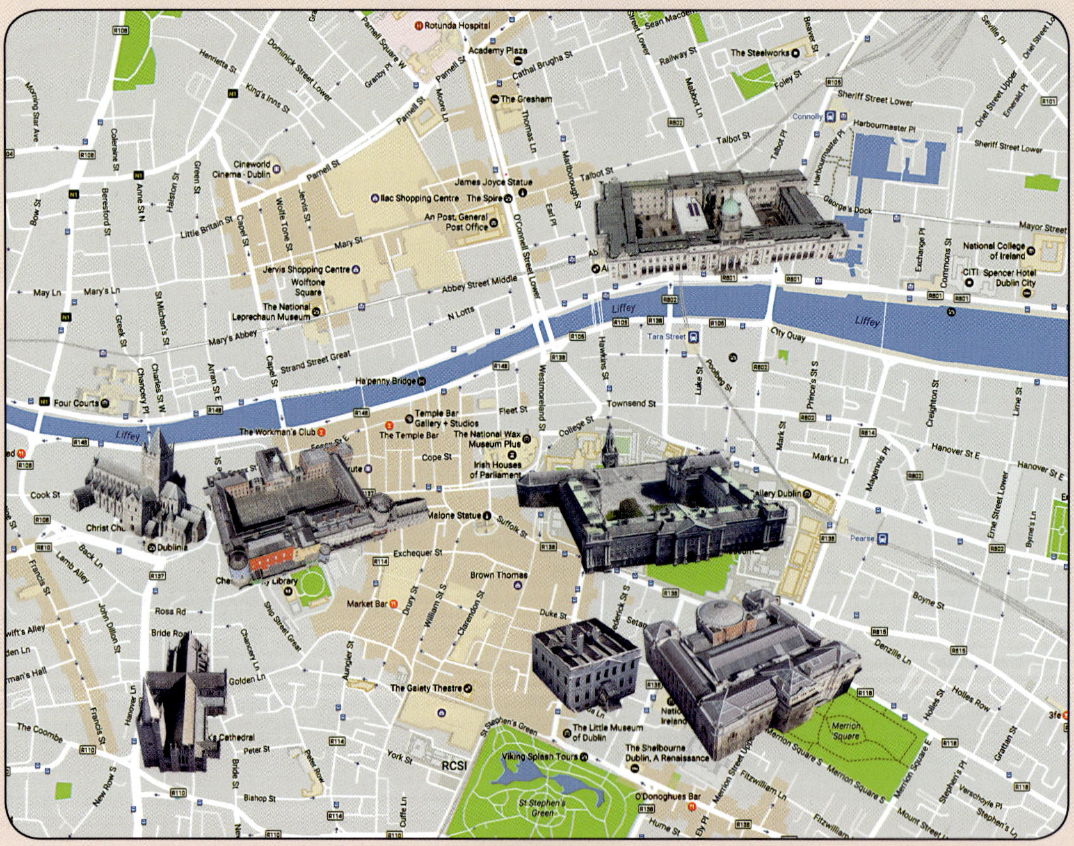

Dublin is the birthplace of famous writers such as *James Joyce*, *Oscar Wilde* and *Jonathan Swift*, author of the popular political satire *Gulliver's Travels*.

Dublin has a population of 527,612 inhabitants.
It's at the mouth of the river *Liffey* and was founded by the Vikings as a settlement for the slave trade. Its original name was in Gaelic *Dubh linn* which means *black pond*.
The *River Liffey* divides the city into two parts, the North side and the South side where

you can see various 17th century Georgian buildings and *O' Connell* and *Liffey Bridges*. Dublin is a beautiful city with a lot of monuments. On the North side you can walk along *O'Connell street* and visit famous places such as the *General Post Office* or the *Dublin Writers Museum*. On the South side you can visit *Dublin Castle*, *St. Patrick's Cathedral*, the *Old Parliament* and *Christ Church Cathedral*, the oldest building of the city.
Dublin is also the seat of the prestigious *Trinity College*, the oldest University in Ireland. It was founded by Elizabeth I in 1592.

Dublin Castle was the seat of English power in Ireland. The original castle was built by *King John Lackland*.

St. Stephen's Green is a public park with beautiful fountains and gardens where people can relax.

The *Guinness Storehouse* is the home of the traditional dark beer or stout.

Christ Church Cathedral is a medieval protestant church founded in 1038 by the first Viking king, *King Sitric Silkenbeard*.

2 Speak about Dublin and mention:

- where Dublin is located;
- some important monuments;
- how many inhabitants it has;
- what you'd like to visit.

The British Flag
The Union Jack, a symbol of unity

The British flag is called the *Union Jack* and is made up of three different national symbols. It is the national flag of the United Kingdom.

The St.George Cross, the flag of England.

St. Andrew's Cross, the flag of Scotland.

St. Patrick's Cross, the flag of Ireland.

The Virgin Queen, *Elizabeth I,* the last monarch of the Tudor dynasty never married and had no children, so when she died on 24th March 1603, King *James VI* of Scotland became King *James I,* King of England.

So there was the union of the two crowns, Scottish and English, under one king and with one flag.

The new flag consisted of the red cross of England superimposed on the white cross of Scotland, on the blue background of the Scottish flag.

It was usually only used at sea until the two kingdoms of Scotland and England united in 1707.

The flag was used in its original form until 1801 when, with the union between Ireland and Great Britain, Ireland was also represented in the Union Flag with the cross of St. Patrick. When the southern part of Ireland became independent in 1921 no alteration was made to the Union Jack.

In 1908 the name *Union Jack* was approved in Parliament which officially stated "the Union Jack should be regarded as the National flag".

DID YOU KNOW?

- In the flag, there isn't the red dragon, the symbol of Wales. The first version of the Union Flag was created in 1606 and Wales had already been united with England.
- It was probably from its use at sea that the flag got the name *Jack* (*Union Jack*).
- It was usually flown at the bow end of the ship, from the jack staff.

ACTIVITIES

1 Translate each word into Italian.

a. Alteration ....
b. Background ....
c. Cross ....
d. Crown ....
e. Dragon ....
f. Flag ....
g. Independent ....
h. National symbol ....
i. Staff ....
j. Superimposed ....

2 Say if the following sentences are True (T) or False (F). Correct the false ones.

a. The British Flag is called the *Union Jack*. T F
b. It is made up of four different national symbols. T F
c. The red dragon is not in the flag. T F
d. Queen Elizabeth I had no children. T F
e. King James VI of Scotland became King of England. T F
f. The *Union Jack* was initially used at sea. T F
g. England and Scotland were united in 1801. T F
h. The cross of St. Patrick was included in 1707. T F
i. The independence of the southern part of Ireland modified the flag. T F
j. The name *Union Jack* was approved in Parliament in 1910. T F

3 Answer the following questions.

1. What is the national flag of the United Kingdom?
2. How many national symbols are in the British Flag?
3. What are they?
4. Who became king of England when Elizabeth died?
5. What was the first English and Scottish flag like?
6. When were the kingdoms of England and Scotland united?
7. What happened in 1801?
8. When did the southern part of Ireland become independent?
9. What is the symbol of Wales?
10. When was the name "Union Jack" approved in Parliament?

4 Fill in each blank using the following words: *flag – cross – red – died – king - crowns – consisted in – sea – form – independent – approved.*

The Union Jack is the national ____________ of the United Kingdom.
St. George's ____________ is the flag of England. It is a __________ cross.
When Elizabeth I _______ on 24th March 1603, King James VI of Scotland became ______ of England.
The Scottish and English __________ united under one king and with one flag.
The new flag __________________ the red cross of England superimposed on the white cross of Scotland, on the blue background of the Scottish flag.
It was usually used at _________ until the two kingdoms of Scotland and England were united in 1707.
The flag was used in its original __________ until 1801.
When the southern part of Ireland became ___________________ in 1921 the Union Jack wasn't modified.
In 1908 the name *Union Jack* was ______________ in Parliament.

THE UNITED STATES OF AMERICA

The USA or US is a very large country in the North of the American Continent. Its states are fantastic places to visit and they are known all over the world for their different and beautiful landscapes.

The USA is a *Federal Republic* of fifty states, it includes the District of Columbia which is the seat of Government. The 49th state is *Alaska* and the 50th is *Hawaii*.

The national flag is called the *Stars and Stripes* and consists of fifty stars, which symbolize the fifty states, and thirteen stripes which represent the original colonies that achieved independence from the *United Kingdom* in 1776.

The national capital is *Washington DC*, where the *White House*, the American President's home and office is located.

American geographical features

The country borders and oceans are:

- *Canada* in the north
- *Mexico* and the *Gulf of Mexico* in the south
- The *Atlantic Ocean* in the east
- The *Pacific Ocean* in the west

The non bordering states are:

- *Alaska*
- *Hawaii*

The USA's territory includes a number of other areas such as

- the *American Samoa Islands* in the *South Pacific Ocean,*
- the *Commonwealth of Puerto Rico* and the *Virgin Islands of the United States* both in the *Caribbean Sea.*

DID YOU KNOW?

In the *Caribbean Sea* there are the *British Virgin Islands* too. They are under *United Kingdom* sovereignty and share the British monarch, *Queen Elizabeth II*, as Head of State.

EXERCISES

1 Translate each word into Italian.

a. Federal Republic;
b. District;
c. Landscape;
d. National Flag;
e. Stars;
f. Stripes;
g. Colonies;
h. Map;
i. Border;
j. Sovereignty

2 Read the text "American geographical features" and complete.
In the USA:

The border countries are ....

....

The border oceans are ....

....

Alaska and *Hawaii* aren't ....

....

The USA's territory includes ....

....

The British Virgin Islands are ....

....

DID YOU KNOW?

American states have nicknames, we include some below:

- Alaska: *Land of the Midnight Sun;*
- California: *The Golden State;*
- Florida: *The Sunshine State;*
- Hawaii: *The Aloha State.*

INCREDIBLE NATURAL PLACES!

The USA is extremely large and is an amazing place to explore! There are different kinds of climates, of time zones and it is considered the land of extraordinary wide plains and deserts, high mountains, picturesque forests, beautiful rivers and lakes.

The *Great Plains* are in the central areas of the country and divide the most important mountain chains, the *Rocky Mountains* in the west and the *Appalachians* in the east.

The *Mississippi River* is one of the longest rivers in the world, it passes through eight different American states. Other rivers include the *Rio Grande*, the *Sacramento*, the *Hudson*, the *Potomac,* that runs through *Washington DC* and the *Colorado* that flows through the *Grand Canyon*.

Huge lakes, called the *Great Lakes*, such as the *Superior,* the *Ontario*, the *Erie* and the *Huron* are located along the Canadian border. Lake *Michigan*, also in the north, is the only lake that lies entirely within the USA territory.

There are also wonderful *National Parks* including *Yellowstone*, one of the largest, the famous *Death Valley,* in the State of California and the *Grand Canyon* which is in the State of Arizona and is visited by many tourists each year for its spectacular views.

> Grand Canyon

> Death Valley

> Yellowstone

DID YOU KNOW?

- The American Indians call the Mississippi River *The Father of Waters.*
- In the USA there is also the *Great Salt Lake*, if you swim in it you cannot sink.
- Many film directors from all over the world have made western films with cowboys and Native Indians, one of them is Sergio Leone, an Italian director.

> Great Salt Lake

EXERCISES

3 Read the text "Incredible Natural places!" and complete the grid.

Plains	Mountains	Rivers	Lakes	National parks

4 Draw on the map: rivers, mountains, lakes and write their names.

CLIMATE, TIME ZONES, POPULATION AND CITIES

The climate of the United States of America is different from north to south and from east to west. It is *tropical* in Hawaii and Southern Florida, *arctic* in Alaska, *desert* in the Southwest. Extreme weather is quite usual in the country and there are often *hurricanes*, *tornadoes* and *floods* caused by *storms* and *heavy rainfalls*.
Earthquakes happen from time to time, especially in California.

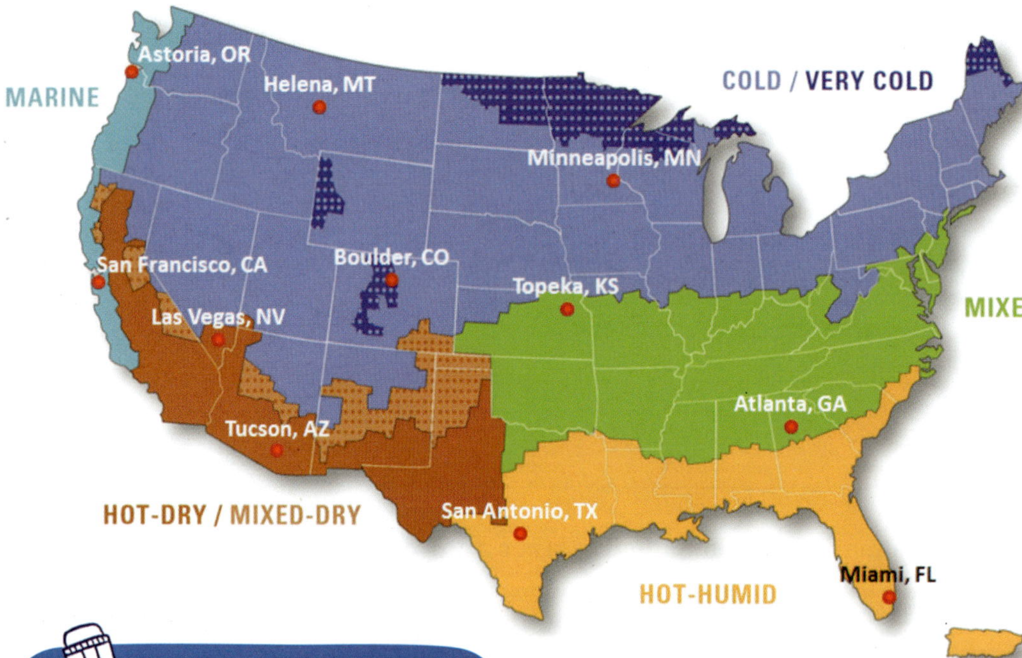

EXERCISES

5 Translate each word into Italian.

Tornado ....
Hurricane........................
Earthquake ....
Floods...........................
Storms ....
Rainfalls ....

6 Connect pictures and words.

1. Hurricane 2. Tornado
3. Earthquake 4. Flood

TIME ZONES

Time zones change as we travel from east (*New York*) to west (*Hawaii*). There are six time zones so we must set our watch back one hour as we enter each new time zone and one hour forward if we travel in the opposite direction.

American people have *Daylight Saving Time* (DST) from March to November.

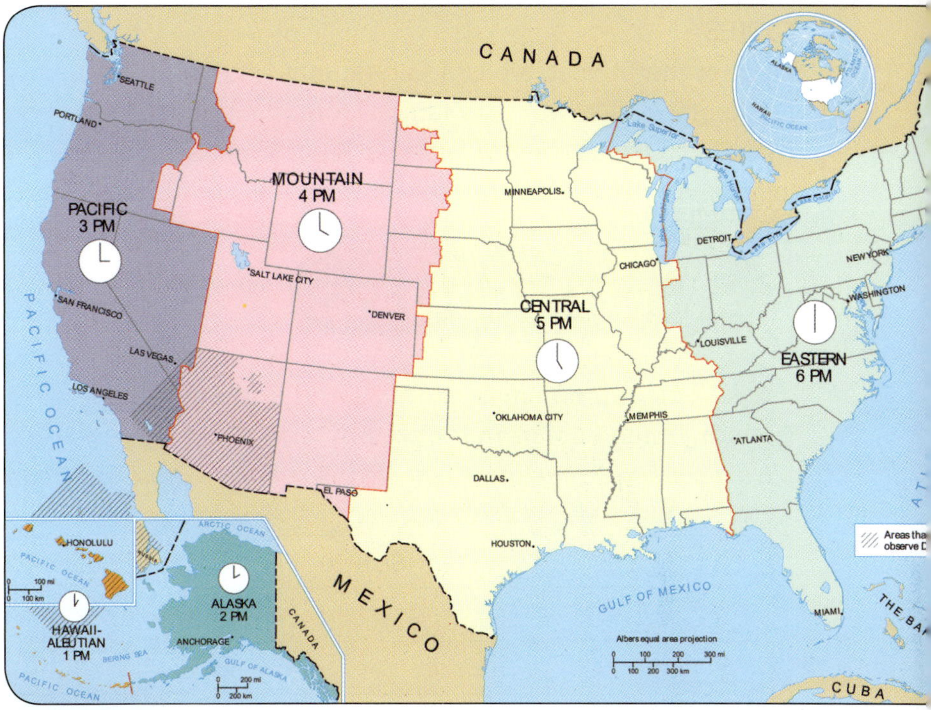

EXERCISES

7 **Look at this grid! Find the cities on the map. Circle the names in red.**

▪ New York	▪ 6:00 (a.m.)
▪ Chicago, IL	▪ 5:00 (a.m.)
▪ Denver, CO	▪ 4:00 (a.m.)
▪ Los Angeles, CA	▪ 3:00 (a.m.)
▪ Juneau, AK	▪ 2:00 (a.m.)
▪ Honolulu HI	▪ 1.00 (a.m.)

DID YOU KNOW?

When it's 12.00 p.m. in Italy it's 6.00 a.m. in New York.

POPULATION

The population of the USA is composed of people from many countries and this is the reason why there are so many different languages, races and cultures. The first language is *English* and the second is *Spanish* but there are also others such as *Italian*, *French*, *German* and *Chinese*. A Melting Pot is a metaphor for a society, city or country where many different types of people blend together as on. The population of the USA is about 325.000.000.

CITIES

Each of the 50 states has a capital city but not all of them are popular among tourists. Some other cities are very famous tourist attractions although they are not capitals. *New York, Los Angeles, Miami, Las Vegas, New Orleans, San Francisco* and many others are interesting places for your next holiday!

EXERCISES

8 Look at the map of the USA and find out if these cities are in the north, in the south, in the east or in the west.
New York, San Francisco, Los Angeles, Washington DC, Miami, New Orleans, Chicago, Honolulu, Las Vegas, Philadelphia.

North	South	East	West

9 You are planning a holiday in the USA next year. Here are ten places that are very popular with travellers choose: *New York, National Parks, Washington DC, Arizona, Los Angeles, South Dakota, San Francisco, Hawaii, New Orleans, Puerto Rico.* Write your top ten cities! Find information and pictures of your holiday destination, glue them on your copybook then speak about your chosen place.

10 Read the texts again and answer the following questions.

1. Where is the USA located?
2. What does USA mean?
3. How many States form the USA?
4. What is the American flag's name?
5. How many stars are there? How many stripes?
6. What is the national capital city? Where is it?
7. What is the longest river in the USA?
8. What are the most important mountain chains?
9. Which lake is entirely in the American territory?
10. Does the USA have extreme weather (hurricanes, floods...)?
11. How many time zones are there in the USA?
12. What does *Melting Pot* mean?
13. What is the first language in the USA?
14. What is the nickname of Alaska?

WELCOME TO WASHINGTON!

Washington D.C. is the capital of the United States of America. D.C. stands for District of Columbia, which is an independent area of the country. The name of the district comes from the Italian navigator, *Christopher Columbus* the city, on the other hand, was called Washington after the first American President, *George Washington* who was elected in 1789. It is a modern city on the *Potomac River*, a lot of tourists go there because there are many interesting and historical places to visit. Walking through Washington one senses a strong political atmosphere due to the presence of important federal buildings. Washington D.C. is also a beautiful place to enjoy music. Along the streets many artists play blues and the city is charming when all the monuments are lit up at night.

The White House

The best known building is the *White House*, home and office of the President of the USA since 1800. The President lives in the White House with his family and works in the *Oval Office,* where he takes all the governmental decisions, the famous *Resolute Desk* is here! When the President makes an official speech to the country, he sits behind this desk and people from all over the world can watch him on television.

The White House is a neoclassical building and has three hundred and thirty-two rooms. There is a blue room, a green room and a red room. On the first floor there are public offices. The President and his family live on the second floor. On the third floor there are rooms for guests and for the people who work there.

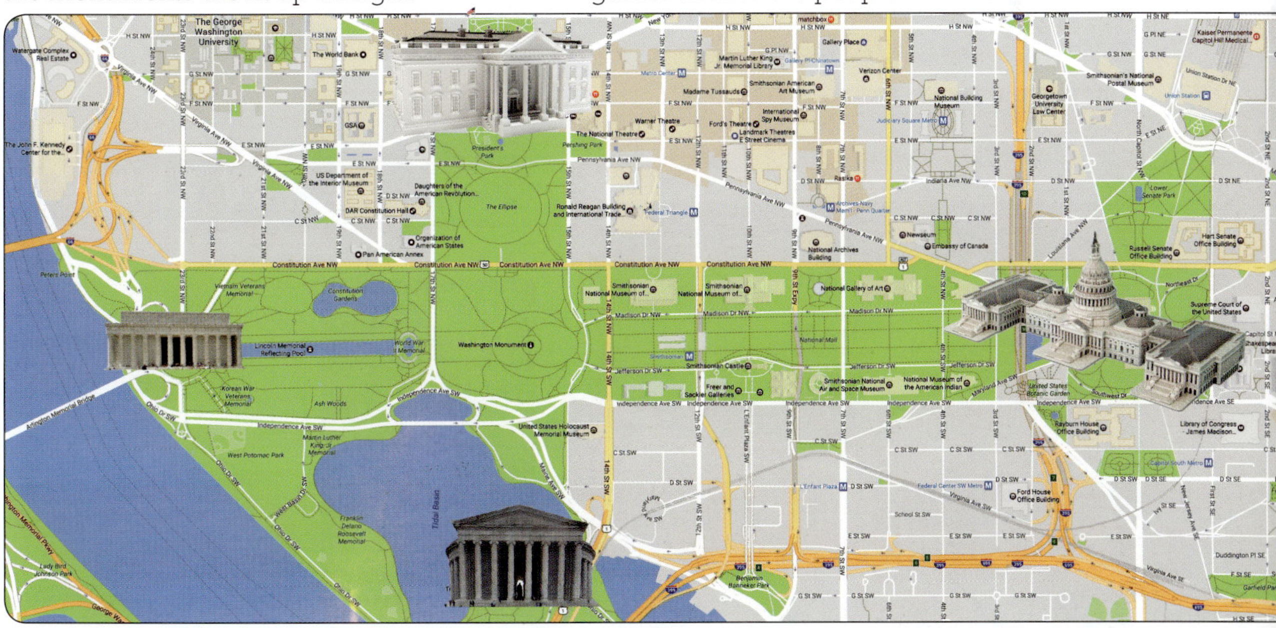

> The Oval Office

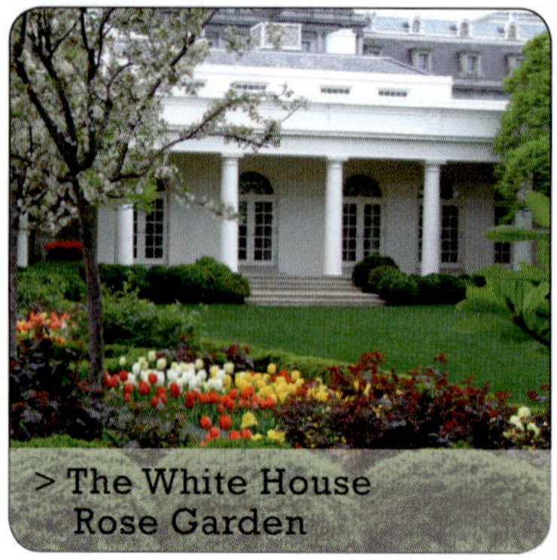
> The White House Rose Garden

> The White House

The house is surrounded by a beautiful park. The magnificent *White House Rose Garden* is used for both official and informal events. The President sometimes holds press conferences there too.

The Capitol

The Capitol, also white and neoclassical, is another important building of American political life. The Capitol is located on *Capitol Hill* and was built in 1800. It is the place where *Congress* meets. Visitors can have an interesting Capitol experience by entering the *Senate* and *House of Representatives Galleries* to see Congress in action. Of course, passes are required!

> The Capitol

Lincoln Memorial

Going around Washington, tourists can be reminded of famous American presidents of the past and of recent times. Different monuments express the history of the USA. The design resembles an ancient Greek temple. There are 36 columns, reflecting the number of states that existed at the time of President Lincoln's death. The large statue of Lincoln was created by *Daniel Chester French*, an American sculptor, and the Memorial opened to the public in 1922. The *National Mall Park*, a national stage where movements and celebrations take place, is nearby.

DID YOU KNOW?

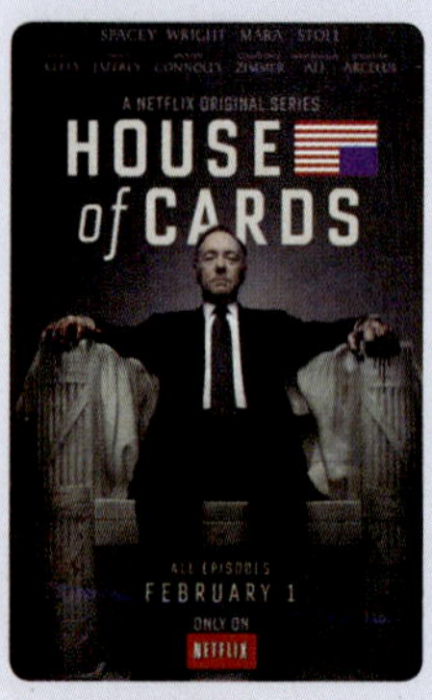

Famous films have been set at the *White House* including *All the President's Men* (1976), *White House Down* (2013) and the recent television series *House of Cards*.

> Lincoln Memorial

The *Washington Monument*, dedicated to President George Washington, is a marble obelisk at the end of the *Lincoln Memorial Reflecting Pool* between the Capitol and the Lincoln Memorial. Tourists can go up in a lift and enjoy a fantastic view of Washington.

Thomas Jefferson Memorial

This circular building was built in honour of *President Jefferson* who was the author of the *Declaration of American Independence* in 1776. The *Memorial* is on the south side of the *Tidal Basin* and houses a bronze statue of the President. White Ionic columns support the roof and the walls are inscribed with important quotations from the President in which he underlines that changing laws represent changing times. It is fantastic to see the Memorial illuminated by moonlight and its shadow reflected in the water!

> Thomas Jefferson Memorial

DID YOU KNOW?

- President *Abraham Lincoln* was a strong opponent of slavery which he abolished. On 15th of April 1865 Lincoln was assassinated.
- *Martin Luther King Jr.* addresses marchers during his *I have a dream* speech, at the Lincoln Memorial, in Washington, on 28th of August 1963. He was assassinated on 4th of April, 1968.
- In the *Arlington Cemetery* many famous American people are buried including President *John F. Kennedy.*
- The *Pentagon* is the USA's *Department of Defense.*
- The *National Air* and *Space Museum* is one of the most visited in the world. Here you can see the *1903 Wright Flyer* and the *Apollo 11 Command Module Columbia*, the only portion of the Apollo 11 spacecraft to return to Earth. Visitors can touch a lunar rock brought back from the *Apollo 17* mission in 1972.

> Martin Luther King Jr.

ACTIVITIES

ESERCIZI ON LINE www.medusaeditrice.it

1 Say if the following sentences are True (T) or False (F) and correct the false ones.

a. New York is the national capital of the USA. T F
b. Washington is in the District of Columbia. T F
c. Christopher Columbus was a Spanish navigator. T F
d. George Washington was the second American president. T F
e. George Washington was elected in 1789. T F
f. The Capitol isn't a neoclassical building. T F
g. The Lincoln Memorial resembles a Greek temple. T F
h. There is a marble statue of Jefferson inside the Jefferson Memorial. T F
i. The Pentagon is the USA's Department of Defense. T F
j. In the *National Air* and *Space Museum* you can see the "*1903 Wright Flyer*". T F

2 Answer the following questions.

1. What is the national capital of the USA?
2. Where is Washington?
3. What river is it on?
4. What does D.C. mean?
5. Who was George Washington?
6. What is the White House?
7. How many rooms are there?
8. What is the Oval Office?
9. Where does the President hold his outdoor conferences?
10. Where do members of Congress meet?
11. Who was Abraham Lincoln?
12. What did he abolish?
13. Where did Martin Luther King give his "I have a dream" speech?
14. What did President Thomas Jefferson write?
15. What are the other important tourist attractions in the city?

3 Read the text "Welcome to Washington!" and translate each word into Italian.

a. Modern ....
b. Interesting ....
c. Historical ....
d. Through ....
e. Breathe ....
f. Atmosphere ....
g. Governmental ....
h. Speech ....
i. Neoclassical ....
j. Marble ....
k. Guests ....
l. Official ....

ESERCIZI ON LINE www.medusaeditrice.it

4 Read the texts again. Complete the exercise below using the following words: *atmosphere, President, city, Oval Office, buildings, capital, Resolute Desk.*

Washington is the national.................... of the United States of America. The American..............lives in the White House with his family. The .... is the place where he works and his desk is the famous...................... The first American president was George Washington and the .... was named after him. Washington symbolizes America's history due to its important historical.................... but it's also a place with a fashionable................. and the sound of music in the streets.

RISORSE ON-LINE
www.medusaeditrice.it

WELCOME TO NEW YORK!

"New York, New York" is one of the most popular songs in the world! Liza Minnelli, a famous American singer, sings. «...I wanna wake up in the city, that doesn't sleep...». This is the idea that everybody has of this breezy city, that it is full of people at every hour of the day and night!

Why is New York so popular? Why is it the major tourist attraction of the USA?

Let's read!

Even if it is a new town, it is known as a place where people from all over the world can find their own style of life. In fact, since the beginning of its history, New York has been a city that has welcomed masses of immigrants. Furthermore it is the financial and cultural capital of the USA and, thanks to the UN, it is also a diplomatic capital.

A great number of tourists go to New York in every period of the year. There are many things to see and do. It's easy to get around because there are different kinds of public transport such as buses, the subway and taxis, that here in New York are yellow! The avenues and streets are numbered so it's very simple to use the city map! Avenues are usually larger than streets.

The Statue of Liberty

The *Statue of Liberty* or "*Lady Liberty*" is on Liberty Island. She is the symbol of the "*American dream of freedom*". The figure wears a toga and holds a book with the date of the American Independence in her left hand, a torch in her right hand and a crown on her head with seven rays that symbolize the seven seas. However the most dramatic element is a broken chain that lies at her feet.

She seems to talk with all these symbols of justice and to ėveryone who is coming to the USA, a light of hope for a new life. Millions of people saw the statue on first arriving in New York. They traveled by boat and their destination was Ellis Island, in New York Harbour. Ellis Island is the site of the *Immigration Museum*.

DID YOU KNOW?

- Tourists can go up to the crown of the Statue of Liberty and see the spectacular view of the city from the top.
- The statue was designed by *Auguste Bartholdi* and the metal framework inside was created by *Alexander Gustave Eiffel* who was later famous for the Eiffel Tower in Paris. Bartholdi and Eiffel were both French.

The boroughs

There are five boroughs in New York: *Brooklyn, Manhattan, Queens, Richmond* and the *Bronx*. Each of them is different from the other. *Manhattan* is the one where a lot of people work. The famous *Rockefeller Center* is here! It was built by John D. Rockefeller, a very rich businessman, in the 1930s, it is popular and fashionable area with its murals and Art Deco statues including the bronze statue of Atlas, carrying the world, and the statue of Prometheus bringing fire to mankind.

In this area there are a lot of skyscrapers. One of them is the *Empire State Building*. It is 443m high and its spire is illuminated by different colours at night. The lights are chosen to celebrate seasonal and other events.

The Bridges

There are important bridges that connect the boroughs to New York. Two of them are: the *Brooklyn Bridge*, built between 1869 and 1883, is one of the most famous

> Prometheus Statue

> Atlas Statue

GOOD MORNING!

HAVE A NICE DAY!

and magnificent landmarks of New York City and the *Verrazano Bridge* which is a double-decker suspension bridge. Its name comes from the Italian explorer of North America, Giovanni Verrazano.

Tourists can visit many other places in New York: the beautiful *Central Park* with its seasonal colours, the museum and the art galleries and fascinating neighbourhoods like *Chinatown*, *Little Italy* and *Wall Street*, the financial capital of the world. But, of course, they can't miss the shopping opportunities on *Fifth Avenue* where they can find New York's most famous fashion shops such as Bergdorf Goodman, Abercrombie & Fitch, Banana Republic, Gucci, H&M, Michael Kors, Prada, Victoria's Secret and Tiffany & Co. or *Times Square* with its fantastic Macy's Store!

And if they like musicals they can go to Broadway and enjoy great shows and discover if somebody still sings "New York, New York!"

> The Brooklyn Bridge

DID YOU KNOW?

- The famous annual Christmas tree lighting ceremony, which marks the beginning of New York's holiday season, takes place here. An enormous tree, decorated with thousands of lights, is placed in the area behind the *Prometheus Statue*. At the same time, the *Lower Plaza* becomes a popular outdoor ice skating rink.
- *Radio City Musical Hall* is in the *Rockefeller Center*! It is known as the country's leading venue for popular concerts, stage shows, special attractions and media events.
- On June 4, 2002, the *Empire State Building's* spire was lit purple and gold, the royal colors of Elizabeth II, in thanks to the United Kingdom for playing the *Star Spangled Banner* during the *Changing of the Guard* at *Buckingham Palace* on September 12, 2001, a show of support after the terrorist attacks of September 11th.

ACTIVITIES

1 Translate each word into Italian.

a. Subway ....
b. Avenue ....
c. Street ....
d. Torch ....
e. Framework ....
f. Businessman ....
g. Fashionable ....
h. Mankind ....
i. Skyscrapers ....
j. Boroughs ....
k. Store ....

2 Answer the following questions.

1. What color are taxis in New York?
2. Why do you think so many people immigrated to New York?
3. Where is the *Statue of Liberty*?
4. What does it symbolize?
5. Who created the *Statue of Liberty's* framework?
6. How many boroughs are there in New York? Write their names.
7. Do the bridges connect boroughs to New York?
8. Who was *John D. Rockefeller*?
9. What does the *Lower Plaza* become in Winter?
10. What is a famous skyscraper in New York?
11. Who was *Giovanni Verrazano*?
12. What are *Chinatown* and *Little Italy*?
13. What are the most important attractions in New York?
14. What is *Wall Street*?
15. What street is famous for designer clothes in the city?
16. Where can tourists enjoy musicals?

3 Multiple choice.
Complete the sentences with the correct ending.

1. *New York is*.................
a. the capital of the USA.
b. the financial and cultural capital of the USA.

2. *The Statue of Liberty is*.................
a. the statue of a woman.
b. the statue of a queen.

3. *Central Park is*.................
a. a bus station.
b. an urban park.

4. *New York is also called*.................
a. the Big Apple.
b. the Small Apple.

One of New York's most popular nicknames is "*The Big Apple*". Find out the meaning and write it in the space below.

....
....
....
....
....
....

LISTENING ACTIVITY

Listen to the song *New York, New York* and complete the text using the words below:

Link: https://youtu.be/GxAnLJwsxII

News, shoes, today, heart, New York, New York, sleep, king, wake up, blues, it, come on, anywhere, hill, old, heap, list.

Start spreading the ......, I'm leaving ....
I wanna be a part of it ...., ...
These vagabond .... are longing to stray
and step around the ....of it, New York, New York
I wanna......... in the city, that doesn't ....,
to find I'm .... of the hill, top of the heap.
My little town .... are melting away
I'll make a brand new start of ...., in old New York
if I can make it there, I'd make it ....
it's up to you, New York, New York
New York, New York
I wanna wake up, in the city that doesn't sleep,
to find I'm king of the ...., head of the ....
cream of the crop at the top of the ....
My little town blues are melting away
I'll make a brand new start of it, in .... New York
if I can make it there, I'd make it anywhere
........., come through New York, New York.

WALT DISNEY'S LIFE

Walter Elias *Walt* Disney was born in Chicago, Illinois, on the 5th December 1901 and died in Burbank, California, on the 15th December 1966.

He was an American entrepreneur, animator, voice actor and film producer.

Disney introduced several developments in the production of cartoons and he is considered one of the main filmmakers of the 20th century; he was a pioneer of the American animation industry.

He created *Disneyland*, the first, and one of the most famous, theme parks in the world.

Disney created the most famous cartoon characters.

In 1928 Walt developed the character *Mickey Mouse*, his first popular success, and provided the voice for his creation.

Walt is as famous as his *mouse* but we know very little about his private life. He never had the child he wanted so much so his wife decided to adopt two daughters.

He was often accused of anti-Semitism: in 1938 he met the German director and Nazi propagandist Leni Riefenstahl in Hollywood in order to promote his film *Olympia*.

Disney was also accused of racism.

When he died, the future President of the USA, *Ronald Reagan,* the governor of California at the time, said: "From now on the world is poorer".

DID YOU KNOW?

- *Mickey Mouse*, a funny animal cartoon character, was created in 1928. He is considered Walt Disney's *alter ego*. Mickey always wears red shorts, large yellow shoes and white gloves. He usually appears alongside his girlfriend *Minnie Mouse*, his pet dog *Pluto* and his friend *Goofy*.
- *"Minnie" Mouse* is a funny animal cartoon character, too. She was created by Walt Disney in 1928, as was Mickey Mouse. Her full name was *Minerva "Minnie" Mouse*; she is presented as the girlfriend of Mickey Mouse, a close friend of *Daisy Duck* and a friend to *Clarabelle Cow*.
- The cartoon character *Donald Duck* was created in 1934. He is a white duck with a yellow orange beak, legs and feet. He usually wears a sailor shirt and cap with a bow tie. He is one of Mickey Mouse's best friends.

ACTIVITIES

1 Translate each word into Italian.

a. Entrepreneur ....
b. Film Producer ....
c. Cartoon ....
d. Filmmaker ....
e. Pioneer ....
f. Animation industry ....
g. Theme park ....
h. Private life ....
i. To adopt ....
j. Director ....
k. Racism ....
l. Governor ....

2 Say if the following sentences are True (T) or False (F). Correct the false ones.

a. Walt Disney was born in California. T F
b. He was a film producer. T F
c. He was the pioneer of the English animation industry. T F
d. He created Disneyland, a famous theme park. T F
e. In 1928, he created the character Minnie. T F
f. His wife decided to adopt two sons. T F
g. He was accused of anti-Semitism and racism. T F
h. Mickey Mouse was created in 1928. T F
i. Minnie's full name was Diana "Minnie" Mouse. T F
j. Donald Duck wears a sailor shirt. T F

3 Answer the following questions.

1. Where and when was *Walt Disney* born?
2. How is he considered?
3. What is *Disneyland*?
4. When did he develop the character *Mickey Mouse*?
5. Who did he receive in Hollywood?
6. What did *Ronald Reagan* say when Walt Disney died?
7. How many children did Walt Disney have?
8. What does *Mickey Mouse* wear?
9. What was *Minnie's* full name?
10. When was *Donald Duck* created?

4 Fill in each blank using the following words: *entrepreneur – film producer – theme parks – Mickey Mouse – daughters - anti-semitism – racism – governor – alter ego – full name – Donald Duck – filmmakers.*

Walt Disney was an American ____________, animator, voice actor and ____ _________.
He is considered one of the main _________ of the 20th century.
He created Disneyland, the first and one of the most famous _____ ____.
In 1928, Walt developed the character ______ _____, his first popular success.
He never had the son he wanted so much, so his wife decided to adopt two _________.
He was often accused of ____________: in 1938 he received the German director and Nazi propagandist Leni Riefenstahl in Hollywood in order to promote his film *Olympia*.
Disney was also accused of ______.
When he died, the ________ of California, Ronald Reagan said *"From now on the world is poorer"*. Mickey Mouse is considered Walt Disney's _____ ___.
Minnie's ____ ____ was Minerva "Minnie" Mouse.
______ ____ wears a sailor shirt and cap with a bow tie.

READING COMPREHENSION

London parks

London is a conurbation of about 7 million inhabitants. It has a lot of monuments but it's also a very green city, too, as there are about 4,000 hectares of green areas and trees. In fact there are a lot of parks that were originally Royal parks: *Green Park, Greenwich Park, Hyde Park, Kensington Gardens, Kew Gardens, Regent's Park, Richmond Park* and *St. James's Park.*

Hyde Park is the favourite park of Londoners who go there in their spare time in order to swim, fish and canoe in a lake called the Serpentine and also for horse riding, cycling, playing tennis or listening to concerts. Moreover there are a lot of meadows where people can sunbathe on a deckchair or have a picnic.

A typical aspect of *Hyde Park* is *Speakers' corner,* which is a corner of the park where people can stand on a wooden box and speak directly to the public and debate a topic of their choice.

The park dates back to *Henry VIII* but *Charles I* transformed it into a public park in 1637.

In *Greenwich Park* there's the *Old Royal Observatory,* one of the most popular monuments in London where you can see

the *Prime Meridian Line*. In this park people can also play tennis, golf, rugby, cricket and hockey. *Greenwich Park* is a *Unesco World heritage site*.

If you go to *Regent's Park* you will have the possibility to visit *London Zoo*, play sport or, from May to September, go to an open air theatre. In August children can also see a puppets' show.

The largest park in London is *Richmond Park*, which was once a hunting ground during Charles's reign. Here people can listen to music, play golf, go sailing or ride a bike, but as it's a *National Nature Reserve* it's possible to see deer roaming freely in the park or other animals such as squirrels, rabbits, snakes and woodpeckers.

Kew Gardens are popular for the collection of gardens, flowers and greenhouses. In fact you can see the wonderful *Royal Botanic Gardens* that became a *Unesco World heritage* site in 2003.

1 Complete the following grid.

PARK	TYPICAL ASPECT
....	It's a nature reserve where animals roam freely.
....	There are gardens, flowers and greenhouses.
Greenwich Park	....
Regent's Park	....
....	It's Londoners favourite park.

2 Read the text and answer the following questions.

1. How many parks are there in London?
2. Write the names of the London Parks.
3. What's the *Serpentine*?
4. Where is it?
5. Why do Londoners prefer *Hyde Park*?
6. What's *Speakers' Corner*?
7. What was *Hyde Park* originally?
8. Who transformed it into a public park?
9. Where is the old *Royal Observatory*?
10. Why is it important?
11. When can children see a puppets' show?
12. Which parks are a *Unesco World heritage site*?
13. Are there any parks in your city?

LISTENING ACTIVITY

Listen to *Hey London* song by Chiddy Bang and complete the text with the words in the box.

Link: http://bit.ly/2fSQagN

London City	Queen
Shakespeare's Globe	Beatles
London Eye	Heathrow
Big Ben	Chiddy Bang

Yeah, uh, yeah
We finally made it, celebration in order, happy belated
this what you waiting for, you know we make it raw .... we love you, that's who we made it for
in my heart you will remain
hope that this trip makes for picturesque change
and we on a jet mayne, platinum dreams gladly go
this that .... feel, remember Abbey Road?
Show out with the words, what an antic?
And we got the Wi-fi, Virgin Atlantic
turbulence can't disrupt my pen
and I swear it's my time, say what up ....
I'm a up this trend and live it up as a teen
to go to the palace to say "what up" to the ....
hit up Westwood, do interviews prolly take calls
University of Cambridge, May Ball
get your ticket ready, it's .... in London
they can never bring me down I'm always up to somethin' contrary to your beliefs I'm still the same dude
only difference is the pilot talkin' plane food.
Hey London
I know you've prob'ly never seen me before
and though I'd love to stay and kick it some more
I gotta get back on my tour
so the only thing I gotta say is
hey London
you gotta know I love you for sure
just let me in could you opened the door?
if I gotta get back on my tour
the only thing I gotta say is
And the boss is on
we head now say "what up" when we across the pond
Yeezy said Jesus Walks, my cross is on
dream of a residence that's heaven-sent, to loft upon
less serious raps, I'm what you call a clown
I'm the raft if ever your bridge fallin' down
drive on opposite I take those roads,
I play right
I'll prolly take her to ....
if the world get cold then we be numb to the reality
I break life into pieces, let's hit the gallery
my, you're platinum baby you're not sterling
rollercoaster ride, ..., Merlin
from you they tried to block me like Berlin
and this that silk flow I bring to you, Persian
uh, my jeans stitched like Lilo
and by the way, meet me at ....
Hey London

STEP BY STEP

How to build up a dialogue

All'Esame di Stato la prova scritta di lingua inglese potrebbe essere un dialogo su traccia.
Ecco le regole da seguire che ti aiuteranno a svolgerla.

- Leggi bene la traccia e i punti da sviluppare.
- Cerca di comprendere la situazione, chi parla e pensa alle funzioni comunicative che si potrebbero usare in quel contesto.
- Stai attento agli errori di grammatica e di ortografia. Fai attenzione all'uso dei tempi verbali: normalmente nelle risposte occorre utilizzare lo stesso tempo delle domande.
- Fai attenzione alle parole interrogative perché le risposte devono essere corrispondenti alle Wh-questions usate.
- Quando hai terminato, ricontrolla tutto prima di consegnare l'elaborato.

OPEN - DIALOGUE

Complete the following open-dialogue.

David is asking a policeman the way to the National Gallery in London.

David: Excuse me! Good morning sir! Can I ask you for some information?

Policeman: ....

David: .... please?

Policeman: You can go by bus, by underground or you can walk there.

David: ....?

Policeman: It's twenty minutes from here to the National Gallery in Trafalgar Square.

David: ....?

Policeman: The nearest underground stations are Charing Cross and Leicester Square.

David: ....?

Policeman: Go along this road, turn on the ....The station is .... the cinema and the stationer's.

David: ....

Policeman: ....

WRITING A DIALOGUE

You want to go to Scotland next Summer. Write a dialogue between the clerk of the Tourist Information Office and you. Follow these points:

- it's your first time in Scotland;
- you would like to rent a two-bedroom house for you and your sister;
- you'd prefer a house in Edinburgh;
- ask how much the rent is;
- don't forget to say what period you're going there;
- ask how you can go to Loch Ness and how far it is;
- ask for some information about Edinburgh monuments;
- don't forget to ask about the weather.

TRINITY GRADE 3

CEFR level A2.1

Total exam time: 7 minutes.

Conversation

Examiner:

- Good morning!
- What's your name?
- How old are you?
- What's the weather like today?
- What was the weather like yesterday?
- What do you do when it's hot and sunny?
- Do your parents drive?
- Do you like bike cycling?
- Have you got a computer?
- Is it a laptop?
- When do you use your computer?
- What's your e-mail address?

Look at the picture!

Examiner:

- What season is this?
- What's the weather like in these pictures?
- Where are they?
- What are they doing?
- How many people are there?
- What are they wearing?
- Are there any animals?
- Are there mountains?

Examiner: OK. Thanks a lot. Bye

You: Goodbye.

CHAPTER 04

THE POLITICAL SYSTEM

DIALOGUE

At Westminster

David: Giovanni, come and see the *Palace of Westminster*, the seat of the British Parliament. It was built in 1840 by Sir Charles Barry and Augustus Pugin.

Giovanni: It is a very old and famous building, isn't it?

David: Yes, the clock tower *Big Ben* is very famous, too. It was planned by Benjamin Hall, a famous architect. The UK is a constitutional monarchy and it is one of the oldest in Europe.

Giovanni: The monarch is a part of Parliament but he/she has no real power.

David: Yes, but he/she is not only the Head of State, he/she is also the Head of the Church of England since *King Henry VIII* separated the Church of England from the Roman Catholic Church.

Giovanni: The Commons have got real power. The MPs make laws. I'd like to be elected to the *House of Commons* as a member of Parliament.

David: Well, I'd like to be a member of the *House of Lords.*

Giovanni: Oh! Nice to meet you Lord David Duran!

David: Nice to meet you Giovanni Rossi MP!

EXERCISE

1 Answer the following questions.

1. What is the seat of the British Parliament?
2. When was it built?
3. Who built the Palace of Westminster?
4. Who planned the clock tower?
5. What kind of monarchy is the UK?
6. What did King Henry VIII do?
7. What do the Commons make?
8. What would Giovanni like to be?
9. What would David like to be?
10. Would you like to live in the UK?

THE BRITISH PARLIAMENT AND GOVERNMENT

The *United Kingdom* or UK is a constitutional monarchy but a parliamentary democracy, too: the *Head of State* is the monarch who reigns but does not rule. Parliament is the real government. It is made up of three parts: the *Queen*, the *House of Commons* and the *House of Lords*.

The seat of the *British Parliament* is the *Palace of Westminster* in London with its popular clock tower, *Big Ben*. It's on the bank of the *River Thames*.

The Queen

The present sovereign of the UK is *Queen Elizabeth II*. The Queen is the *Head of State* but she has no real power. She appoints the Prime Minister and opens and closes Parliament. Moreover she is the Head of the Armed Forces and of the Church of England. She lives in *Buckingham Palace* in London.

The House of Commons

The *House of Commons* has 650 members called *Members of Parliament* or MPs elected by people who are over 18. The president of this house is the *Speaker*.

The House of Commons makes laws. The chamber where it meets is green.

The House of Lords

The *House of Lords* has 826 members called *Peers*. Most of them are not elected by the people but are hereditary members such as the bishops of the Church of England who are *Lords Spiritual* and nobles who are *Lords Temporal*. The president of this house is the *Lord Speaker*.

The House of Lords checks and passes laws. It also controls the activities of the Government. The chamber where it meets is red. When the two Houses come to an agreement the bill becomes State law after it is sent to the Queen who signs it and gives her Royal Assent.

Government

The *Head of Government* is the *Prime Minister* who is appointed by the Queen. He is the leader of the majority party that has won the elections. The general elections in the UK take place every five years.

He or she chooses a Cabinet of twenty ministers to form the government.

The Prime Minister lives and works at *Number 10 Downing Street* in London.

The present Prime Minister is *Theresa May*, leader of the Conservative Party.

Political parties

There are two main political parties in the UK: the *Labour party* that represents the left-wing and the *Conservative party* that represents the right-wing.

In 1988 another party was born, the *Liberal Democrats* which is centrist. This is the smallest party and has never won an election.

ACTIVITIES

ESERCIZI ON LINE www.medusaeditrice.it

1 **Tick the corretct answer.**

1. *The UK is*
a. a federation of states
b. a republic
c. a constitutional monarchy

2. *The Head of State is*
a. the Prime Minister
b. the Queen
c. the President of the Republic

3. *The Queen*
a. appoints the Prime Minister
b. doesn't sign bills
c. makes laws

4. *The British Parliament is made up of*
a. three houses
b. two houses and the sovereign
c. a cabinet

5. *The Prime Minister is*
a. the Head of Government
b. the Head of State
c. the Head of Parliament

6. *In the UK there are*
a. two political parties
b. two political parties and a group of democrats
c. three political parties

2 **Complete the following grid.**

Parts of Parliament		**Task**		**Residence**	
The Queen Name:..........		....		....	
Parts of Parliament	**Task**	**Members**	**President**	**Residence**	**Colour of the chamber**
House of Commons	....	Name: .... Number:	....	....	....
House of Lords	....	Name: .... Number:	....	....	....
Government		**Task**		**Residence**	
The Prime Minister		....		....	

3 **Answer the following questions.**

1. What's the seat of the British Parliament?
2. Where is it?
3. Who opens and closes parliamentary sessions?
4. Who is the Speaker?
5. Why aren't Peers elected by the people?
6. When does a bill become a State law?
7. Who appoints the Prime Minister?
8. When do the British elections take place?
9. What are the political parties in the UK?

10 DOWNING STREET

Downing Street is a famous street in the centre of London.

It takes its name from *Sir George Downing*, a soldier and a diplomat who served under the government of Oliver Cromwell and under the reign of Charles II of England.

The most important address of Downing Street is *Number 10*. It is the headquarters of Her Majesty's Government and the official residence and office of the First Lord of the Treasury that is the Prime Minister.

The current Prime Minister is Theresa May, the so called Ice Queen, the second woman in the history of the UK to lead the British government after Margaret Thatcher.

Number 10 Downing Street is located along *Whitehall*, in the city of Westminster, near Buckingham Palace, the London residence of the sovereign, and the Palace of Westminster, the seat of the two houses of Parliament.

DID YOU KNOW?

- The construction of *10 Downing Street* started in 1682 and was completed in 1684.
- It contains one hundred rooms.
- George II offered Number 10 to Sir Robert Walpole in 1732. Walpole accepted on the condition that it was the office of the First Lord of the Treasury.
- *10 Downing Street* has been the residence and the office of the Prime Minister since 1732.
- In 1985, *Margaret Thatcher*, the *Iron Lady*, said *Number 10* had become *one of the most precious jewels in the national heritage*.

GOOD MORNING!

HAVE A NICE DAY!

ACTIVITIES

1 Match the words.

a. Address	1. Regina di ghiaccio
b. Entitled	2. Soldato
c. Headquarters	3. Che guida
d. Ice Queen	4. Sede
e. Leading	5. Sovrano
f. Residence	6. Strada
g. Seat	7. Intitolata
h. Soldier	8. Quartier generale
i. Sovereign	9. Residenza
j. Street	10. Indirizzo

2 Answer the following questions.

1. Who is Downing Street named after?
2. Who was Sir George Downing?
3. What is Number 10 Downing Street?
4. Who is the current British Prime Minister?
5. Where is Number 10 located?
6. How many rooms are there in Number 10?
7. How long has 10 Downing Street been the residence of the Prime Minister?

3 Now use the answers to write a summary in the copybook.

4 You are in London, walking along *Whitehall*. Complete the drawing below and colour it in.

THE POLITICAL SYSTEM IN THE USA

The United States of America is a *Presidential Republic*, in fact the President is Head of State and the Head of Government. He is also the Commander-In-Chief of the armed forces. People elect him every four years and he can be re-elected only once.

The government of the USA is based on a written Constitution that defines the federal system as the country has both central and local government. The division of power means that states have a self-government for taxes, schools and police but the rules of the central government, based in Washington, can control and modify local laws.

The interpretation of the American Constitution has changed over time, that's why it is considered a *living document*. It includes: a *Preamble, seven Articles* and *23 Amendments*. According to the Constitution, there are three separate branches of government and each of them has its own power and area of influence. Let's see!

The Legislative Power

The *Legislative Power* is represented by the *American Congress*. Through debates and votes it makes federal laws that become effective after the President's approval.
It is divided into two houses: the *Senate* and the *House of Representatives*.

DID YOU KNOW?

The President's election is an important event! American people take part in the electoral campaign by organizing parades, concerts and creating gadgets.

Senate

- The Vice President of the USA presides.
- The Senators are 100, two Senators represent each State.
- They are elected every six years.

House of Representatives

- The Speaker presides.
- There are 435 Members.
- They are elected every two years.

The Executive Power

The President of the USA embodies the *Executive Power*, he enforces and administers the laws and government. In times of emergency and in foreign affairs he can act on his own.

The Judicial Power

The Supreme Court and the federal courts represent the *Judicial Power*. They interpret and apply American laws.

The Parties

In the USA the two main political parties are: the *Democratic Party* and the *Republican Party*. The Democratic Party is considered the centre-left and its symbol is an elephant. The Republican Party is considered the centre-right and its symbol is a donkey.

> **Donald Trump is the 30th Republican President of the USA.**

The sentences *Justice the Guardian of Liberty* and *Equal Justice Under Law* are written on the front of the Supreme Court Building.

ACTIVITIES

ESERCIZI ON LINE www.medusaeditrice.it

1 **Read the text "The political System in the USA" and translate the following words into Italian.**

a. Republic ....

b. Election ....

c. Electoral campaign ....

d. Power ....

e. Preamble ....

f. Articles ....

g. Amendments ....

h. Branches ....

i. Legislative ....

j. Executive ....

k. Judicial ....

l. Law ....

m. Party ....

n. Democratic ....

o. Front ....

2 **Read the texts and then answer the following questions.**

1. What is the American form of government?
2. What is the USA's government based on?
3. What is a federal system?
4. What does the American Constitution consist of?
5. How many branches of government does the Constitution include?
6. How is the Congress divided?
7. What are the major parties in the USA?
8. What does the American President embody?
9. Is the President the Commander-In-Chief of the armed forces?
10. Which party is the centre-right?
11. Which party is the centre-left?
12. Does Donald Trump come from the Democratic Party?
13. Where is the residence of the Supreme Court?

3 **Translate the sentence: "Equal Justice Under Law". Are there similar sentences in the Italian Courts? Find out and then write them in your copy book.**

4 **Reflecting on the text that you have read, write a short summary about the Italian governmental system. Find and glue images of the Italian political residences into your exercise book.**

READING COMPREHENSION

The Oval Office

The *Oval Office* is the official study and workspace of the President of the USA. Here, the American President confers with Heads of State, diplomats and his staff.

The Oval Office is situated in the West Wing of the White House. The *office* has an elliptical shape, three large windows behind the *Resolute Desk* and a chimney in the north of the room.

The Oval Office has four doors: the door in the east leads into the garden of roses of the White House; the door in the west leads into a smaller private study; the door in the north east leads into the main corridor of the West Wing and the door in the north West leads into the office of the President's secretary.

The *Resolute Desk* is considered the President's desk because many Presidents have used it in the Oval Office. The famous *desk* was made from the wood of the ship *HMS Resolute*. In 1880, Queen Victoria of England gave the wood of the ship to President Rutherford Hayes.

ACTIVITIES

1 Complete with the words in the box.

Resolute Desk	President
Oval Office	Wood of the ship

----

2 Answer the following questions.

1. What is the Oval Office?
2. What does the President generally do in the Oval Office?
3. Where is it located?
4. What is the shape of the Oval Office?
5. What is there behind the Resolute Desk?
6. What is the Resolute Desk?
7. Who gave the wood of the ship to President Rutherford Hayes?
8. How many doors are there in the Oval Office?
9. Where are the doors?
10. What is there in the north of the room?

READING COMPREHENSION

The Commonwealth of Nations

The Commonwealth is an association of 53 countries that were part of the British Empire whose extension arrived to all five continents in the 19th century under Queen Victoria.

Then in the 20th century and after the World War I many of colonies obtained independence. However theses ex-British colonies decided to maintain a connection with Britain and formed a free association whose official language is English.

The Queen is the Head of the Commonwealth and is also the Head of State of 16 of the countries that belong to the association including Canada, Australia and New Zealand. In the countries where the Queen is Head of State, she is represented by a Governor General. The remaining countries either have their own republic, such as Cyprus and Malta, or their own monarchy, such as Malaysia and Tonga. Some countries, like Mozambique and Rwanda, chose to be part of the Commonwealth even if they weren't ex-colonies of Britain.

The main aims of the Commonwealth are to promote social development and human rights. Other important objectives are cultural, economic and international cooperation and to help people of different cultures in areas such as agriculture, the environment, health, law and education. It was founded as the British Commonwealth in 1926 and as the modern Commonwealth in 1949. Its headquarters are in London where the Secretary General is located.

There is also a flag of the Commonwealth: it is a yellow globe on a blue background.

The Commonwealth of Nations also organises an important sporting event that unites all member states every four years. The *Commonwealth Games* are similar to the Olympic Games and amongst the various events are two famous British sports, rugby and cricket.

ACTIVITIES

1 Read the text and answer the following questions.

1. How many countries are there in the Commonwealth?
2. What is the Commonwealth of Nations?
3. What is the official language of the Commonwealth countries?
4. Who is the Head of the Commonwealth?

5. Who represents the Queen in 16 countries of the Commonwealth?
6. What are the aims of this association?
7. When was it founded?
8. Where are the headquarters of the Commonwealth?
9. Describe the flag of the Commonwealth of Nations.
10. Which countries were not ex-colonies of Britain?
11. What is the Commonwealth's main sport event?
12. When does it take place?

2 Complete the grid by placing the Commonwealth countries in the correct box.

America	Africa	Asia	Europe	Oceania

The population of the Commonwealth is about two billion and covers an area of 12.1 million square miles. *India*, *Pakistan*, *Bangladesh* and *Nigeria* are the largest nations of the Commonwealth by population.

LISTENING ACTIVITY

Listen to "God Save the Queen", the British National anthem that was played for the first time on 28th September 1745 in London and complete the text with the missing words.

http://bit.ly/19xBzmz

GOD SAVE THE QUEEN
(The British national anthem)

1.
.... save our gracious Queen,
Long live our noble Queen,
God save the ....!
Send her victorious,
Happy and glorious,
Long to .... over us;
God save the Queen!

2.
O Lord our God, arise,
Scatter her enemies
And make them fall;
Confound their................,
Frustrate their knavish tricks,
On Thee our hopes we fix,
Oh, save us all!

3.
Thy choichest gifts in store
On her be pleased to pour;
Long may she reign;
May she defend our ....,
And ever give us cause
To sing with .... and voice,
God save the Queen!

DIO SALVI LA REGINA
(Inno nazionale britannico)

1.
Dio salvi la nostra graziosa Regina,
lunga vita alla nostra nobile Regina,
Dio salvi la Regina!
Donale la vittoria,
la felicità e la gloria,
possa regnare a lungo su di noi;
Dio salvi la Regina!

2.
O Signore, nostro Dio, sorgi,
disperdi i suoi nemici
e falli cadere;
confondi i loro intrighi,
frustra le loro manovre disoneste,
su di te sono riposte le nostre speranze,
oh, salvaci tutti!

3.
I regali più preziosi che conservi,
sii disposto a riversarli su di lei;
possa regnare a lungo;
possa difendere le nostre leggi
e sempre darci l'occasione
di cantare col cuore e con la voce,
"Dio salvi la Regina!"

OPEN - DIALOGUE

1. Complete the following open-dialogue.

Oliver has just arrived in Cardiff from London. Now he is going to the Tourist Information Office to find somewhere to stay for the night.

Oliver: ....

Assistant: Good morning! Can I....... you?

Oliver: Yes, ... I'd like to book a .... in a bed and breakfast for ....

Assistant: How .... do you want to ....?

Oliver: Well, between 20 and 30 ....

Assistant: Ok! Let's see, do you want a double or a ....?

Oliver: A single, please!

Assistant: That's all right! There's a single room at the Welsh Guest House bed and breakfast in Cathedral Road not far from the City centre. .... 25 pounds a ....What's ...., ...?

Oliver: Fine, ... Smith. Thank ....! Bye!

Assistant: ....

BUILDING UP A DIALOGUE

1. You are in a restaurant with your friend Mark. Write a dialogue between the waiter, Mark and you. Follow these points:

- the waiter greets you and asks what you'd like to eat;
- you and Mark respond to the greeting and order a hamburger for you and fish for Mark;
- the waiter asks you if you want salad or chips;
- Mark wants some chips and you a salad
- he asks for the dessert;
- answer you don't want the dessert and thank him;
- he asks for drinks;
- you want a coke and Mark a sprite;
- after your lunch ask for the bill;
- pay, take your change and say good bye.

STEP BY STEP

How to write a letter

All'Esame di Stato la prova scritta di lingua inglese potrebbe essere la produzione di una lettera.

Ecco le regole che ti aiuteranno a svolgerla.

- Leggi bene la traccia e i punti da sviluppare.
- Stai attento agli errori di grammatica e di ortografia. Fai attenzione all'uso dei tempi verbali: si usa il *past simple* per parlare di un evento passato e il futuro per un evento che deve ancora accadere, negli altri casi puoi usare il *present simple*.
- All'inizio della lettera ringrazia per una lettera, una telefonata, una foto o un regalo ricevuti.
- Alla fine spiega il motivo per cui termini la lettera.
- Una lettera è formata da sei parti: *indirizzo*, *data*, *saluti iniziali*, *messaggio*, *saluti finali* e *firma*. Controlla di averli inseriti tutti e al posto giusto.
- Quando hai terminato, ricontrolla se hai sviluppato tutti i punti della traccia e il layout della lettera prima di consegnare l'elaborato.

WRITING A LETTER

1. Leggi la lettera di Kate alla sua amica di penna alla pagina seguente e osserva le parti che la formano.

2. Write a letter to a pen-friend and include:

1. your name;
2. your age;
3. your school year and the type of school;
4. your nationality and where you live;
5. the colour of your hair and eyes and your personality;
6. your parents' jobs;
7. inform your friend if you have any brothers or sisters and their age or if you're an only child;
8. your likes and dislikes;
9. your possessions;
10. ask some questions.

Kate Bercow 11, Liverpool Street EC2 London	**Sender's address (indirizzo del mittente)** Si scrive in alto a destra. Quando si scrive l'indirizzo in inglese, si mette prima il numero civico, poi il nome della strada e infine street per via, avenue per viale oppure road per strada.
21st July, 2016	**Date (la data)** Si scrive in alto a destra sotto l'indirizzo. La data in inglese si scrive con i numeri ordinali, il mese e l'anno. In americano si scrive prima il mese e poi il giorno
Dear Robert,	**An opening greeting (saluto iniziale)** Si scrive all'inizio del messaggio, sul lato sinistro sotto la data.
Thanks for your letter. I received it last week. I'm very happy to have a pen-friend. I'm thirteen and I'm in Year 8 of Secondary School. My father is a lawyer and my mother is a fashion designer. I've got a brother, Joe. He's 8. I've got blond hair and brown eyes, I'm friendly and talkative but I'm stubborn. I've got a black and grey dog. His name's Falcon. I love him. Have you got a pet? I like rugby and rock music, and you? Now it's dinnertime, my mum is calling me. Bye for now. Write soon!.	**Body of the letter (corpo della lettera)** Contiene il messaggio e si scrive sotto i saluti iniziali.
Yours,*	**A closing salutation (saluti finali)** Si scrivono in basso a destra sotto il messaggio nella lettera inglese, a sinistra in quella americana.
Kate	**Signature (firma)** Si scrive in basso a destra sotto i saluti finali, a sinistra in quella americana.

*Si possono usare anche altri saluti finali come: yours faithfully, with love, love and kisses, best wishes, from.

TRINITY GESE GRADE 3

CEFR level A2.1

Total exam time: 7 minutes.

Conversation

Examiner:

- Good morning!
- What's your name?
- Where do you live?
- Do you live in a house or a flat?
- How many rooms are there in your home?
- What's your favourite room? Why?
- Is your school far from home?
- Are there any shops nearby?
- What kind of shops are there?
- What do you buy there?
- What can you see from your bedroom window?

Look at this picture!

Examiner:

- How many shops are there?
- What are they?
- Where are the girls?
- What are they doing?
- What is the old man doing?
- What colour is his jacket?
- Where is the woman with the child?
- What is the child doing?
- Where is the florist's?
- Is there a man with a dog?
- Can you see any boys? How many?

Examiner: OK. Thanks a lot. Bye

You: Thanks. Goodbye.

CHAPTER 05

BRITISH AND AMERICAN HISTORY

DIALOGUE

I love History

Mary: Hi, Ted!

Ted: Hi, Mary!

Mary: How is school?

Ted: Very good.

Mary: What's your favourite subject, Ted?

Ted: I love studying History. It's one of my favourite subjects. In particular, I love British History.

Mary: I agree with you. British History is very interesting and rich in events and famous characters. What historical period do you like?

Ted: I like the *Victorian Age*. It was a period of progress, expansion and social reforms. A time of great industrial development and scientific and technological progress.

Mary: I love the Victorian Age, too. I love reading Victorian novels because they are the mirror of Victorian society. My favourite writer is *Charles Dickens*, a great critic of the society of his time. He attacked the hypocrisy of the people that ruled the country and denounced the exploitation of children. I think his best novel is *Oliver Twist*.

Ted: I prefer reading *Rudyard Kipling*'s novels. I love the animals of *The Jungle Book*.

Mary: OK, Ted. It's time to go back home. See you tomorrow.

Ted: See you, Mary.

EXERCISE

1 Answer the following questions.

1. Is Mary a good student?
2. What subject does Ted love studying?
3. What historical period does Ted like?
4. Why is the Victorian Age interesting?
5. Why does Mary love reading Victorian novels?
6. Who is Mary's favourite writer?
7. What did he denounce in his novels?
8. What is Dickens's best novel in Mary's opinion?
9. What does Ted like reading?

FROM THE CELTS TO THE NORMANS

> Stonehenge

First the Celts

The *Celts* were among the first inhabitants to arrive in Britain around the year 600 B.C. (Before Christ). They came from the centre of Europe, lived in tribes and were warriors, farmers and shepherds. Druidism was their religion and their priests were called *Druids* and were famous for their magic arts. *Stonehenge* with its great circles of stones, was probably a religious place used by Druids. It was probably built 5,000 years ago. Their language, Gaelic, is still spoken in Scotland and Wales today.

...then the Romans

The *Romans* invaded Britain in 55 B.C. led by *Julius Caesar* but they conquered it in 43 A.D. (after Christ) under *Emperor Claudius*. They brought their civilization and built a lot of roads and towns such as *Colchester*, *Chester* and *Winchester* for military purposes. *Chester* derives from the Latin word *castra* that means *military camp*.

They were farmers but also merchants so they built other towns for commercial purposes such as Londinium, an important centre of communication and port, *York* and *Bath* with its Roman thermal baths.

In 122 A.D. *Emperor Hadrian* built a huge wall, called *Hadrian's Wall*, between Scotland and England to defend the frontier

> Hadrian's Wall

> Roman thermal baths

> Anglo-Saxon helmet

from the attack of Picts and Scots who lived in the North of Britain.

> Anglo-Saxon writing

The Anglo-Saxons after the Romans

After the Romans left Britain to defend the Roman Empire from the attacks of the German tribes in 410 A. D., some peoples from central Europe invaded the island. Among them there were the *Angles* and the *Saxons*, strong warriors, hunters and farmers. They lived in villages and grew cabbages, onions and corn.

Later they united and became the Anglo-Saxons. The first Anglo-Saxon king was *Edward the Confessor*. They conquered most of Britain and divided the country into 7 kingdoms.

> Bayeux Tapestry

The part in the South of Britain was *Angleland* from which derives the word England, the land of the Angles.
Old English was born from the West-Saxon dialect.

Finally the Normans

In 1066 the *Normans* led by *William the Conqueror*, Duke of Normandy, from France arrived in Britain. They defeated the Saxon King Harold at the *Battle of Hastings* and conquered England. William became king and introduced feudalism, the French language and culture in the new land.
The Normans built castles and cathedrals such as the *Tower of London,* which is an old Norman fortress, and a prison where eight ravens have lived since the Norman conquest. A legend says that "*if the ravens go away from the Tower, the British monarchy will come to an end*".

DID YOU KNOW?

- There are thirty-eight guards at the *Tower of London* and they are called *Beefeaters*, probably because they used to eat beef that was a part of their salary. Their uniform is black and red and goes back to the Tudor period.
- *Edward the Confessor* is a Saint. His tomb is on the altar in Westminster Abbey.
- *King Arthur* and the *Knights of the Round Table* were the legendary heroes of the Anglo-Saxon period. Arthur was King of Albion in the year 600 and his castle was, according to the legend, at Tintagel in Cornwall. The legend says that *Merlin*, the magician put the sword "*Excalibur*" into a stone in order to find the king of England and Arthur extracted it.
- The *Vikings* arrived in Britain from Scandinavia in 789 A.D. Their capital was *York*. Their ships were the strongest and fastest ones of their time.

ACTIVITIES

1 Match the letters with the numbers.

a. hut	1. cipolle
b. straw	2. corvo
c. ground	3. terme
d. cattle	4. bestiame
e. roof	5. capo
f. Druid	6. villaggio
g. onions	7. grano
h. shepherd	8. agricoltore
i. thermal baths	9. pastore
j. raven	10. terreno
k. hunter	11. tetto
l. chief	12. capanna
m. village	13. paglia
n. corn	14. Druido
o. farmer	15. cacciatore

2 Read the text "From the Celts to the Normans" and write T (true) or F (false) near the following sentences. Correct the false ones.

a. The Celts arrived in Britain 500 years B.C. T F
b. Stonehenge was probably a temple. T F
c. Gaelic is a Celtic language. T F
d. The Romans were merchants and farmers. T F
e. Bath is an old Roman military camp. T F
f. The Romans left Britain in 409 A.D. T F
g. The Anglo-Saxons grew vegetables. T F
h. The Old English language derives from the West-Saxon dialect. T F
i. The Normans came from central Europe. T F
j. The Tower of London was a Norman cathedral. T F

ESERCIZI ON LINE www.medusaeditrice.it

3 Complete the text.

The Celts came from .... and arrived in Britain .... They were ....
Their priests were ....
After them.................... conquered Britain in .... They built .... and ....
One of the most important cities they founded was .... , an important .... on the river Thames.
When the Romans left Britain, ... arrived on the island, in .... They were ...., ... and .... After they ...., they divided Britain in ....
The English language derives from ....
Finally in 1066 .... arrived in Britain and conquered it. .... became king and introduced .... and .... in the island. The Normans built .... and .... such as the .... of London.

FROM THE MAGNA CHARTA TO THE INDUSTRIAL REVOLUTION

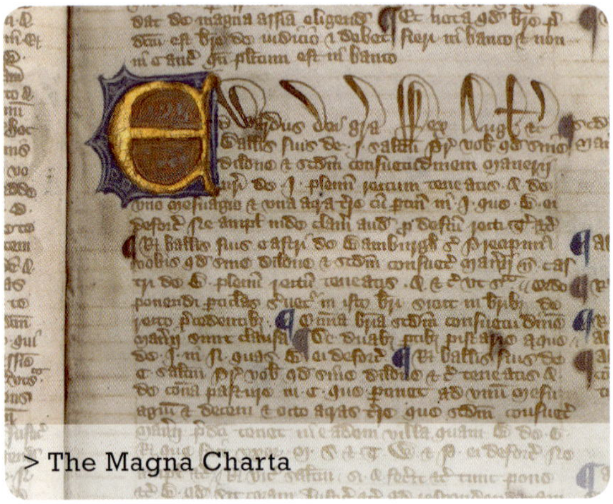
> The Magna Charta

Magna Charta

Richard, nicknamed the *Lionheart* for his great courage, and *John,* nicknamed *Lackland* for the loss of the Norman lands in France, belonged to the Norman dynasty of Plantagenets. The former was always busy fighting in the 3rd Crusade, the latter, Richard's brother, signed the *Magna Charta Libertatum*. During his reign, in 1215, John was forced, by very angry noblemen, to sign this document after he increased taxes and ignored the law. Magna Charta limited the powers of the king and was a step towards democracy.

Robin Hood was the legendary hero who was born in this period. He was an outlaw who lived in Sherwood forest in Nottingham and stole from the rich to help the poor who couldn't pay the taxes imposed by King John. His popular supporters were his friends Friar Tuck and Little John.

The Tudors

The *Tudor* dynasty came to the throne of England after the *War of the Roses* between two families: the *House of York,* whose

>Kevin Kostner as Robin Hood

> Henry VIII

> Invicible Armada

symbol was a white rose, lost the war against the *House of Lancaster*, whose symbol was a red rose. The Tudors ruled England from this moment on.

Henry VIII was king from 1509 to 1547. He was a despotic king but a clever and cultured man who loved music and sport. In 1534 he proclaimed himself *Supreme Head of the Anglican Church* with the *Act of Supremacy* which legalized the separation of England from the Roman Catholic Church when *Pope Clement VII* didn't allow Henry to divorce his first wife *Catherine of Aragon*. He had six wives and three children: *Mary* nicknamed *Bloody Mary*, *Elizabeth I* and *Edward VI*.

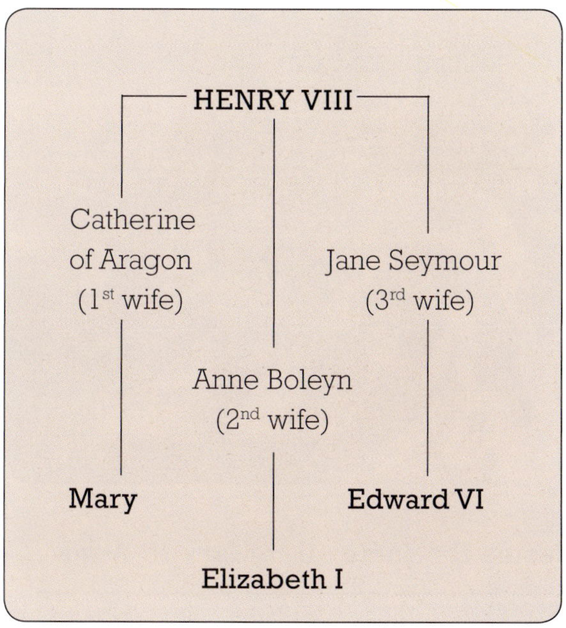

After Henry, his son Edward was king but he died at 15 because he was sick and after him Mary became queen. Elizabeth was the last Tudor monarch. She was a great queen who encouraged pirates such as *Francis Drake* and *Walter Raleigh* to create colonies and to fight against *Philip II of Spain*, her brother-in-law. In 1588 Francis Drake defeated Philip's "*Invicible Armada*". Queen Elizabeth I then proclaimed herself Supreme Governor of the Anglican Church.

The Stuarts

When Elizabeth I died, *James of Scotland*, Mary Stuart's son, became king. James I

united the Crowns of Scotland and England. In this way the British flag was born even if it was adopted two centuries later. His mother was imprisoned in the Tower of London and beheaded by her cousin Elizabeth I for treason. James was an unpopular and an intolerant king. In fact a group of Puritans called the *Pilgrim Fathers* who were protestant, emigrated to America on the *Mayflower*, a large ship, in order to profess their religion freely.

When James died, his son *Charles I* became king. He was beheaded in 1649 after a war broke out in 1642 between the Crown and Parliament. This was the start of a republic known as the *Commonwealth*. Its leader was *Oliver Cromwell*, a general in the army.

The Commonwealth came to an end in 1660, the year of the Restoration, when Parliament decided that a monarch was important for England and *Charles II* became king.

The Industrial Revolution

The *Industrial Revolution* transformed Britain into the first industrial country in the world.

> Oliver Cromwell

The Stuarts: James I — Charles I — Charles II — James II — Mary II — Anna

The main aspect of the revolution was that new machines replaced manual labour. As a consequence a lot of people moved from the country to the town where they worked in factories and mines. The most important inventions were *James Watt's* steam engine and *James Hargreaves'* Spinning Jenny.

The Industrial Revolution changed Britain from a social point of view too: working class people lived in slums in terrible conditions and worked up to 16 hours a day for very low wages. A lot of women and children died because of the hard work and bad living conditions.

In 1830 the first railway line opened: the Liverpool-Manchester line thanks to the invention of *George Stephenson's* steam locomotive.

ACTIVITIES

1 Crossword. Complete.

ACROSS

1. A person who doesn't respect laws.
2. Robin Hood shot it from a bow.
3. A small hat.
4. A place full of trees and grass.
5. An agent of the Sherwood forest.

DOWN

1. Robin Hood used it.
2. A tariff you must pay.
3. A person who has got a lot of money.
4. The opposite of rich.
5. A person who steals.

2 Use different colours, match and find out information about Henry VIII's wives.

Catherine of Aragon (1st wife)

Anne Boleyn (2nd wife)

Jane Seymour (3rd wife)

Anne of Cleves (4th wife)

Catherine Howard (5th wife)

Catherine Parr (6th wife)

- Anne Boleyn was beheaded for treason. Henry and Anne had a daughter, Elizabeth.
- She was repudiated by Henry.
- Henry divorced Catherine. They had a daughter, Mary.
- She was beheaded
- Jane died when she bore her son Edward. She was Henry's favourite wife.
- She survived Henry.

3 **Match the letters with the numbers.**

a. Restoration	**1.** Repubblica
b. Commonwealth	**2.** Guerra civile
c. Civil war	**3.** Restaurazione
d. Puritans	**4.** Padri pellegrini
e. Army	**5.** Intollerante
f. General	**6.** Capo
g. Intolerant	**7.** Decapitato
h. Beheaded	**8.** Generale
i. Leader	**9.** Puritani
j. Pilgrim fathers	**10.** Esercito

4 **Write true (T) or false (F) next to the following sentences. Correct the false ones.**

a. The Industrial Revolution changed the aspect of Britain. T F

b. New machines supported manual labour. T F

c. The working classes worked 8 hours a day. T F

d. Workers didn't earn much money. T F

e. Women and children didn't work. T F

f. People moved from the countryside to the city. T F

5 **Read the text "From the Magna Carta to the Industrial Revolution" and complete the summary with the following words:**

1215 – powers – became – united – negative – worked – country - Charles II – civil – republic – the Commonwealth - Magna Charta – Roses – Church – Cromwell – agricultural – ruled - Roman Catholic Church – monarchy – changed - Anne Boleyn - reign (x 2) - steam engine – industrialized – Watt – Head – six - spinning jenny – lived – proclaimed - Hargreaves

In .... King John Lackland was obliged to sign the ...., a document that limited the .... of the monarch.

After the War of the .... the Tudors .... England. Henry VIII separated the .... of England from the .... and .... himself .... of the Anglican Church. He had .... wives. Under Elizabeth I, the daughter of Henry VIII and .... England became a rich and powerful .... Her .... is called "The Golden Age".

When Elizabeth I died, James I Stuart .... king. Under his reign the Union Jack flag was born because he .... the crowns of England and Scotland.

During Charles I's .... there was .... war and as consequence the .... was born. The leader of the .... was Oliver .... In 1660 .... was restored and .... became king.

The Industrial Revolution .... Britain from an .... country to an .... country thanks to the inventions of new machines like the .... of James .... and the .... by .... This event had .... aspects, too. The working class .... up to 16 hours a day and .... in terrible conditions.

FROM QUEEN VICTORIA TO THE 20th CENTURY

Queen Victoria was queen of Britain from 1837 to 1901. She belonged to the German House of Hanover. Victoria married a German prince, *Albert of Saxony*, and had nine children.

During her reign Britain became a global power with a very large Empire that extended from India to Canada. Factories that were born during the Industrial Revolution needed rubber, cotton, tea, sugar and cocoa that were found in Africa, Asia and Latin America. Moreover in England nationalism and the idea that a western country had to civilize an underdeveloped one were very strong.

The Prime Minister under Victoria was *Disraeli* who worked to extend British colonial dominions. In fact in 1876 Queen Victoria became *Empress of India*.

When Victoria died Britain was the richest country in the world. It was highly industrialized thanks to new inventions such as the railway, the steamship and the telegraph. But there were a lot of poor people and much social injustice.

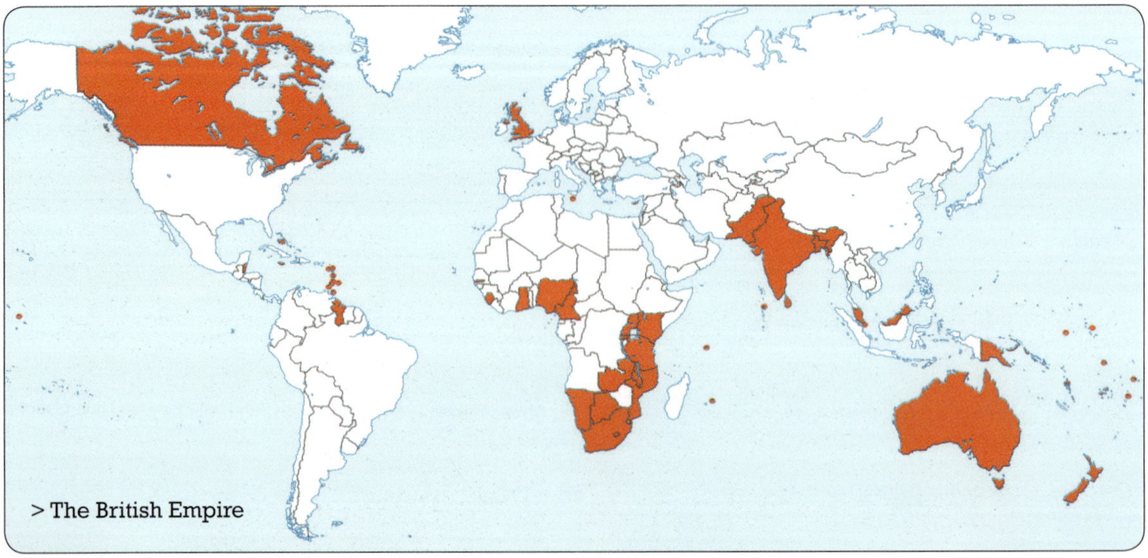

> The British Empire

The Great War

When Victoria died, her son Edward VII came to the throne of Britain and later her grandson *George V.*

During *George V's* reign *World War I* broke out. It lasted from 1914 to 1918 and the king was obliged to change his German surname from Saxe-Coburg and Gotha to the English surname *Windsor* because of the anti-German campaign of Great Britain and its colonies.

The war was between two opposing alliances: the *Triple Entente* made up of the alliance of France, the British Empire and the Russian Empire and the *Central Powers* that was made up of the German Empire, Austria-Hungary, the Ottoman Empire and Bulgaria. Britain declared war on Germany in 1914 after it invaded Belgium.

The war ended with the victory of the *Allied Forces* and peace was declared on 28th June 1919 with the signing of the Treaty of Versailles.

The First World War was characterized by the use of trenches. Soldiers dug holes in the ground to protect themselves against machine guns and giant guns that fired shells. These powerful weapons were being used for the first time in a war and explains why more than 400,000 British soldiers lost their lives.

Winston Churchill and the Second World War

After *George V*, his son *Edward VIII* became king but he abdicated because he fell in love with an divorced American woman, Wallis Simpson. For this reason his brother, *George VI*, *Queen Elizabeth II's* father, ascended to the British throne.

During his reign *World War II* broke out. It was fought between the *Allies* consisting of the USA, the UK and the Soviet Union and the *Axis* that was formed by Germany, Japan and Italy. Britain declared war on Germany after Hitler invaded Poland in 1939. The British Prime Minister, Winston Churchill, led the nation to victory.

He was very good at speaking to the British people during the war. From a bunker under 10 Downing Street Churchill encouraged people to resist, just like St Paul's Cathedral that wasn't struck during the heavy bombing of London on 29th December 1940.

London was attacked many times during the Blitz, a German word that means *"lightning war"*. This was the strategic bombing of the UK by Nazi Germany from September 1940 to May 1941. Britain resisted thanks to its *Royal Air Force* that won an air battle called the *Battle of Britain*.

The war finished in 1945 with the Allies victorious. In the war Britain lost about 300,000 soldiers and 40,000 civilians.

In 1952 George VI died and *Elizabeth II* became queen.

ACTIVITIES

1 Imperialism

Write the capitals of some popular British colonies and the continent on which they are located.

British colonies	Capitals	Continent
South Africa		
Egypt		
Kenya		
Nigeria		
Somaliland		
Sudan		
The Bahamas		
British Honduras		
Canada		
Falkland Islands		
Jamaica		
West Indies		
India		
Malaysia		
Pakistan		
Cyprus		
Gibraltar		
Malta		
Australia		
New Zealand		

2 Write true (T) or false (F) next to the following sentences. Correct the false ones.

a. Queen Victoria's reign was marked by Imperialism. T F
b. In 1877 Queen Victoria was named Empress of India. T F
c. World War I broke out under Edward VII. T F
d. During World War I George V changed the German surname of his House into an English one. T F
e. Great Britain won World War II. T F
f. Winston Churchill was Prime Minister under George V. T F
g. St Paul's cathedral resisted the bombs of World War II. T F
h. World War II finished in 1945. T F
i. Elizabeth II is George VI's daughter. T F
j. Elizabeth II became queen seven years after World War II. T F

3 Read the text "From Queen Victoria to the 20th Century" and answer the following questions.

1. How long did Queen Victoria reign?
2. When did she receive the title of Empress of India?
3. Who was her husband?
4. What were the reasons for Imperialism?
5. When did World War I start?
6. Who was king of Britain during World War I?
7. Which countries did the *Triple Entente* include?
8. Why did Edward VIII leave the throne of Britain?
9. Who was king of Britain during World War II?
10. What did Winston Churchill say to the British people during the war?
11. When did Nazi Germany bomb the UK?
12. Who ascended to the throne of Britain in 1952?

4 Speaking

Say:

- when Victoria reigned;
- reasons for Imperialism;
- when World War I started;
- who was the king and why he changed his surname;
- who won the Great War;
- when World War II started;
- who fought the war;
- who was the Prime Minister during World War II;
- what he did;
- who won the war.

AMAZING NEW WORLD!

The History of the USA is rich in events that allowed the constant growth of the country. We usually start from the *New World's* discovery in 1492 by Christopher Columbus but it is from the first permanent settlements that we can consider the beginning of *American history*. That's because when the Europeans arrived on the American continent they imposed their culture and inventions in each field of knowledge, radically changing the native inhabitants' world.

> Mayan calendar

At the time of the European discovery of the New World, there were *Native Americans*, also called *Indians*, who lived as nomads in tribes and were good hunters and fishermen. Most of them lived in Central and South America. They had a democratic society, advanced agricultural techniques and acquired important skills in Astronomical Science especially the *Maya* who created the *Mayan calendar*. They didn't know that their way of life would change drastically with the arrival of the European conquerors repressed them and forced them into reserves.

DID YOU KNOW?

- There were other important communities of Native Americans like the *Inca* in Peru and the *Aztecs* in Mexico.
- *Christopher Columbus*, who thought he had reached the East Indies (in Asia), called the Native Americans "Indians".
- The name *America* derives from *Amerigo Vespucci*, an Italian sailor and explorer.
- *Giovanni Caboto* and *Giovanni da Verrazano* were famous Italian explorers of the New World too.

The European settlements and "The Pilgrim Fathers"

The European kings and queens decided to send their explorers to the *New World* in order to extend their possessions and create successful trade links but they were also curious about what they could find by sailing the unknown seas. When their brave sailors came back with tobacco, potatoes, tomatoes and sugar and reported that the new territories were rich in gold, an intense land rush began.

The colonization created new places for Europeans to live, villages that, in time, became the towns that we know today. Spanish settlements were in the South of the USA whereas the French, Dutch and British arrived on the coasts of North America where they and their families started a new life.

The first permanent English settlement was founded in 1620 when the Pilgrim Fathers, a religious Protestant group known as the Puritans, left England because of religious problems with the intolerant *King James I* who was persecuting them. *Puritanism* encouraged the spirit of adventure in the name of liberty and the idea that handwork improves an individual's social and financial situation.

The Pilgrim Fathers travelled to America on a ship called the *Mayflower* and landed on the coast of Massachusetts where they founded the colony *New Plymouth*. Their aim was to profess their religion freely in a new land.

The journey was long and very hard. They lost food while crossing the ocean and when they finally arrived the weather was extremely cold and many of them died during the first Winter.

The native Indians welcomed them and taught them how to hunt and to plant corn. After the first harvest in October they decided to have a feast in order to thank God. They celebrated together with their Native American friends who had helped them to survive. The three day feast was called *Thanksgiving*.

> The Mayflower

> The Pilgrim Fathers and Indians

ACTIVITIES

1 Decide if the following sentences are True (T) or False (F). Correct the false ones.

a. The New World was discovered in 1640. T F
b. Native Americans were inhabitants of the New World. T F
c. They were called Indians. T F
d. They weren't nomads. T F
e. They were good hunters but weren't good fishermen. T F
f. Inca, Aztec and Maya were important Native American communities. T F

2 Find out information about the New World's European explorers and write them in your copybook, then complete the grid.

Name	Country

3 Translate each word into Italian.

a. Explorer
b. Handwork
c. Freely
d. Survival
e. Unknown
f. Brave
g. Colonization
h. Possessions
i. Aim
j. Harvest
k. Trades
l. Sailors
m. Rush
n. Settlement

4 Answer the following questions.

1. Did the European kings and queens send explorers to the New World? Why?
2. Why did the land rush start?
3. What kind of products did the explorers find in the New World?
4. Were there Spanish settlements in the South of the American continent?
5. Who arrived on the coast of Massachusetts in 1620?

5 Read the text again, find the information and complete the summary using the words below:

first, religious persecution, Mayflower, religious group, Thanksgiving, 1620, New Plymouth, Native Americans.

The Pilgrim Fathers were a .... of Puritans that left England because of...................... by the king James I. The name of their ship was .... and they landed in North America in............... They founded the .... colony. They met the............................... who helped them. They celebrated .... to thank God for their survival.

THE COLONIES AND INDEPENDENCE

Colonization at this time allowed the expansion of the *British American Empire*. In fact Britain controlled a large part of the eastern coast of North America with its *Thirteen Colonies* along the Atlantic Ocean. They were founded between 1607 and 1733, the first was *Virginia*, named after *Queen Elizabeth I*, the unmarried queen of England. Very soon the relationship between the thirteen colonies and England became difficult because of the increasing taxes that American colonists had to pay to the mother country.

In December 1773 a group of colonists raided a British ship and threw the cargo of tea into the *Harbor of Boston*. It was called the *Boston Tea Party* and marked the start of the bloody *American War of Independence*. The colonies united to defeat England.

The commander-in-chief of the American forces, *George Washington*, led them to victory and in 1776 the *Declaration of Independence* of the USA was announced. It was recognized by Britain in 1783 and in 1788 the USA adopted the first written *Constitution*. George Washington became the first president of the United States of America.

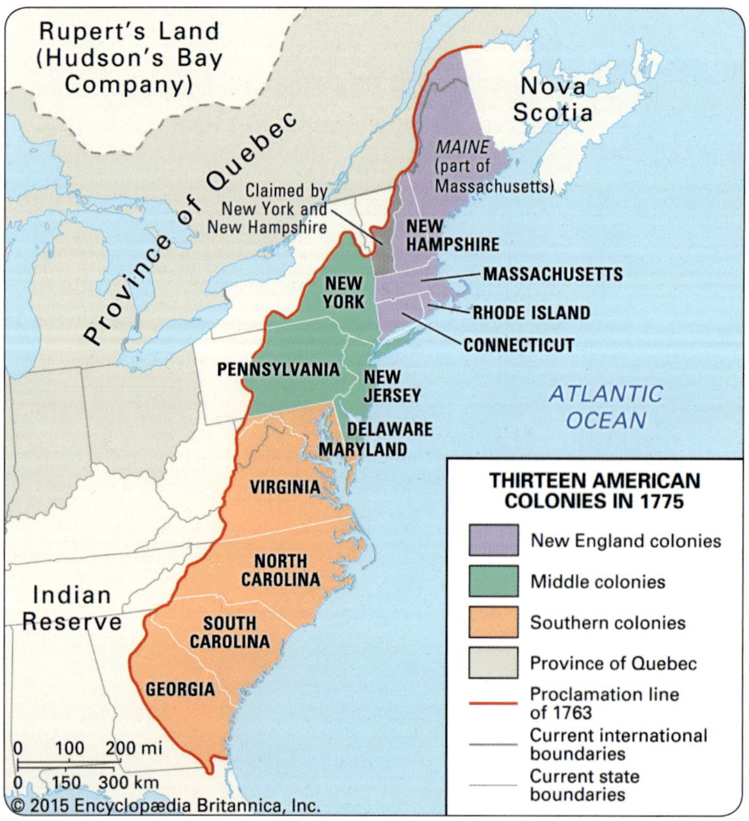

> The *Stars and Stripes* flag.

> The Boston Tea Party.

ACTIVITIES

1 Translate each word into Italian.

a. Founded ....
b. Unmarried ....
c. Soon ....
d. Relationship ....
e. Increasingly ....
f. Recognized ....
g. Overseas ....
h. Trading activities ....

ESERCIZI ON LINE www.medusaeditrice.it

2 Choose the correct answer.

1. *Great Britain had .... colonies in the New World.*
a. twelve
b. seventeen
c. thirteen

2. *The colonies had ....*
a. to pay a lot of taxes to the English.
b. a good relationship with Great Britain.
c. an easy life under British rule.

3. *The "Boston Tea Party" was ....*
a. a big feast.
b. the reason for the conflict between the Americans and the British.
c. an American document for the Independence of the country.

4. *The American War of Independence ended in ....*
a. 1771
b. 1776
c. 1802

3 Read the text and answer the following questions.

1. How many colonies were there on the American Atlantic coast?
2. What was the name of the first colony? Why?
3. When did the American War of Independence begin?
4. Why did Americans protest with their mother country?
5. What happened during the Boston Tea Party?
6. Did George Washington take command of the American Army?
7. Did the colonies obtain independence? When?
8. When did Americans adopt the Constitution?
9. Who was the first American President?
10. Who was Francis Drake?

DID YOU KNOW?

- During the Elizabethan Age England expanded its overseas trade; *Francis Drake* was the most famous English explorer of Elizabeth's reign which was known as: *The Golden Age.*
- *New Amsterdam* was the name the Dutch gave to New York.

FROM THE GOLD RUSH TO THE SECOND WORLD WAR

The West

After the *War of Independence*, American history continued to be full of events.

There were pioneers, animated by the spirit of adventure that went *West* and occupied territories known as the frontier. In many cases the Native American Indian communities, who rightfully owned those territories, became hostile. They tried to defend their homelands and fought terrible battles with the white man. The discovery of gold in California encouraged more Europeans to come to America.

The Government gave the new colonists land for a few dollars. The new arrivals hoped to make their fortune in the New World.

The Civil War

During the 19th century, the problem of slavery was the cause of the *Civil War*. Black people worked in the cotton plantations as slaves without any civil rights. Gradually a part of American society became more sensitive towards the problem and tried to solve it.

The southern states, that produced cotton and tobacco, based their economy on slavery while the northern states began to protest against it. The tensions between the two parts of America culminated in the *Civil War* of 1861 that saw the North emerge victorious.

President *Abraham Lincoln*, who supported the abolition of slavery, declared the *Emancipation Proclamation* in 1863. A southern fanatic assassinated him and unfortunately racial problems remained a feature of the South.

DID YOU KNOW?

Uncle Sam has been the personification of the American Government since 1812 and this poster was used to recruit soldiers for the *American Army* during both World War I and World War II.

The First World War and the "Great Depression"

In the following years important events involved the United States of America.

During the *First World War* the USA supported the *Allies* and gave a decisive contribution to the final victory.

In 1929, after a period of great prosperity, Americans got to know the *Great depression* and the *Wall Street Market Crash* that saw many banks in great crisis.

DID YOU KNOW?

Britannia with *Uncle Sam* symbolizes the British-American alliance in World War I.

DID YOU KNOW?

- Most slaves were African because slave traders considered them stronger than white men.
- *The Last of the Mohicans* (1826), is one of the most famous novels written by *James Fenimore Cooper*. It is part of a series of novels entitled *The Leather Stocking Tales*. He created the first great epic of the American frontier.
- Cowboys are the symbol of the American frontier, they rode horses and their work was to drive the cattle from the *West* to the meat markets of the *North*.
- There are many *cowboy* songs and frontier ballads as is often shown in western films.
- In the *Black Hills*, South Dakota, one can visit the *National Memorial* in Mount Rushmore with the carved faces of four American presidents: *George Washington, Thomas Jefferson, Theodore Roosevelt* and *Abraham Lincoln*. A *Crazy Horse Memorial* in honour of Indian warriors is currently under construction.

> Franklin Delano Roosevelt

President *Franklin Delano Roosevelt* was able to help the country by his economic program known as the *New Deal*.
The USA entered World War II in 1941 when the Japanese bombed the American naval base of *Pearl Harbour* in Hawaii. Once more America had joined the Allies to defeat Nazi Germany.
In 1945 America dropped the first atomic bombs on Hiroshima and Nagasaki in order to put an end to World War II. After seeing the destructive power of the atomic bombs Japan surrendered.
After the Second World War the USA emerged as a world leader. Its supremacy was both political and economic and its culture, music and films have had a huge influence on people's lifestyle, especially the young generation.

DID YOU KNOW?

In 1969 America became the first country to land on the Moon.

ACTIVITIES

1 Translate each word into Italian.

a. Pioneers ....
b. Frontier ....
c. Owners ....
d. Homelands ....
e. Colonists ....
f. Slavery ....
g. Plantations ....
h. Fanatic ....
i. Abolition ....
j. Supremacy ....

2 Answer the following questions.

1. Why did pioneers go to America?
2. Did the Indians defend their homelands?
3. What was the main problem for Americans in the 19th century?
4. Which part of America was against slavery?
5. Who worked in the cotton plantations?
6. Who was Abraham Lincoln?
7. What was his attitude towards slavery?
8. Who won the Civil War?
9. What happened in 1863?
10. Did the USA take part in the First World War?
11. Did the Wall Street Crash in 1929 produce an economic crisis in the USA?
12. Who was Franklin Delano Roosevelt?
13. Why did America support the Allies in the Second World War?
14. Did America drop the first atomic bomb? Where?

3 Speaking

Look at these pictures. They show historic scenes of friendship and of slavery. What do you think? Work with your friends and talk about immigration today.

READING COMPREHENSION

Hampton Court Palace

If you go on a trip to London, you'll be able to visit Hampton Court, a historic royal palace that achieved its greatest heights in the Tudor period.

It's in the south-west of London near the river Thames and was open to the public under Queen Victoria. This was a wonderful country residence that Cardinal Thomas Wolsey acquired for himself in 1514.

Cardinal Thomas Wolsey was Henry VIII's personal advisor and minister and he transformed the building into a magnificent palace.

Later the residence became Henry VIII's Royal Palace. King Henry appropriated it to seek revenge on the Cardinal who didn't

help him to divorce his first wife Catherine of Aragon. King Henry approved of the residence. In fact as he loved sport he had a tennis court built, a park for hunting, a Great Hall and Royal Kitchens, too. All these areas of the residence are open to the public.

There's also an astronomical clock located precisely on Anne Boleyn's gate. It indicates the hours, the day, the month and the phases of the moon.

According to a legend a ghost lives in the palace. Apparantly it's the ghost of Catherine Howard, Henry's fifth wife who was beheaded. It is said that while the guards were taking her to the Tower for the execution, she managed to escape and went to Hampton Court. In the palace, thanks to a secret doorway, she reached the Chapel where her husband was at mass. But there, just at the door, she was caught and while the guards were carrying her away she screamed. It's said that the ghost appears screaming at the door every night.

This area of the building is called the *Haunted Gallery*. The Chapel Royal is also open to the public.
Some parts of the palace were rebuilt by the architect Christopher Wren who was called by King William and Queen Mary in 1689. Wren built elegant Royal Apartments that can be visited today. One of the best attractions of the palace that was built in that period is the popular maze. It is 300 years old and is the oldest in the UK. George II was the last monarch who lived here.

EXERCISES

1 Write True (T) or False (F) next to the following sentences. Correct the false ones.

a. Hampton Court Palace is an old fortress. T F
b. Henry VIII acquired Hampton Court. T F
c. Cardinal Wolsey was Henry VIII's minister. T F
d. Henry VIII improved the residence. T F
e. There's a football pitch in the residence. T F
f. The maze is 300 years old. T F
g. The astronomical clock is on Anne Boleyn's gate. T F
h. Catherine Howard, Henry VIII's fifth wife, was repudiated. T F
i. You can't visit the Chapel Royal. T F
j. You can visit the Great Hall and the Tudors' Royal Kitchens. T F

2 Read the text and answer the following questions.

1. When did Hampton Court Palace reach its splendor?
2. Where is Hampton Court?
3. Who was the original owner?
4. Why did Henry VIII appropriate the palace?
5. What are the most important attractions?
6. What is the mysterious presence in the palace?
7. Why is it said that Catherine Howard's ghost visits the castle?
8. Who built the Royal Apartments?
9. Who called Sir Christopher Wren to rebuild parts of the palace?
10. How old is the maze?
11. Who opened the palace to the public?
12. Would you like to visit it?

WRITING A SUMMARY

STEP BY STEP

How to write a summary

All'Esame di Stato la prova scritta di lingua inglese potrebbe essere la produzione del *riassunto* di un testo (in inglese *summary*). Per riassumere (*to summarize*) un testo, è necessario acquisire una tecnica che prevede delle operazioni da compiere prima, durante e dopo la lettura del brano. Ecco le fasi da seguire che ti aiutano a scrivere il riassunto:

1st step

- Leggi il titolo e gli eventuali sottotitoli per capire di cosa tratta il brano.
  Es.: *Hampton Court Palace*

2nd step

- Leggi il brano più di una volta per farti un'idea generale e durante la lettura soffermati sulle parole che non conosci. Usa il dizionario per trovare il significato. Es.: *be able to* = potere; *achieved its greatest heights* = raggiunse il massimo splendore; *advisor* = consigliere; *to appropriate* = impossessarsi; *to improve* = migliorare, etc.

3rd step

- Puoi utilizzare gli avverbi interrogativi per riconoscere i punti fondamentali o dividere il testo in paragrafi e dare a ciascuno un titolo. Es.:
  who = Cardinal Wolsey, Henry VIII, William and Mary, Wren, Catherine Howard.
  what = Hampton Court Palace is a historic Royal Palace.
  when = in the Tudors' time.
  where = in the south-west of London.
  why = because Wolsey didn't help Henry to divorce Catherine of Aragon.

4th step

- Sottolinea nel testo le frasi che contengono le idee principali. In genere corrispondono alle risposte del questionario. Poi scrivile in ordine sul quaderno. Scrivi risposte intere alle domande. Es.:

1. *Hampton Court Palace reached its splendour in the Tudor period.*
2. *Hampton Court Palace is in the south-west of London.*
3. *The original owner was Cardinal Thomas Wolsey.*
4. *Henry VIII appropriated the palace because Cardinal Wolsey didn't help him to divorce his first wife Catherine of Aragon.*
5. *The most important attractions are the maze, the gardens, the park, the Royal Apartments, the Tudors' Royal Kitchens and the Chapel Royal.*
6. *In the palace there is a mysterious presence, the ghost of Catherine Howard, Henry VIII's wife.*

5th step

- Infine per scrivere il riassunto, unisci le

frasi tra di loro utilizzando i connettori, cioè le congiunzioni, gli avverbi e le locuzioni che servono a metterle in relazione: *above all* (soprattutto), *firstly* (innanzitutto), *after*, *and*, *because of* (a causa di), *besides* (oltre a), *but*, *however* (comunque), *consequently*, *finally* (infine), *in fact*, *instead* (invece), *or*, *then* (poi), *moreover* (inoltre), *because*, *that*, *as*, *even if* (anche se), *in spite of* (nonostante), *later*, etc.

- Evita le ripetizioni utilizzando i relativi *that*, *which*, *who*, i pronomi personali e i sinonimi.
  Es.: *palace* = *building*; *king* = *monarch*; *appropriate* = *size*, etc.
- Rielabora il testo in modo personale ponendo attenzione agli eventuali errori di grammatica e di ortografia. Fai attenzione all'uso dei tempi verbali. Ricorda che il riassunto deve essere pari alla metà del brano originale.

Summary

Hampton Court Palace

Hampton Court Palace is a historic Royal Palace in the south-west of London, which reached its splendour in the Tudor period. The original owner was Cardinal Thomas Wolsey, Henry VIII's minister. Henry VIII seized the palace when the Cardinal refused to help him divorce his first wife Catherine of Aragon.

The most important attractions are the maze, the gardens, the park, the Royal Apartments, the Tudors' Royal Kitchens and the Chapel Royal. Queen Victoria opened the palace to the public.

There is a mysterious presence at the Palace, the ghost of Catherine Howard, Henry's fifth wife who, before her execution at the Tower, managed to escape. She returned to Hampton Court where, thanks to a secret doorway, she reached her husband who was at mass in the Chapel Royal. There, at the door, she was caught and carried away screaming. According to legend every night the ghost appears screaming at the doorway.

In the 17th century King William and Queen Mary called Architect Christopher Wren to rebuild parts of the palace. In fact he built the Royal Apartments. During this period the popular maze was built, too. It's 300 years old.

- Quando avrai terminato, rileggi l'elaborato prima di consegnarlo.

In short (in breve) the steps to write a summary:

1. title and subtitles;
2. reading and meaning of the unknown words;
3. 5 wh to find out the main ideas;
4. answers to the questions;
5. summary.

1. Read the text "British history: from Queen Victoria to the 20th Century" and summarize it.

LISTENING ACTIVITY

Listen to the "OO-DE-LALLY" song taken from the "Robin Hood" cartoon by Walt Disney and complete the text with the following words.

Link: http://bit.ly/1RsafZk

day – fences – sheriff – danger
good time – back – escape – forest

Robin Hood and Little John, walking through the ....
Laughing .... and forth at what the other one has to say
Reminiscing this and that and having such a ....
Oo-de-lally, oo-de-lally, golly, what a day
Never ever thinking there was .... in the water
They were drinking, they just guzzled it down
Never dreaming that a scheming .... and his posse
Was a-watching them and gathering around
Robin Hood and Little John, running through the forest
Jumping ...., dodging trees and trying to get away
Contemplating nothing but .... and finally making it
Oo-de-lally, oo-de-lally, golly, what a ....
Oo-de-lally, oo-de-lally, golly, what a day.

OPEN - DIALOGUE

1. Read the text "BRITISH HISTORY: from the Celts to the Normans" on page 110 and complete the following open-dialogue.

Teacher:....................................?
Oliver: The Celts arrived in Britain about 600 years B. C..
Teacher: ....?
Oliver: They came from the centre of Europe.
Teacher: How did they live?
Oliver: ....
Teacher: What was their religion?
Oliver: Well! ....
Oliver: And their priests ....
Teacher: Do you remember why they were famous?
Oliver: Yes, ...
Teacher: What's Stonehenge?
Oliver: ....
Teacher: This temple was probably built 5,000 years ago.
Oliver: Very interesting! Mr Smith, what was their language?
Teacher: ....
Today ....
.... and Wales.

BUILDING UP A DIALOGUE

2. Write a dialogue between Daniel and Elizabeth following these instructions:

Daniel: Chiede dove andrà in vacanza questa estate.
Elizabeth: Risponde che andrà negli Stati Uniti.
Daniel: Chiede com'è il clima.
Elizabeth: Risponde che in genere è bello e caldo.
Daniel: Chiede che cosa vuole vedere negli Stati Uniti.
Elizabeth: Risponde che vuole vedere la Statua della Libertà e New York e poi visitare Washington.
Daniel: Chiede se vuole andare alle Cascate del Niagara.
Elizabeth: Risponde che sarebbe bellissimo, ma non può perché resterà per pochi giorni.
Daniel: Chiede se ha dei parenti in America.
Elizabeth: Risponde di no, ma i suoi genitori hanno degli amici a Boston.
Daniel: Chiede se può portargli un souvenir.
Elizabeth: Risponde che gli porterà un berretto da baseball.

WRITING A LETTER

3. Write a letter to a pen-friend following these suggestions:

1. thank him/her for the letter that you received;
2. where you live;
3. do you live in a flat or in a house?
4. describe your flat or house;
5. have you got a garden?
6. have you got a balcony?
7. do you share your bedroom?
8. describe your bedroom.

TRINITY GRADE 4

CEFR level A2.2

Total exam time: 10 minutes.

Conversation:

- Good morning
- What's your name?
- How are you?
- Where is your school?
- Were you at the same school last year?
- What time does school start?
- Which subjects do you study at school?
- What are your favourite subjects?
- How often do you have English lessons?
- What do you do in your school break?
- Which subject are you best at?
- Can you play a musical instrument?
- Is there a choir at your school?

Look at the picture!

- Where are these students?
- What are they doing?!
- Are there any CDs in the classroom? Where?
- What is the teacher doing?
- Are there any photos on the wall? How many?
- Are there any books on the chairs?
- How many instruments are there in the music lab?
- Which one is your favourite?
- What colour is the CD player?
- What are the students wearing?
- Ask me if I studied Music at school.

You: Did you study Music at school?

Examiner: OK. Thanks a lot. Bye

You: Thanks. Goodbye.

CHAPTER 06

FESTIVALS

DIALOGUE

One month, one festival!

Martha: Hello, Giacomo!

Giacomo: Hello, Martha!

Martha: Today is the 31st October and in Britain we celebrate Halloween.

Giacomo: Our teacher told us about the British festivals. Great Britain is a very interesting country. One month, one festival!

Martha: Yes. It's true. We celebrate a different festival each month. In September we celebrate *The Harvest Festival* to wish good luck for the following year's harvest. In October we celebrate *Halloween,* the Eve of All Saints' Day and in November we commemorate the *Gunpowder Plot*, the plot planned by the Catholic *Guy Fawkes* to blow up the Protestant *King James I*.

Giacomo: I bet you prefer Halloween, don't you?

Martha: Yes, I do. We are having our Halloween party tonight. Let's go and put on our costumes.

Giacomo: I'm dressing up as a ghost. And you?

Martha: I am dressing up as a bat.

Giacomo: Ok. Let's go now. It's late.

EXERCISE

1 Answer the following questions.

1. What is the date today?
2. What do they celebrate in Britain?
3. What did the teacher tell his students?
4. Why is Great Britain a very interesting country?
5. Why do they celebrate *The Harvest Festival*?
6. What do they celebrate in November?
7. What festivity does Martha prefer to celebrate?
8. What are Martha and Giacomo doing tonight?

THE BRITISH FESTIVALS

The Harvest Festival

The word *harvest* is from the old English *hærfest* meaning *Autumn*.

The *Harvest Festival* is a British tradition with pagan origins.

It is usually celebrated in churches and schools, on a Sunday near the *Harvest Moon*, at the end of September.

It is a special day to celebrate the end of the harvest and farmers are very busy at this time of the year.

The tradition of celebrating the *Harvest Festival* in churches began in 1843, when the *Reverend Robert Hawker* organized a special thanksgiving service for the harvest at his church in Cornwall.

Schools have special assemblies to celebrate the *Harvest Festival*. During the assembly students listen to talks about the harvest and sing traditional songs.

They also bring food that is given to a local charity at the end of the assembly.

At school, students make *Corn Dolls* for the *Harvest Festival*. They are straw dolls and bring good luck.

Students sell the dolls and give the money to charity.

DID YOU KNOW?

- The full moon nearest the autumnal equinox is called the *Harvest Moon*.
- The *Harvest Festivals* are celebrated at different times, in different places, around the world.
- In the USA it falls on a specific day and has become a national holiday. It is called *Thanksgiving Day* and is celebrated on the 4th Thursday of November.
- In Asia, the *Harvest Festivals* include the *Chinese Mid-Autumn Festival*, one of the most widespread harvest festivals in the world.

ACTIVITIES

ESERCIZI ON LINE www.medusaeditrice.it

1 Match the words.

a. Harvest	1. Buona fortuna
b. Moon	2. Agricoltore
c. Farmer	3. Beneficenza
d. Thanksgiving	4. Grano
e. Assembly	5. Raccolto
f. Talk	6. Luna
g. Food	7. Ringraziamento
h. Charity	8. Discorso
i. Corn	9. Assemblea
j. Good luck	10. Cibo

2 Say if the following sentences are TRUE (T) or FALSE (F). Correct the false ones.

a. The word *harvest* is from old English. T F
b. The *Harvest Festival* is celebrated at the end of October. T F
c. It is a special Thanksgiving Day. T F
d. Schools organize assemblies for the *Harvest Festival.* T F
e. Students bring food to eat during the assembly. T F
f. Corn Dolls are made at home. T F
g. Corn dolls bring good luck. T F
h. Students sell the dolls and give the money to charity. T F
i. *Harvest Festival* in the UK is Thanksgiving Day in the USA. T F

3 Answer the following questions.

1. When is the *Harvest Festival* celebrated?
2. Where is it celebrated?
3. What is the *Harvest Moon*?
4. When did the tradition begin in churches?
5. How do schools celebrate the *Harvest Festival*?
6. What do students do during the assembly?
7. Who is the food given to after the assembly?
8. Who makes the *Corn Dolls*?
9. What are they?
10. Why do students sell the dolls?

4 "All things bright and beautiful".

This is a Victorian hymn written by the hymn writer and poet *Cecil F. Alexander.* Students sing it to celebrate the *Harvest Festival.*

Complete the poem with the words below and learn it.

Beautiful, flower, sings, small, their, wings.

All things bright and ________________.
All creatures great and ________________.
All things wise and wonderful, The Lord God made them all.
Each little ________________ that opens,
Each little bird that ________________,
He made ________________ glowing colours,
He made their tiny ________________.

Guy Fawkes

In Britain, they celebrate *Guy Fawkes Day* or *Bonfire Night* on 5th November.

After Queen Elizabeth I died in 1603, King James VI of Scotland became King of England as James I. He was a Protestant and was not tolerant of Catholics.

Guy Fawkes, by contrast, was Catholic and both the king and the members of Parliament were making life difficult for Catholics.

For this reason Guy Fawkes and his friends planned to blow up the king and the *Houses of Parliament* on 5th November 1605.

Their plan is also known as the *Gunpowder Plot.*

Guy Fawkes was in the cellar of Parliament with 36 barrels of gunpowder when he was caught.

Their plan failed, they were arrested and executed.

Today, the British usually celebrate *Guy Fawkes Day* with a traditional bonfire party. Students make a *'guy'* from old clothes and newspapers and on *Bonfire Night* they put the *guy* on the fire. The *guy* represents Guy Fawkes.

During the party people usually eat sausages and burgers and set off a lot of fireworks.

ACTIVITIES

1 Match the words

a. Tolerant	1. Barile
b. Plan	2. Cantina
c. Blow up	3. Complotto
d. Gunpowder	4. Falò
e. Plot	5. Fuochi di artificio
f. Cellar	6. Programmare
g. Barrel	7. Fantoccio
h. Bonfire	8. Tollerante
i. Guy	9. Far esplodere
j. Fireworks	10. Polvere da sparo

ESERCIZI ON LINE www.medusaeditrice.it

2 Say if the following sentences are TRUE (T) or FALSE (F). Correct the false ones.

a. Bonfire Night is celebrated on 5th December. T F
b. James I became king in 1603. T F
c. He was Catholic. T F
d. Guy Fawkes planned to blow up the king. T F
e. The gunpowder was in the cellar of the Parliament. T F
f. Students make guys from old clothes. T F
g. The guy on the bonfire represents the king. T F
h. People set off fireworks during Bonfire Night. T F

3 Answer the following questions.

1. When is *Bonfire Night* celebrated?
2. When did James become king of England?
3. Why did Guy Fawkes plan the plot?
4. What's the name of the plot?
5. Where was Guy Fawkes when he was arrested?
6. How many barrels of gunpowder were in the cellar?
7. How do people celebrate *Guy Fawkes Day* now?
8. What do students make?
9. Where do they put the *guy*?
10. What do people do during the bonfire party?

4 This is a traditional rhyme about Bonfire Night. Read and learn it.

Remember, remember, the fifth of November.
Gunpowder, treason and plot.
We see no reason, why gunpowder, treason
Should ever be forgot!
Guy Fawkes, 'twas his intent.
To blow up King and Parliament.
Three score barrels were laid below
To prove old England's overthrow.
By God's mercy he was catch'd
With a darkened lantern and burning match.
So, holler boys, holler boys,
Let the bells ring.
Holler boys, holler boys, God save the King.
And what shall we do with him?
Burn him!

Halloween

Halloween is celebrated on 31st October that is the night before All Saints' Day. The word *Halloween* is from "All Hallows' Eve", that is "All Saints' Eve".

It is a Christian festival with pagan origins and comes from the Celtic festival of Samain that celebrated the end of Summer and the beginning of Winter.

The Celts believed that the souls of the dead visited Earth on the last day of October.

Now *Halloween* is a fun festival. Children usually dress up as ghosts and witches: they celebrate *Halloween* with parties and usually go from house to house and say *'trick or treat?'*. If people do not give them sweets or chocolates, they play some tricks like dumping dustbins.

People also make *Jack O' Lanterns* from pumpkins. They put a candle inside the pumpkin and put it at the window to keep away evil spirits.

Halloween is celebrated in the Western world, in the USA, Canada, the UK, Ireland and also Australia and New Zealand.

ACTIVITIES

1 Match the words.

a . Festival	1 . Pattumiera
b . Soul	2 . Festeggiare
c . Dead	3 . Candela
d . Dress up	4 . Scherzo
e . Celebrate	5 . Festività
f . Trick	6 . Anima
g . Dumping	7 . Zucca
h . Dustbin	8 . Morti
i . Pumpkin	9 . Mascherarsi
j . Candle	10 . Svuotare

2 Say if the following sentences are TRUE (T) or FALSE (F). Correct the false ones.

a . Halloween is celebrated ~~in November.~~ T F

b . Halloween has got pagan origins. T F

c . The Celtic festival celebrated the end of ~~Winter.~~ SUMMER T F

d . Halloween is a fun festival. T F

e . People celebrate Halloween with parties. T F

f . Children play trick or treat. T F

g . The pumpkins keep away ~~good~~ spirits. EVIL T F

h . Halloween is celebrated ~~all over the world.~~ T F

3 Answer the following questions.

1 . When is Halloween celebrated?
2 . What does the word Halloween mean?
3 . What did the Celtic festival celebrate?
4 . What did the Celts believe?
5 . What do children dress up as at Halloween parties?
6 . When do children play tricks?
7 . Why are pumpkins put at the windows?
8 . Where is Halloween celebrated?
9. Do you like celebrating Halloween?
10. How do you celebrate it?

4 "Trick or treat"

This is a nursery rhyme about Halloween. Children say it on Halloween day. Read the rhyme and learn it.

Trick or treat! Trick or treat!
Give me something nice to eat.
Give my friends something too,
Or we'll play a trick on you!

DID YOU KNOW?

- *Celts* used to carve turnips and put a light inside because they didn't know what pumpkins were.
- When *Irish* people arrived in America in the VIII and IX centuries, they discovered pumpkins and saw that they were more suitable for making *Halloween* lanterns.

Christmas

In Britain most people decorate their houses two weeks before *Christmas*. All houses have a *Christmas tree* with lights. They also hang mistletoe on the door.
On *Christmas Eve* children usually hang their *Christmas stockings* on their beds.
Father Christmas comes at night!
On Christmas morning, children find presents in their stockings and under the Christmas tree.
Families usually go to church in the morning and then they have the traditional *Christmas dinner* of roast turkey with carrots, peas, potatoes and Brussels sprouts.
As dessert they have *Christmas pudding* and mince Pies.
In the afternoon families watch the Queen's Christmas message on TV.

ACTIVITIES

1 Translate each word into Italian.

a. Christmas tree
b. Mistletoe
c. Stocking
d. Roast Turkey
e. Brussels sprouts
f. Pudding
g. Mince pies

2 Say if the following sentences are TRUE (T) or FALSE (F). Correct the false ones.

a. In Britain, houses have a Christmas tree. T F
b. Children hang stockings on the doors. T F
c. At night they find presents under the tree. T F
d. Families go to church in the afternoon. T F
e. They have roast turkey for lunch. T F
f. They watch the Queen's message on TV. T F

3 Answer the following questions.

1. When do the British decorate their house?
2. When do we decorate our house in Italy?
3. What do British children do on Christmas Eve?
4. What do Italian children do on Christmas Eve?
5. What do British families have for lunch?
6. And what do Italian families have?

4 Now write a paragraph about Christmas in England and in Italy.

Hogmanay

In Scotland they celebrate the New Year with music, parties, parades and fireworks.

The Scottish name for the New Year celebrations is *Hogmanay*.

On 31st December thousands of people go to Edinburgh, the capital of Scotland, to celebrate Hogmanay. The party lasts for four days.

At midnight on New Year's Eve people sing "*Auld Lang Syne*". *Auld Lang Syne*[1] is based on a Scots poem written by *Robert Burns* in 1788 and set to the tune of a traditional folk song.

According to tradition it brings good luck if the first person to enter the house after midnight is a tall, dark haired man.

[1] *Auld Lang Syne* = The good old days.

ACTIVITY

1 Complete the traditional song with the following words and then translate it into Italian.

Forgot mind days dear syne cup auld

Auld Lang Syne

Should auld acquaintance be ______________,
And never brought to ______________
Should auld acquaintance be forgot,
And ______________ of auld lang syne?
For auld lang syne, my ______________,
For auld lang ______________,
We'll take a ______________ of kindness yet
For ______________ lang syne!

Valentine's Day

Who was *St. Valentine*?

What's his story?

Valentine, a Christian martyr, lived in the 3rd century A.D. in Rome under Emperor Claudius who oppressed Christians.

There are a lot of legends about St. Valentine. One says that he was arrested by the Roman soldiers because he secretly married many couples even though Emperor Claudius had prohibited it.

According to another legend Valentine met a girl called Julia who was blind. He taught her many things, read her some stories and spoke to her about God. When Valentine was arrested he met Julia's father who was his jailer. Before his execution he wrote a message to Julia signing it "*from your Valentine*" and gave it to the jailer. After some days Valentine was killed, precisely on 14th February 273 A.D.. When Julia read the message a miracle took place and she could see.

Since then, on this day all over the world, lovers send messages to each other.

In the UK people usually send cards and exchange chocolates or flowers with their Valentine.

The tomb of St Valentine is in Italy, in the Cathedral of Terni.

ACTIVITIES

1 Read the text "Valentine's Day" and find the words with these meanings.

a. The leader of an empire:

....

b. Everyone who believes in Christ:

....

c. A person who cannot see:

....

d. A person that is in the army:

....

e. A place where a person is put as a punishment:

....

f. Body of a letter:

....

g. A supernatural event:

....

h. Someone who imprisons a person:

....

2 Say if the following sentences are TRUE (T) or FALSE (F). Correct the false ones.

a. Valentine was a Roman Emperor. T F

b. Claudius was tolerant of Christians. T F

c. Valentine was arrested. T F

d. He wrote a letter to Julia before his death. T F

e. Julia was no longer blind after reading Valentine's message. T F

f. Valentine's Day is on 14th February. T F

3 Complete the poem with the words below and learn it.

Love sea beach seagull

On the rocks a .... is free
On the .... only you and me.
The .... is blue
I .... you

4 Complete the poem with the words below and write another one.

Vase bijou dove love you

My heart is a ....
full of ....
In the sky there's a flying ....
I'm in love.
You are a ....
I miss ....

5 Who's your Valentine? ....

Valentine isn't only a boyfriend or a girlfriend, but he/she can be a person that you particularly love in your family or your best friend.

Pancake Day

In the UK *Shrove Tuesday* is also called *Pancake Day* and is the day before the beginning of *Lent*. On this day in Britain people love eating pancakes. They are round cakes made of butter, milk, flour and eggs and are cooked in a pan.

Pancake Day is a very funny day because in some British towns and villages a pancake race is organized. During the race the participants, who are generally women, run and toss or throw pancakes in the air from a frying pan. Some of them can't catch them.

This tradition dates back to the 15th century and was born in a British town called Olney, not far from London in the south-east of England. It's said that on Shrove Tuesday a woman was making pancakes when the bells of the church began to ring for confession. The woman wanted to confess and didn't want to be late. So she went to church running with a frying pan in her hands.

Activities

1 Match the following words.

a. Shrove Tuesday	1. Lanciare
b. Lent	2. Frittelle
c. Pancakes	3. Burro
d. Butter	4. Quaresima
e. Egg	5. Gara
f. Pan	6. Padella
g. Toss	7. Campane
h. Race	8. Confessione
i. Bells	9. Uovo
j. Confession	10. Martedì Grasso

2 Say if the following sentences are TRUE (T) or FALSE (F). Correct the false ones.

a . *Pancake Day* is the first day of Lent. T F

b . British people eat pancakes on Shrove Tuesday. T F

c . Pancakes are cakes of egg, flour, milk and butter. T F

d . In a Pancake race women hold a frying pan from which they toss pancakes in the air. T F

e . *Pancake Day* is a tradition of the 15th century. T F

f . It was born in Olney in the south-east of England. T F

3 Answer the following questions.

1 . What's *Pancake Day*?

2 . Why is *Pancake Day* a funny day?

3 . What's a Pancake race?

4 . When was it born?

5. Where was it born?

6. What is its story?

Easter

Easter, that comes from the word Eastre, the Anglo-Saxon goddess of fertility and new life, is an important Christian festival which is on the first Sunday after the first full moon of *spring*. It celebrates the Resurrection of Jesus Christ.

In the UK three particularly important days of the Holy Week are called Maundy Thursday, Good Friday and Easter Sunday.

On *Maundy Thursday*, when Christians remember the Last Supper of Jesus, the Queen gives Maundy money to poor and old people in Westminster Abbey in London. *Good Friday*, the day of Christ's death, is a national holiday. All bakeries sell *hot cross buns*, sweet bread rolls with a cross on the top that British people eat on this day.

On *Easter Sunday* people go to church and then exchange chocolate chicks and eggs. Children take part in egg hunts, because

they believe that the *Easter Bunny* brings and hides the eggs for them. They're symbols of rebirth and life. Women wear characteristic spring hats and in some villages children decorate hard-boiled eggs and let them roll downhill during organized games. At lunch British people eat lamb with mint sauce and vegetables then in the afternoon they watch TV and play board games.

ACTIVITIES

1 Read the text "Easter" and find the words with these meanings.

a. The Christian festival of Resurrection: ....

b. The season that begins on 21st March: ....

c. The fourth month of the year: ....

d. Young chickens: ....

e. They're made of chocolate: ....

f. Young sheep: ....

g. Sweet bread rolls with a cross on the top: ....

2 Answer the following questions.

a. What is Easter? **b.** Where does the word Easter come from? **c.** When is Easter? **d.** What does it celebrate? **e.** What do children do at Easter? **f.** How do British people spend Easter Sunday?

3 CROSSWORD

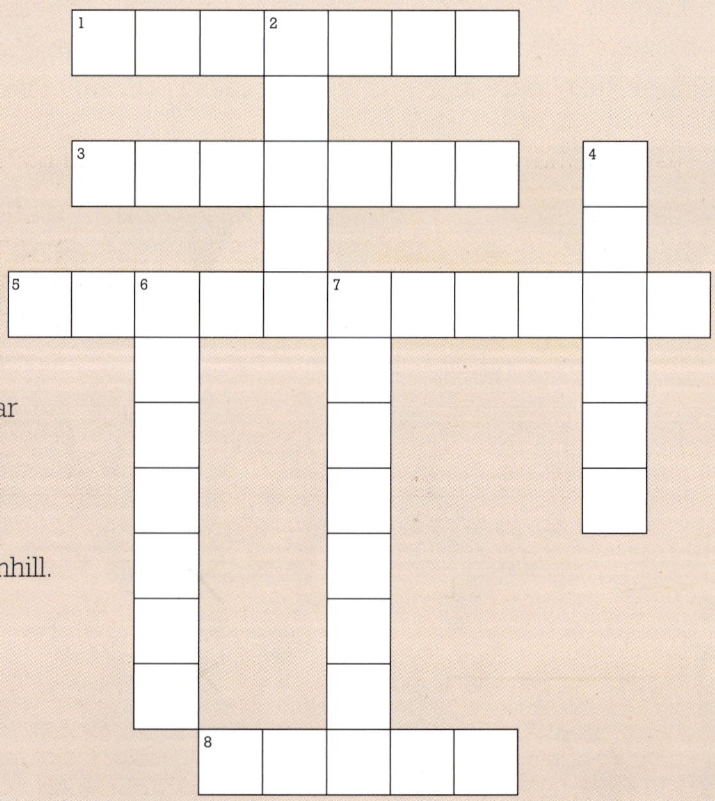

Across

1. Children do this at Easter.

3. A female divine being.

5. He died on Friday.

8. Little Easter rabbit.

Down

2. *To hide* in 3rd person singular of the present simple.

4. A Christian spring festival.

6. An emblem or a sign.

7. They play rolling eggs downhill.

Notting Hill Carnival

Notting Hill Carnival is a very popular event that takes place in Notting Hill, a district in the west of London. It takes place in August because the weather is better than in February. It's the second largest street festival in the world after the Rio de Janeiro Carnival. It was born in 1965 thanks to Caribbean immigrants who had arrived in Great Britain in the 1950s because of the bad economic conditions of the Caribbean Islands after World War II.

At the beginning the immigrants suffered racial attacks by whites so at first the carnival was organized as a response to these race riots and to celebrate the Caribbean culture and traditions.

Nowadays this festival is characterized by parades of children and people from the Caribbean community, all wearing traditional costumes. The festival takes place on the bank holiday weekend at the end of August and the parades are accompanied by percussionist bands and colourful floats.

The streets of Notting Hill are full of stalls selling Caribbean food.

The event is a reflection of the Caribbean carnival of the 19th century. It's a particular tradition of Trinidad, an island in the Caribbean, that celebrated the abolition of slavery and the slave trade.

ACTIVITIES

1 Match the following words.

a. Costume parade	1. Carnevale
b. Floats	2. Dei Caraibi
c. Stalls	3. Bancarelle
d. Immigrants	4. Percussionisti
e. Race riots	5. Tumulti razziali
f. Percussionist	6. Immigrati
g. Caribbean	7. Carri
h. Carnival	8. Sfilata in costume

2 Say if the following sentences are TRUE (T) or FALSE (F). Correct the false ones.

a. *Notting Hill* is a London district. T F
b. The *Notting Hill Carnival* is in July. T F
c. In 1965 Caribbean immigrants went to London. T F
d. Colourful floats go through the streets of Notting Hill. T F
e. Bank Holiday is on the last Monday of August. T F
f. Trinidad is a British island. T F

3 Answer the following questions.

1. When was Notting Hill Carnival born?
2. Why did Caribbean immigrants go to the UK?
3. What did immigrants suffer from initially?
4. How is this carnival organized?
5. What did the 19th century Caribbean Carnival celebrate?

FESTIVALS IN THE USA

There are popular and traditional holidays in the USA. Let's start with *Halloween, Thanksgiving* and *Independence Day!*.

Halloween

Halloween was celebrated for the first time by *Celts* who performed pagan rituals at the beginning of Winter. They believed that Winter was the season of darkness because of its long nights whereas Spring, Summer and Autumn were those of light. *Dark* as *dead* and *light* as *birth* meant the end of a year and the beginning of another. *Halloween* was on 31st October, therefore the first of November, called *Samhain*, was the Celtic New Year. They used to make bonfires and danced around them to frighten ghosts, witches and spirits.

In A.D. 601, *Pope Gregory I*, in order to spread Christianity, issued an edict instructing his missionaries to convert the natives, but to allow them to keep their traditions.

The Catholic approach was built on these ancient traditions; church holidays were purposely set to coincide with native holidays, for example the Christian feast of *All Saints* was assigned to the 1st November. The day honored every Christian saint and was meant to substitute Samhain. That did not happen, however, and the Celtic rituals transformed into the modern tradition of Halloween.

Today Americans make pumpkin lanterns, called "*Jack o' lanterns*", and place them at their windows or outside the house. Children wear scary costumes, and go from door

to door reciting rhymes and asking "*trick or treat?*" with a basket to collect candies. If neighbours don't give them sweets they play tricks on them! Many families organize parties at home and play games like "*Halloween apple bobbing*", adults wear costumes too!

DID YOU KNOW?

- The *Druids* were Celtic priests. They believed that giving food to the spirits on Halloween night placated them. Maybe this is the origin of "*trick or treating*"; if the spirit wasn't "*treated*" he played a trick on people.
- It is said that the origin of "*Halloween apple bobbing*" dates back to the Roman annual festival in honor of *Pomona*, the goddess of fruits, trees and gardens that was held every 1st November.
- The word holiday stands for "*holy day*", but many American holidays aren't religious.

>Pomona, Nicolas Fouché, Budapest

ACTIVITIES

1 Translate each word into Italian.

a. Celts ....
b. Pagan ....
c. Rituals ....
d. Darkness ....
e. Scary ....
f. Dead ....
g. Birth ....
h. Light ....
i. Bonfires ....
j. Frighten ....
k. Goddess ....
l. Holy day ....
m. Edict ....
n. Purposely ....

2 Answer the following questions.

1. When is Halloween?
2. What did the Celts celebrate?
3. Why was Winter the season of darkness?
4. Did the Celts make bonfires? Why?
5. When did *Pope Gregory I* issue his edict?
6. What are the *Jack o' lanterns* made of?
7. Do children wear costumes?
8. Do Americans organize any parties?
9. What do children wear?
10. What is the name of a popular Halloween game?

3 Find out information about the Halloween apple game. Write simple sentences to describe it.

Thanksgiving

In 1863 President *Abraham Lincoln* declared *Thanksgiving,* the English *"Harvest Feast",* a National holiday. Since then, every year on the last Thursday of November, it is celebrated all over the United States of America. In memory of the first English colonists, the *"Pilgrim Fathers"*, American families have a special meal on *Thanksgiving Day*: turkey with cranberry sauce, corn on the cob, potatoes, pumpkin and apple pie! People still keep alive the tradition of praying to thank God for all they have in their lives. They usually spend the holiday going to parades or spending their time at home with family and friends. They traditionally watch football matches on television in the evening.

ACTIVITIES

1 Translate each word into Italian.

a. Turkey .... TURCHIA
b. Cranberry sauce .... SALSA DI MIRTILLI
c. Corn on the cob .... PANNOCCHIE
d. Potatoes .... PATATE
e. Pumpkin pie .... TORTA DI ZUCCA
f. Apple pie .... TORTA DI MELE

2 Answer the following questions.

1. Why do Americans celebrate Thanksgiving?
2. Is it a National Holiday?
3. Who declared it?
4. When is it?
5. Do Americans stay with their families?
6. What does the traditional meal consist of?
7. Do Americans go to parades?
8. What is the most famous parade in New York?
9. Are there football matches on television on *Thanksgiving Day*?
10. What season starts on Thanksgiving weekend?

3 Find out and write information about the history of *Macy's Thanksgiving Parade* in New York. Imagine, draw and colour your parade. Glue pictures too.

DID YOU KNOW?

- *Thanksgiving* weekend is the official beginning of the Christmas season in the USA.
- *Macy's Thanksgiving Parade* is the traditional New York annual parade. It is fun; there are giant balloons, floats, cheerleaders, clowns and marching bands! Macy's is one of the most popular stores in New York.

Independence Day

Independence Day is on 4th July and is considered of the United States of America's birthday as it celebrates the separation from Britain. *George Washington*, who was the first American President, declared the country's Independence in 1776 with an important document called the *Declaration of Independence*. On this day Americans don't stay at home but have a special outdoor meal. They usually have picnics and barbecues and love eating typical American food like grilled hamburgers and sausages, fried chicken, ribs, hot dogs, potatoes, corn on the cob with butter and of course the American flag pie which substitutes the traditional apple pie because it's made of ingredients that are the same colours as the American flag! There are parades during the day and firework displays at night. The President of the USA gives a speech on television and marching bands play the American national anthem or the patriotic song *"God Bless America"* that people love to sing.

> American Flag Pie with strawberries, blueberries and cherries.

DID YOU KNOW?

On *Independence Day* American families decorate their houses with the national flag and many red, white and blue ribbons.

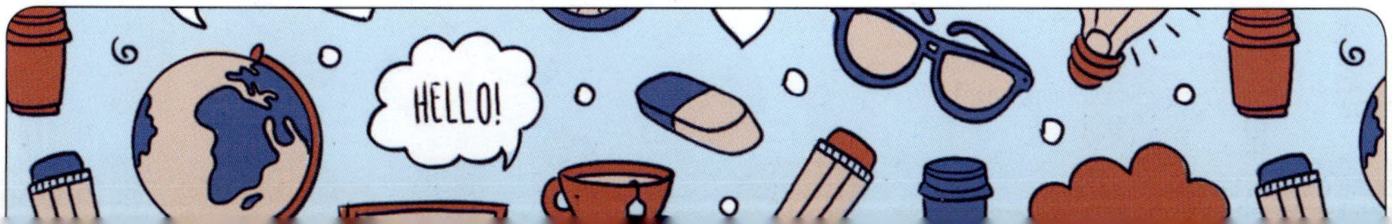

DID YOU KNOW?

Celine Dion, a Canadian pop singer, performed the song *God Bless America* following the terrorist attack on 11th September 2001 as tribute to heroes.

ACTIVITIES

1 Translate each word into Italian.

1. Outdoor ....
2. Ribs..........................
3. Marching bands ....
4. Strawberry....................
5. Blueberry.....................
6. Cherry ....
7. Ribbons ....
8. National anthem ....
9. Floats ....
10. Terrorist attack ....
11. Heroes ....
12. Tribute ....

2 Answer the following questions.

1. When is *Independence Day*?
2. What do Americans celebrate?
3. When was the *Declaration of Independence*?
4. Where do Americans go on this holiday?
5. What typical food is eaten on *Independence Day*?
6. Why do they make the American Flag pie?
7. What is the name of the USA anthem?
8. What does *God Bless America* mean?
9. Do Americans decorate their houses? How?
10. What happened on 11th September 2001?

3 Say if the following sentences are True (T) or False (F) and correct the false ones.

a. *Independence Day* is considered the birthday of the USA. T F
b. It is a religious holiday. T F
c. *Independence Day* celebrates the independence from France. T F
d. On this day Americans usually stay at home. T F
e. The typical food of the day is grilled meat. T F
f. On 4th July there are parades and firework displays. T F
g. *God Bless America* is the USA's national anthem. T F
h. Celine Dion is a Spanish singer. T F

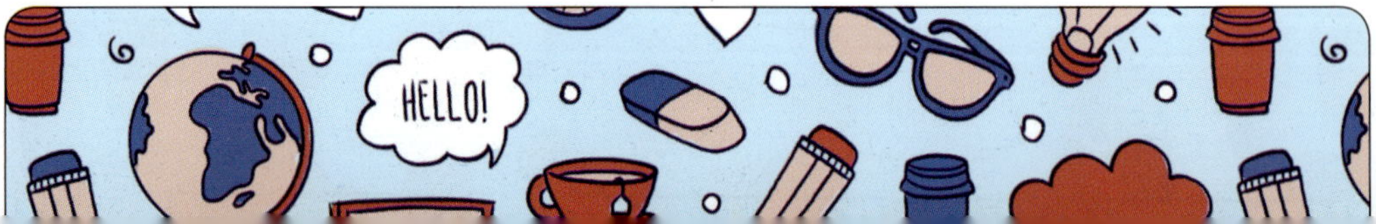

LISTENING ACTIVITY

Read and listen to the song "God Bless America" then translate the lyrics.

Link: http://bit.ly/1KphqAc

God bless America
Land that I love
Stand beside her
And guide her
Through the night
With the light
From above
From the mountains
To the prairies
To the oceans
White with foam
God bless America
My home sweet home

God bless America
Land that I love
Stand beside her
And guide her
Through the night
With the light from above

From the mountains
To the prairies
To the oceans
White with foam
God bless America
My home sweet home
From the mountains
To the prairies
To the oceans
White with foam
God bless America
My home sweet home
God bless America
God bless America

(whispering:)
God bless America
My home sweet home

Americans celebrate Christmas...

Christmas and *Easter* are two important holidays for American people, both are celebrated in traditional ways.

Christmas is really a special time for Americans. They adorn their houses with coloured lights and big Christmas trees. They love shopping so they run from one shop to another to buy gifts. In each shop, there are beautiful decorations, Christmas music and *Father Christmas* or *Santa Claus*, as they call him, who is there to meet children. The Christmas shopping begins on *"Black Friday"* which is the day following Thanksgiving and in which there are promotional sales.

A popular tradition is to send Christmas cards. Americans use the Christmas cards that they receive as decorations in the house and hang Christmas stockings that Santa Claus will fill with sweets! On Christmas day there is a special dinner and traditional desserts such as *Christmas Pudding* and *Mince Pies* which, according to the tradition are Santa Claus's favourites!

...and Easter too!

Easter is egg painting time! All the children start decorating their eggs some weeks before Easter. When the eggs are ready on *Easter Sunday*, they are put in a basket, which usually has a rabbit shape, in the centre of the table. Another symbol that can't be missed at Easter is the *Easter Bunny*! Children call rabbits "*bunnies*" and they can be seen in every toy shop. Families enjoy hiding chocolate eggs that children believe the Easter bunnies have left during the night. In the morning the egg hunt begins, with children going around the house and garden with their baskets looking for the eggs and candy that the Easter Bunny has bought them. Every year the USA President celebrates the holiday too. This American Easter celebration, which is held at the White House, includes a visit by the Easter bunny, an egg roll and an Easter egg hunt!

DID YOU KNOW?

- Prince Albert, the German husband of Queen Victoria, brought to Britain, his country's tradition of decorating *Christmas trees*.
- The first *Christmas cards* were sent in the Victorian period.
- *Santa Claus's* picture, shaped into the jolly character that we know and love today, has changed the colour of his outfit over time. During the Victorian Age and before, he wore a range of colours such as green, brown, blue and red. In the 1930s a certain American soft drinks company decided that Santa Claus should be dressed in red as a part of their marketing campaign.
- The *Easter Bonnet* is a type of hat that people wear during the Easter day parades.
- Valentine's Day is largely celebrated in the USA. Shops sell a great variety of cards and people share lovely moments with friends, lovers and families. Houses are decorated with flowers and there are heart shaped lights in the windows. Many families may even have evening parties with special food. The most popular presents are, of course, heart shaped chocolates!

Write your love note!

....

....

....

....

....

ACTIVITIES

1 Answer the following questions.

1. What are two important American religious holidays?
2. Do Americans decorate their houses and gardens? How?
3. Do they like to send Christmas cards?
4. When do they start Christmas shopping? Why?
5. What is the traditional Christmas dessert?
6. Who comes during the night with presents and toys?
7. What do children call the Easter rabbit?
8. What do children prepare for Easter Sunday?
9. What does the Easter Bunny bring to children?
10. Does the USA President celebrate Easter at the White House? How?

2 Find the following words about Christmas and Easter. There are two wish messages, try to discover them! *Christmas - Tree - Cards - Gifts - Eggs - Rabbit - Pudding - Bunny -Toys - Lights - Stockings - Basket - Happy.*

Q	W	E	R	T	Y	U	I	O	P	A	S	D	F	G	H	J	K	L
M	N	B	V	C	X	Z	S	D	F	G	G	X	V	B	N	M	I	O
L	I	G	H	T	S	E	S	D	F	G	I	L	P	O	I	U	Y	T
R	E	W	E	O	T	F	G	H	J	K	F	U	E	Y	T	R	E	D
M	E	R	R	Y	G	C	H	R	I	S	T	M	A	S	M	N	P	O
G	H	J	K	S	T	A	R	E	S	D	S	V	S	C	X	D	U	R
Z	X	C	V	B	N	R	T	Y	U	I	O	K	T	J	H	G	D	F
R	T	Y	U	I	O	D	P	B	L	K	J	H	E	G	F	D	D	S
A	Z	X	E	G	G	S	V	A	B	N	M	K	R	A	B	B	I	T
Q	W	R	T	Y	U	I	L	S	M	N	B	V	C	X	U	Z	N	L
K	J	H	G	S	T	O	C	K	I	N	G	S	F	D	N	S	G	A
W	E	R	T	Y	R	U	I	E	O	L	K	J	H	G	N	F	D	S
Q	C	E	R	D	E	F	G	T	K	L	H	A	P	P	Y	N	H	Y
T	R	D	F	G	E	H	J	K	L	P	O	I	H	F	G	H	V	N

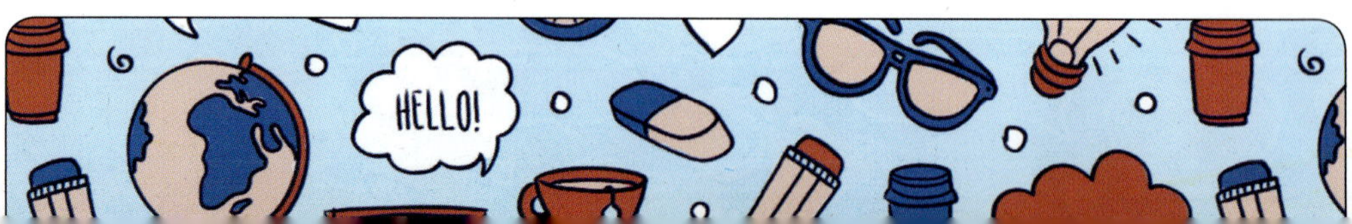

READING COMPREHENSION

Trooping the Colour

Trooping the Colour is one of the most important ceremonies that take place in London every year. It celebrates the Queen's birthday and is really spectacular. Queen Elizabeth II's birthday is on 21st April, but it is celebrated in public on the second Saturday of June when the weather is better.

The ceremony is performed by Foot Guards and the Household Cavalry on Horse Guards parade in Whitehall, a main road in the city of Westminster, Central London. The Foot Guards band plays music too. Lots of ordinary people and members of the Royal family go to watch it.

The origins of the ceremony date back to the 17th century exactly with the Stuart king, King Charles II. The name of the event derives from the fact that under his reign a single battalion used to troop the colours during battle so that they could be seen and recognized by the other soldiers. Flags were used on the battlefield as a rallying point for the army.

Every year during the ceremony a different battalion of the Brigade of Guards has the honour of trooping its own colours while marching past the Queen. The Queen travels on an old carriage and carries out an inspection of the troops while the national anthem "God Save the Queen" is played and blank shots are fired in Green Park and from the Tower of London in her honour. Queen Elizabeth II leads the troops along the Mall, a road between Buckingham Palace and Trafalgar Square, and up to her Palace where she goes onto the balcony to greet people and to watch the Royal Air Force show.

The parade first took place in 1748 thanks to King William III of Orange. In 1760 George III decided that the Sovereign's birthday would be celebrated on that date every year.

EXERCISES

1 Write True (T) or False (F) next to the following sentences. Correct the false ones.

a. Trooping the colour takes place in Spring. T F
b. This ceremony is really spectacular. T F
c. The parade is in the courtyard of Buckingham Palace. T F
d. During the ceremony the band of the Foot Guards plays. T F
e. People can't watch the ceremony. T F
f. Trooping the Colour dates back to Charles II's reign. T F
g. The Queen travels on an old carriage during the ceremony. T F
h. The Mall is an ancient building in London. T F

2 Read the text and answer the following questions.

a. When does the *Trooping the Colour* ceremony take place?
b. Is the Queen's birthday in June?
c. Why does the *Trooping the Colour* ceremony take place in June?
d. Where does the ceremony take place?
e. Who has the honour of trooping its own colour?
f. What does the Queen do during the ceremony?
g. What happens while Queen Elizabeth II is carrying out an inspection of the troops?
h. How does the Queen get to Buckingham Palace?

WRITING A SUMMARY

STEP BY STEP

Some tips on how to write a summary.
A volte la stesura di un riassunto potrebbe essere richiesta da una consegna contenente la traccia, che, in genere, ne facilita la produzione perché aiuta a capire e a scrivere i punti salienti del brano.

1st step
Leggi il brano. Poi segui la traccia e sottolinea le frasi utili per scrivere il riassunto. Esse indicano le idee principali.

2nd step
Usa i connettori per unirle e scrivere il riassunto.

Example: read the text "Trooping the Colour" and write the summary. Mention:

1 what Trooping the Colour is;
2 what it celebrates;
3 when it takes place;
4 who performs Trooping the Colour;
5 what its origins are;
6 who organized the first parade;
7 who decided to celebrate the Monarch's birthday with this parade;
8 what the Queen does during the ceremony.

Dopo aver sottolineato questi punti nel brano unisci le frasi con i connettori rielaborandole in modo personale.

Summary
Trooping the Colour
Trooping the Colour is an important ceremony that celebrates the Queen's birthday on the second Saturday of June. During the ceremony there is a parade of Foot Guards and Household Cavalry in Whitehall. A battalion of the Brigade of Guards has the honour of trooping its own colour while marching past the Queen.
This event goes back to Charles II's reign when a single battalion used to troop the colours during a battle so that they could be seen and recognized by their own soldiers.
The first parade was organized under King William III of Orange but George III decided that it should celebrate the Monarch's birthday every year.
During the ceremony Elizabeth II carries out an inspection of the troops, then she leads them along the Mall travelling on an old carriage and finally she arrives at Buckingham Palace from where she greets the crowds and watches the *Royal Air Force* show.

WRITING A SUMMARY

Write a summary about Easter and give the following information:

- when Easter occurs;
- what it celebrates;.
- what people do on Good Friday.;
- what people do on Easter Sunday.

/12

WRITING A LETTER

Write a letter to a pen-friend and describe how you spend your Christmas Day:

- where you spend Christmas;
- who you spend it with;
- what you do on Christmas Day;
- what you eat;
- ask your pen-friend about his/her Christmas Day.

/15

BUILDING UP A DIALOGUE

Write a dialogue between a British boy called John and yourself following these instructions. Read the texts *Bonfire Night*, *Christmas* and *Notting Hill Carnival*:

You: Chiedi a John la data di *Notting Hill Carnival*.

John: Risponde che è intorno alla fine di agosto.

You: Chiedi perché questo carnevale si festeggia ad agosto.

John: Risponde che a febbraio fa troppo freddo.

You: Chiedi quand'è Bonfire Night.

John: Risponde che Bonfire Night è il 5 novembre.

You: Chiedi che cosa fa per Bonfire Night.

John: Risponde che fa una festa con i suoi amici e mangia salsicce e patate. Adesso sta costruendo un fantoccio che brucerà sul falò quella sera.

You: Chiedi che cosa fa alla vigilia di Natale.

John: Risponde che appende la calza al caminetto.

You: Chiedi che cosa mangia il giorno di Natale.

John: Risponde che mangia tacchino e poi il Christmas pudding. /24

OPEN - DIALOGUE

Complete the following dialogues with the words in the boxes.

does	tall	hair	eyes	who	look

Fiona 1________ is Miss Candle?
Sheila She's our new English teacher.
Fiona What 2_______ she 3___________ like?
Sheila She's 4______ and she's got blond 5_____ and brown 6__________.

shall	would	I'd love to	let's	good

A 1_________ you like to come for a walk?
B Oh yes, 2_______________!
A 3______ we go this afternoon?.
B Yes, OK. 4_______meet at 5 pm. Is that OK?
A 5_________ idea! /11

LISTENING ACTIVITY

Listen to "The Addams Family" song and complete the text with the following words.

Link: http://bit.ly/1RsafZk

witch	broomstick	creepy
together	sweet	mysterious
scream	museum	

The Addams Family

They're ________ and they're kooky.
____________ and spooky.
They're all _________ ooky.
The Addams Family.
Their house is a ___________ .
When people come to see'em.
They really are a _________ .
The Addams Family.
Neat
____
Petite
So get a _________ 's shawl on.
A ___________ you can crawl on.
We're going to pay a call on.
The Addams Family.
They're creepy and they're kooky.
Mysterious and spooky.
They're altogether ooky.
The Addams Family.

1. Sing it now and at your Halloween party too.

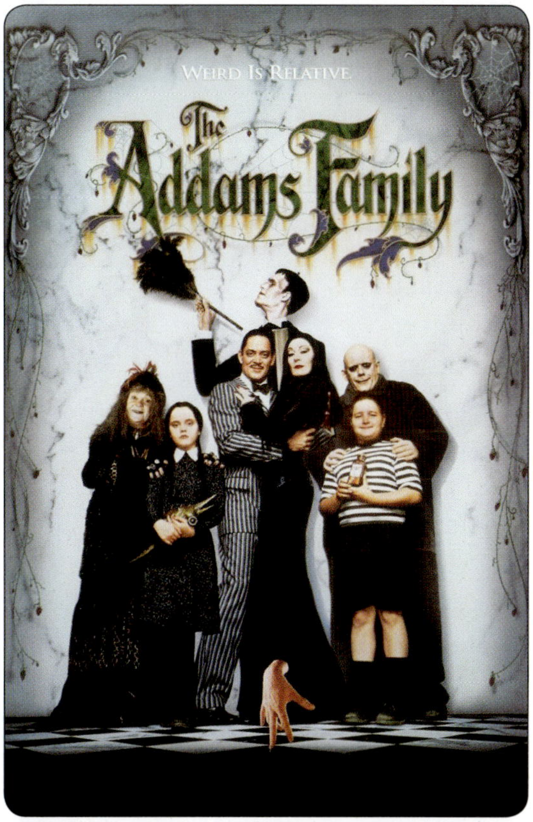

TRINITY GRADE 4

CEFR level A2.2

Total exam time: 10 minutes.

Conversation

Examiner:

- Good morning!
- What's your name?
- Where are you from?
- Do you like travelling?
- What type of holidays do you like?
- Where did you go on holiday last year?
- How did you get there?
- Where did you stay?
- Do you usually go sightseeing?
- Did you go on a school trip last year?
- Did you enjoy it?
- What was the weather like?
- Did you take photos?

Look at this picture!

Conversation

- Where are these people?
- How many children are there?
- Are they playing?
- What colour is the boat?
- How many people are swimming?
- Is there a woman?
- What is she doing?
- Is she wearing sunglasses?
- Are there beach umbrellas? How many?
- What colour is the man's hat?
- What is he reading?
- Ask me about my last holidays.

You: Where did you go and what did you do on your last holiday?

Examiner: OK. Thanks a lot. Bye

You: Thanks. Goodbye.

CHAPTER 07

LIFE IN BRITAIN AND THE USA

DIALOGUE

Birthday party

Caroline: Hello, Martina!

Martina: Hello, Caroline!

Caroline: In a few days it will be my birthday. I'd like you to come to my birthday party.

Martina: I'd love to come. Where is the party?

Caroline: I'll have my birthday party at home. I have got a very large house.

Martina: Do you live in a house or in a flat?

Caroline: I live in a detached house. It has got a large garden so we can celebrate my birthday outdoors.

Martina: That is a good idea. But, when is your birthday?

Caroline: It's next Thursday. I was born on 10th November.

Martina: I prefer having my birthday party in a pub, where I can meet my friends. Also because I live in a flat and it is rather small.

Caroline: And when is your birthday?

Martina: My birthday? It's on 11th May. See you on Thursday at your party, Caroline!

Caroline: See you, Martina.

EXERCISE

1 Answer the following questions.

1. When is Caroline's birthday?
2. Where will Caroline celebrate her birthday?
3. Where does Caroline live, in a house or in a flat?
4. Has the house got a garden?
5. Is Martina going to Caroline's birthday party?
6. When was Caroline born?
7. When is your birthday?
8. Do you usually celebrate your birthday?
9. Do you usually have a birthday party?
10. Where do you celebrate your birthday?

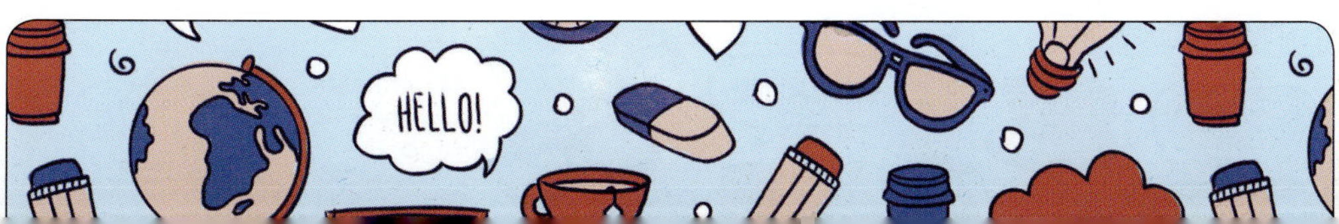

1st LESSON

BRITISH HOUSES

In the UK there are different types of houses: *detached houses, semi-detached houses, terraced houses, bungalows, flats* and *cottages*.

Detached houses are single houses with a front and back garden and a garage. They have two floors, called an upstairs and a downstairs. Upstairs you can find bedrooms, a bathroom and a study; downstairs there is usually a hall, a kitchen, a dining room, a living room and a bathroom. This type of house is generally in the outskirts of towns.

Semi-detached houses consist of one building that is shared between two families, each with its own house. In short the two houses are attached on one side and have a garden and a fence. Their structure is similar to detached houses. They are very popular in the UK and are also in the outskirts of towns and villages.

Bungalows are houses which have only one floor. In towns and cities you can find blocks of flats, which are apartments, or terraced houses that are identical houses built in

ACTIVITIES

1 Read the text and place the correct words under the drawings.

Block of flats   cottage   detached house   terraced houses
semi-detached houses   houseboats

----

rows, each one next to the another. Terraced houses have two floors: there are bedrooms and a bathroom upstairs, while downstairs there is a hall, a dining room with a kitchen, a living room and a toilet.

Cottages are small houses. Some of them have a thatched roof that is made of straw. You can find them in the countryside. Some of them have only one floor.

Some people in the UK live on houseboats on rivers or canals.

ACTIVITIES

2 True or false

Read the text "British houses" and write T (true) or F (false) next to the following sentences. Correct the false ones.

a. In Britain there is a mixture of house types. T F
b. Detached houses are single houses. T F
c. In British villages there are blocks of flats. T F
d. In British towns there are streets with houses in rows. T F
e. Cottages are very large. T F
f. In Britain there aren't any houseboats. T F

3 Read the text "British houses" again and answer the following questions.

1. How many floors have detached houses got?
2. What is there upstairs? And downstairs?
3. Is there a garden?
4. What are semi-detached houses?
5. Where can you find apartments?
6. What are terraced houses?
7. Where are they?
8. Which houses have got thatched roofs?
9. Where can you find houseboats?
10. What type of house is yours?

4 SPEAKING

Describe your house. Mention:

a. where you live, in a house or in a flat;
b. what type of house it is;
c. where it is;
d. how many bedrooms there are;
e. how many bathrooms there are,
f. if there is a living room;
g. if there is a cellar or an attic;
h. where you eat, in the kitchen or in the dining room;
i. if there is a garden;
j. if you share your bedroom.

BRITISH FOOD

Breakfast, *lunch* and *dinner* are the three main meals in England.

Breakfast is a rich meal. British people usually drink tea or coffee or have milk with cornflakes and some toast with butter and jam or marmalade. The typical and popular English breakfast that foreign people want to try is less common than in the past because students and people who work choose to have a standard breakfast in order not to waste too much time before school or work. However on Sundays some British people have the traditional breakfast that consists of milk, coffee or tea, orange juice, bacon, toast with butter and jam or marmalade, eggs, sausages and cakes.

Lunch is a very quick meal. Generally people have a sandwich and fruit at work or school, in a canteen or in a pub. Students take a packed lunch to school or eat at the school canteen.

The main meal of the day is dinner for most people who usually have it around 6 or 6.30 p.m.. They eat meat or fish with vegetables and then a dessert: some ice cream, a piece of cake or apple pie. They drink wine or

ACTIVITIES

1 **Complete with the correct word.**

....

....

....

....

....

....

water. Some people start dinner with a vegetable soup.
On Sundays they may have one main meal called brunch which is a fusion of breakfast + lunch, this meal is usually eaten late in the morning but it can be extended to the early afternoon. Another typical Sunday meal is the very popular *Roast Dinner,* consisting of Roast chicken, roast potatoes, steamed vegetables and gravy. Meals usually end with a dessert called pudding.
Teenagers love eating hamburgers and chips or the famous *fish and chips.*
In the UK there are a lot of take-away restaurants where you can buy food and eat it at home. Chinese, Indian and Italian restaurants are very popular.

Teatime

Teatime is an important moment of the day. It's generally at 5 p.m. and it is a break for a cup of tea and home-made pastries.
The typical teapot is a popular souvenir that you can take back home when you visit the UK.

DID YOU KNOW?

When British people are at table for lunch or dinner they use the expression «Enjoy your meal» or «Bon appétit» that corresponds to the Italian «Buon appetito».

ACTIVITIES

ESERCIZI ON LINE www.medusaeditrice.it

2 Look at the following drawings, add the missing words and learn the vocabulary.

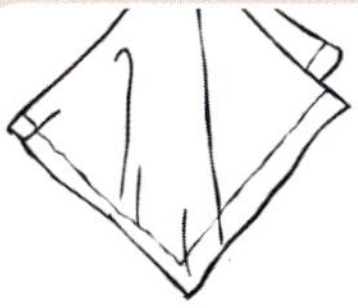

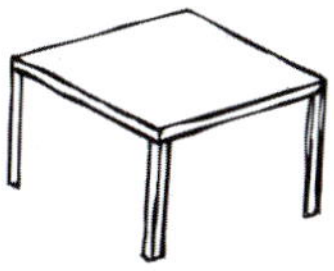

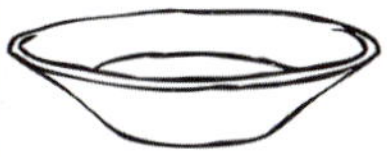

ACTIVITIES

ESERCIZI ON LINE www.medusaeditrice.it

1 True or false? Correct the wrong sentences.

a. The most important meal in Great Britain is dinner. T F
b. Breakfast is a quick meal. T F
c. British people usually have the typical English breakfast. T F
d. Dinner is at 6 or 6.30 p.m. T F
e. Teenagers favourite food is fish and chips. T F
f. Tea time is at 7 p.m. T F
g. Some British people eat pudding on Sundays. T F
h. The typical teapot is a popular souvenir from the UK. T F

2 Read the text "British food" and answer the following questions.

1. How many meals do British people have?
2. What do British people eat for breakfast?
3. And for lunch?
4. What does the typical English breakfast consist of?
5. Why is lunch a very quick meal?
6. Where do British people have lunch?
7. What do teenagers prefer eating?
8. What do British people have for dinner?
9. What do they have for dessert?
10. What do some people have on Sundays?

3 SPEAKING

Talk about your meals and say.

- What time do you have breakfast?
- What do you have for breakfast?
- Do you have a snack at school?
- What time do you have lunch?
- Where do you have lunch?
- What do you have for lunch?
- What time do you have dinner?
- What do you have for dinner?
- What's your favourite food?

3rd LESSON

RISORSE ON-LINE
www.medusaeditrice.it

SPORTS IN THE UK

British people love sport and they like practicing it in their daily lives .
In the UK the most popular sports are *football, cricket, rugby* and *tennis*. But there are also other sports such as *golf, swimming, rowing* and *horse-racing*.

Read and then study the drawings and complete them with the correct word.

Golf

Golf is the sport most loved by Scottish people. It originated in Scotland in the 15th century. It is played on grassy fields where players use long sticks called clubs with which they hit a small ball into holes.

Read and then study the drawings and complete them with the correct word.

Cricket

Cricket is the *national sport* of England, it probably started in the 14th century. It's played on a ground called a pitch by two teams of eleven players. Each team is on an area of the pitch, either the larger oval area or the smaller rectangular part. The *bowler* has to throw the ball and try to hit the batsman's *wicket* which is a set of wooden stumps, *the batsman* has to prevent this by trying to hit the ball with a bat. After hitting the ball the batsman has to run and go towards the opposite end of the pitch in order to score a run. The batsman wears a helmet and gloves.

Read and then study the drawings and complete them with the correct word.

Rugby

Welsh people particularly like rugby. It is played by two teams with an oval ball. A legend says that a student from Rugby, a town in England, invented the game in 1823. During a football match he picked up the ball and ran to score a goal. On the rugby pitch there are two H-shaped goalposts that consist of two poles connected by a horizontal crossbar above the ground.

Read and then study the drawings and complete them with the correct word.

Tennis

Modern tennis started in England in 1874. Every year in Wimbledon, between June and July, the famous British championship is played.
Tennis matches are played on a lawn called a tennis court. The players use tennis rackets.

Football

Football is the sport that British people like more than any other. The rules of modern football were invented in England in 1863. Each country in the UK has its own national team and Football leagues. Matches are played every Saturday afternoon from August to April. There are two important competitions, the Premier League and the Football Association Cup. The final of the latter is played at Wembley Stadium in London in May.
Some of the most popular British football teams are:

Arsenal

Chelsea Football Club

Leicester City Football Club

Manchester United

Manchester City

ACTIVITIES

1 True or false? Correct the wrong sentences.

a. British people love sport. T F
b. Football is the most popular sport in Great Britain. T F
c. Cricket is played on a court. T F
d. The bowler uses a bat to hit the ball. T F
e. Golf originated in Scotland. T F
f. Welsh people love playing basketball. T F
g. The Wimbledon tournament is very popular all over the world. T F
h. Football matches are played on Saturdays. T F

2 Read the text "Sports in the UK" again and answer the following questions.

1. What sports are popular in Great Britain?
2. What's the national sport of England?
3. What does the batsman do?
4. What does a bowler have to do?
5. When did golf originate?
6. What do golf players use?
7. Where did rugby originate?
8. What does the legend say about its origins?
9. When did modern tennis start?
10. Where were football rules invented?
11. Where is the Cup Final played?
12. Mention some popular British football teams.

3 SPEAKING

Talk about sport and say:

- what your favourite sport is;
- if you do any sports;
- who your favourite player is;
- who your favourite team is;
- if you do sport at school.

BRITISH TRANSPORT

Transport in the UK

Britain can be easily reached by plane. London has four international airports: *Heathrow*, the largest one, *Gatwick*, *Luton* and *Stansted*. But there are airports in Manchester and Birmingham, too. In Scotland the most important international airport is Glasgow. The national airline company is *British Airways*. There are also popular low cost airline companies such as *Easy Jet*.

Britain can also be reached by train. From Calais in France to Folkstone near Dover in England you can travel by train through the Channel tunnel. There are two trains, one for passengers and another one for cars.

You can also reach Great Britain by ferry.

As regards to traffic in Britain people drive on the left like in Japan, India, Australia and New Zealand.

Unlike other European cars, British cars have the driving wheel on the right. The choice of driving on the left probably dates back to the middle ages when knights used to walk on the left so that in case of danger they could easily take out their swords with their right hands, and then subsequently to the rules imposed by Napoleon. In France nobles used to travel by carriage on the left side of the road while other people were obliged to travel on the right. After the Revolution this habit changed and in 1794 they established a new law to keep the right. French customs were imposed by Napoleon to most of Europe but the English and their colonies refused to accept the enemy's customs.

ACTIVITIES

ESERCIZI ON LINE www.medusaeditrice.it

1 Look at the pictures and match them with the correct words.

Runway platform baggage check-in desk pier gate boarding pass Traffic Light

London transport

In London there are various means of transport: trains, buses, taxis and ferries. Some of them are particularly popular as, for example, the *Underground* called *the tube* by Londoners because of the tubular shape of some of its tunnels, and the typical red double-decker buses. The first underground line was opened between Baker Street and the City in 1863.

There are eleven main train stations in London and King's

Cross station is one of these. Today a lot of tourists go there to see platform $9^{3/4}$ because it is the place where Harry Potter caught the train to Hogwarts School.
London taxis are very popular, too. They're black.
As the river Thames flows through London, another form of transport used to visit the city is the *ferry*. There's also an amphibious vehicle that travels both on land and water, it is called the *Duck*.

ACTIVITIES

2 **Complete the crossword.**

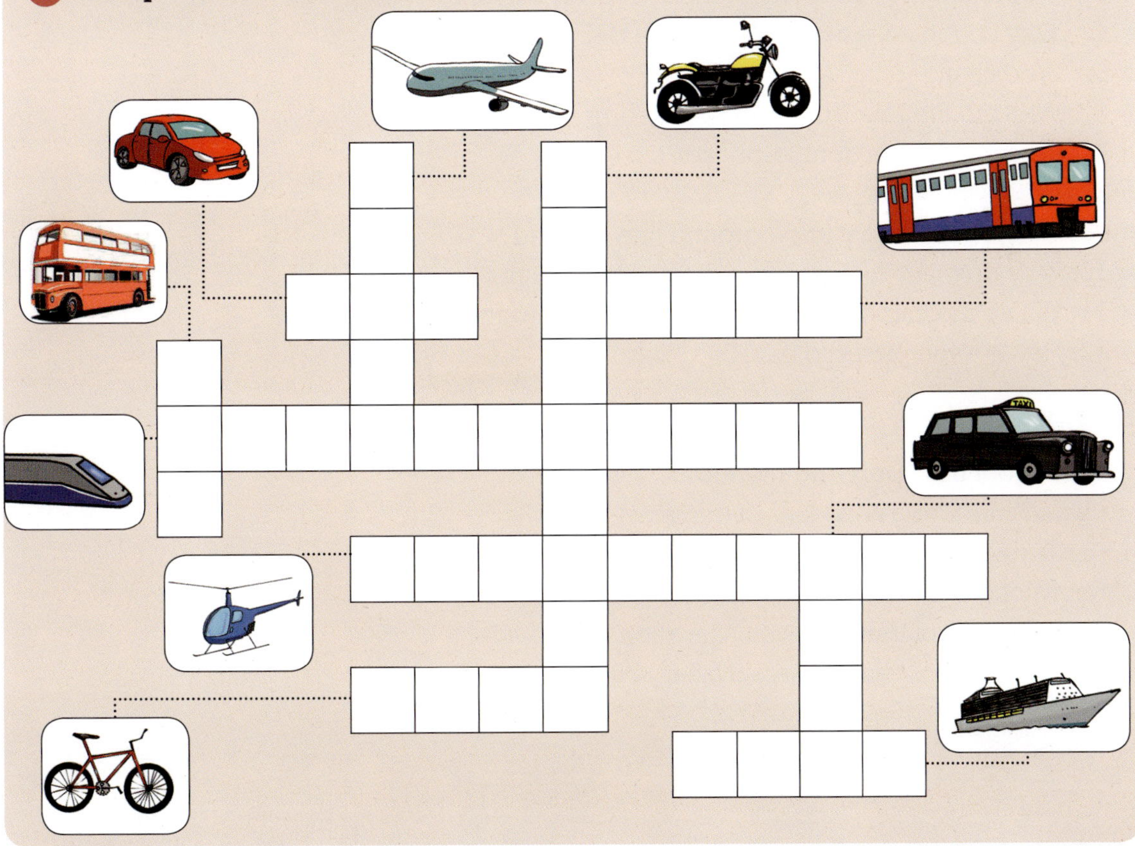

ACTIVITIES

3 True or False? Correct the false sentences.

a. You can go to the UK by plane. T F
b. Easy Jet is a popular low cost airline company. T F
c. Two trains go through the Channel tunnel. T F
d. British people drive on the right. T F
e. The *tube* tunnels have a rectangular shape. T F
f. King's Cross is one of the main London stations. T F
g. London taxis are green. T F
h. The *Duck* is an amphibious vehicle. T F

4 Read the two texts again and answer the following questions.

1. How many airports are there in London?
2. Which is the UK's national airline company?
3. Where are the two Channel tunnel railway stations?
4. Why do they drive on the left in the U.K.?
5. Who changed this habit?
6. Why did the English refuse Napoleon's decision?
7. What colour are double-decker buses?
8. What's the Tube?
9. When was the first underground line opened?
10. Why do many tourists go to King's Cross station?
11. What's the name of the river which flows through London?
12. How do you prefer to travel?

5 SPEAKING

Talk about transport and mention:

- what your favourite means of transport is;
- how you go to school;
- how long it takes you to go to school;
- what means of transport you use when you travel;
- what means of transport are available in your town.

THE CHANNEL TUNNEL

Fact file
English name: Channel Tunnel.
French name: Le Tunnel sous la Manche.
Shortened to: Chunnel.
What is it: The longest undersea tunnel in the world.
Length: 31 miles/50 km.
Importance: It links Folkestone in Kent (UK) to Coquelles in Pas de Calais, in France.
Tunnelling started: 1988.
Tunnel opening: The tunnel was opened on 6th May 1994 by Queen Elizabeth II and the French President Francois Mitterrand.

DID YOU KNOW?

- To determine where to place the Channel tunnel a contest was held.
- Both the British and French started to dig from each side at the same time.
- At the opening of the tunnel, the Queen travelled through the tunnel to Calais on a Eurostar train, which stopped nose to nose with the train from Paris on which the French President Francois Mitterrand was travelling on.
- In 1994, the Chunnel was elected as one of the seven modern WONDERS of the WORLD.

ACTIVITIES

1 Match the words.

a. Tunnel — 1. Viaggiare
b. Channel — 2. Inaugurazione
c. Undersea — 3. Meraviglia
d. Opening — 4. Canale
e. Travel — 5. Galleria
f. Wonder — 6. Sottomarino

2 Say if the following sentences are TRUE (T) or FALSE (F) and correct the false ones.

a . The Chunnel is the longest undersea tunnel in the world. T F
b. It is 50 miles long. T F
c. It links Folkestone with Coquelles. T F
d. Tunneling started in 1987. T F
e. The tunnel was opened in 1994. T F
f. Queen Elizabeth and President Mitterrand opened the tunnel. T F
g. The Queen travelled on a Eurostar train. T F
h. The French President travelled from London. T F

3 Answer the following questions.

1. What is the English name of the tunnel?
2. And the French one?
3. What is its nickname?
4. How long is the tunnel?
5. Which countries does the Chunnel link?
6. When did tunneling start?
7. When was it opened?
8. Who opened the tunnel?
9. What title was the Chunnel given?
10. Would you like to travel through the Channel?

4 Write a paragraph about the Chunnel using the points of the fact file.

5 Talk about the Chunnel using the points of the fact file and mention:

- what the English name of the tunnel is;
- what the French name of the tunnel is;
- its nickname;
- how long the tunnel is;
- what the tunnel links;
- when it was opened;
- who opened it;
- the title it was given;
- if you would like to travel through the tunnel.

FOOD IN THE USA

Let's read about the lifestyle of Americans! Their food, sport, leisure time, housing and transport habits.

Food
We all know that the history of America is based on immigration and that the country is a *melting pot* with different cultures living together, in this respect food is the mirror of the USA's social reality. Shops that sell foreign products for the preparation of ethnic dishes are everywhere and a wide range of restaurants, Italian, Chinese, Greek, Indian and Mexican, can be found in American towns.
There are suburbs whose inhabitants are people who come from the same country, the most famous are *Little Italy* and *Chinatown* in New York, where communities have kept their food traditions alive. Americans share their typical dishes with their foreign food eating habits. However, despite the different origins, almost all Americans have three main meals: *breakfast, lunch* and *dinner.*

Breakfast
Americans believe that it is very important to face the day by having a good breakfast, so it is a hearty meal. Many have scrambled eggs with bacon or toast with ham and cheese and a fruit salad but others prefer something lighter like a bowl of cereal with milk or some toasted bread with jam or pancakes with maple syrup. They usually drink American coffee or orange juice.

DID YOU KNOW?

- *Brunch* is a meal that Americans have between breakfast and lunch time.
- Americans drink their long coffee many times a day and wherever they are, so *take-away coffee* is very popular.

ACTIVITIES

1 Translate each word into Italian.

a. Scrambled eggs ....
b. Ham............................
c. Fruit salad......................
d. Cereal..........................
e. Bread ....
f. Maple syrup......................
g. Bacon ....
h. Cheese..........................
i. Bowl ....
j. Milk............................
k. Jam ....
l. Juice ....

2 Read the text and complete the words under each picture.

C....................
B....................

O..................
J..................

P..................

S..................
E..................

F....................
S....................

T..................
C..................

T ....

J..................

Lunch

The famous American invention of fast food by Richard and Maurice McDonald gave life to the well-known *Mc Donald's fast-food* chain, which is famous all over the world! In time, other fast food restaurants like *Burger King*, *KFC*, *Pizza Hut* and the *Hard Rock Cafè* became just as popular. Americans often have their lunch in these places because they have very short breaks from work or school. Fast food restaurants are meeting places mainly for young people because food is cheaper than in other restaurants.

What's clear is that Americans love fast food! Many families with children spend their free time eating, talking and watching sport events on big TV screens in these places. Fast food restaurants sell hot dogs and different types of burgers, French-fries, pizza, salads and drinks like coke, beer and milk shakes. They usually offer various desserts like cakes or ice cream. Fast food restaurants also sell takeaway food. Tourists generally enjoy eating fast food and also try traditional American hot dogs which they can buy at hot dog stands while going around the streets of the city they are visiting.

ACTIVITIES

1 Answer the following questions.

1. Who invented the Mc Donald's chain?
2. What are the names of other popular fast food chains?
3. Why is American lunch a quick meal?
4. Where do Americans generally have it?
5. Are fast food restaurants cheaper than other kinds of restaurants?
6. What do Americans eat there?
7. Do fast food restaurants sell drinks?
8. Where do tourists stop to buy hot dogs?

2 This is the first McDonald's Corporation logo.
Look for more pictures about its evolution up to the present day.

ACTIVITIES

ESERCIZI ON LINE www.medusaeditrice.it

3 Read the text, look at the pictures and insert the correct words.

Hot dog stand, pizza, hot dog, cheeseburger, French fries, fast food restaurant.

Dinner

Dinner is not only a meal but also a moment for families to get together. People get home from work and school in the evening so they have this meal at about 6 p.m. The influence of culture creates differences from one family to another but, generally, most families have meat or fish with tomatoes, salad, green beans, or potatoes. When it is very cold they often have soups with either beans or vegetables or even chicken. Their favourite drink is coke but they also have water or wine that is usually served with ice. On Sundays families usually enjoy picnics, especially in springtime.

DID YOU KNOW?

- *Cheesecake* is one of America's favourite Desserts. Americans love handmade biscuits too.

- One of the most popular American soups is *Chicken noodle soup.*

ACTIVITIES

1 Read the following recipe and then translate it.

Chicken noodle soup.

"On a cold winter day, this hearty soup is practically a meal in itself".

Ingredients	
6 cups of canned low-salt chicken broth	....
8 ounces of chicken, cut into 8 pieces	....
1/2 cup chopped onion	....
2 carrots, peeled and thinly sliced	....
2 celery stalks, sliced	....
2 tablespoons (1/4 stick) of butter	....
1 cup of sliced mushrooms	....
1 tablespoon of fresh lemon juice	....
8 ounces of dried wide egg noodles	....
chopped fresh parsley	....

Preparation.
Combine chicken broth and chicken in a large pot. Bring to boiling point. Reduce heat; cover partially and simmer until chicken is cooked through, about 20 minutes. Using tongs, transfer the chicken to a large bowl. Cool the chicken and broth slightly. Discard skin and bones from the chicken. Cut the chicken meat into bite-size pieces and put aside. Spoon fat off the top of chicken broth.
Return broth to simmer. Add onion, carrots and celery. Simmer until vegetables soften, about 8 minutes. (Can be prepared one day ahead. Cover chicken meat and broth separately and refrigerate. Bring broth to boiling point before continuing.)
Melt 2 tablespoons of butter in a heavy large skillet over medium-high heat. Add mushrooms and sauté until beginning to brown, about 5 minutes. Stir in the lemon juice. Add mushrooms to the broth; stir in noodles, parsley and chicken pieces, salt and pepper. Simmer until the noodles are tender, about 5 minutes.

2 Translate each word into Italian.

1. Cup ....
2. Canned ....
3. Low salt ....
4. Pot ....
5. Broth ....
6. Chopped onion ....
7. Carrots ....
8. Peeled ....
9. Thinly ....
10. Sliced ....
11. Celery stalks ....
12. Simmer ....
13. Butter ....
14. Mushrooms ....
15. Bones ....
16. Dried ....
17. Wide ....
18. Egg noodles ....
19. Finely ....
20. Parsley ....

3 Find the recipe of your favourite Italian dish. Write down the main ingredients in the grid below, look for their pictures, glue and match them to the words.

1. ....
2. ....
3. ....
4. ....
5. ....
6. ....
7. ....
8. ....

ACTIVITIES

4 SPEAKING

Work in pairs. Describe your favourite dish to your partner.

5 Compare American and Italian breakfast food.

American	Italian

DID YOU KNOW?

Pound and *ounce* are American units of weight.
Cup is used for recipes.

1 pound = 453,59 grams
1 ounce = 28.35 grams
1 ounce = 28,349.52 milligrams

SPORT IN THE USA

Sport activities are top of Americans' daily habits. People love *jogging* at least once a day in the parks or even just around their house. They also like playing America's main national sports which are *football*, *baseball*, *basketball* or *ice hockey*. Of course, there are many other sports like *athletics*, *swimming* and *tennis*. Sport is an important part of school life in the American Education System; many famous players once played in school teams! Students practice different sports and need to have good school marks if they want to be part of a school team. Each school has its own teams and which take part in annual competitions.

In the USA there are national and local sports teams that people support with passion, celebrating the sport events with great enthusiasm. American sport culture has its own style and fashion that is expressed through popular sportswear brands that many people use every day and all over the world!

Baseball is a popular Summer sport. It derives from the English game of cricket. There are two teams of nine players each; who use a ball and bat. The field is called a *diamond* and has four bases. The teams take it in turn to bat. The batters have to hit the ball and then run between the bases in order to score runs. When a player goes round all four bases and returns to the home base, the team scores points. The *American League* and the *National League* are important sporting events.

Basketball is a Winter game. It is played on a court where there are two baskets, two teams of five players and of course a basketball. The teams score points if the players land the ball in the opponents' basket. Americans love playing basketball everywhere in their free time so they often have a basket in their gardens at home and there are many basketball courts in town parks. Basketball players are very tall!

American football is an Autumn and Winter sport and it is much more popular than other sports in the USA today. It developed from rugby and attracts many Americans. There are two teams, eleven players each and an oval ball. The sport field is called a *Gridiron* and is rectangular. The players have to cross the opponents' goal line carrying the ball and score a touchdown or kick the ball between the goal posts. The players protect their bodies with pads on their shoulders, elbows and knees. They also wear a helmet and mask.

DID YOU KNOW?

- The *"New York City Marathon"* is an annual running event! It is very popular; a large number of participants run through the five boroughs of New York City.
- *Super Ball Sunday* is the *American Football Champions League*. It is the biggest USA annual sporting event. There is a spectacular concert of famous singers or bands before the match.

Ice hockey is a Winter sport and it takes place in a rink. It is most popular in North American areas like Canada and the northern United States. There are two teams of six players each; they use hockey sticks and a puck to play. They skate up and down the rink trying to take the puck and score a goal against the opposing team. Players wear ice skates and special equipment to protect their bodies from bruises and severe fractures.

ACTIVITIES

1 Read the text "Sport in the USA" and answer the following questions.

1. What are the main American sports?
2. What do almost all Americans do every day?
3. Is sport an important part of the American Education System?
4. Do students practice different sports?
5. What do schools do every year?
6. How many players are in a baseball team?
7. What do they need to play?
8. Where do the baseball players play?
9. Do they protect their bodies?
10. Is basketball a Winter game?
11. Are basketball players very tall?
12. What is an American football 'ball' like?
13. What is the Gridiron?
14. What is the name of the football Champions League?
15. What do ice hockey players need to play and what do they wear?
16. Where is this Winter sport popular?

2 Find some information about an American athlete of your favourite sport and write below.

3 Do you know the names of any important American stadiums? Complete the grid in your exercise book.

Names	Places

MUSIC IN THE USA

A song, a tune, are often frames of memories and that's why some of them are timeless! There is no right age to listen to music, everybody does it, and each one has a special song and favourite music. Today, like in the past, people love listening to music and enjoy going to live concerts. Some kinds of music were born in the USA and some singers have made history. American music, past and present, is well known all over the world through famous singers like *Elvis Presley, Louis Armstrong, Bob Dylan, Bruce Springsteen, Joan Baez, Michael Jackson, Madonna* and many others that represent different kinds of music.

> Bruce Springsteen

American singers *USA for Africa (United Support of Artists for Africa)* recorded the famous song "We Are the World" in 1985.

> Madonna

DID YOU KNOW?

Blues

It is a type of American black music originally sung by slaves. It is generally slow and sad. Blues stands for "*Blue note*" that is a particular way of playing a musical instrument. Americans think blue is the colour of sadness and melancholy.

Pop

Pop stands for *popular* and means that a large number of people love this kind of melodic music.

Folk

Folk songs deal with politics, society and pacifism.

LISTENING ACTIVITY

Listen to and read the song "We Are the World" (USA for Africa), then complete the text using the words below.

link: https://youtu.be/Zi0RpNSELas

World, brighter, choice, day, saving, lives, better, just, heart, family, stronger, free, stone, lend, dying, truth, giving, believe, heed, all.

There comes a time
When we .... a certain call
When the world must come together as one
There are people.........
And it's time to ....a hand to life
The greatest gift of.........

We can't go on pretending day by day
That someone, somewhere will soon make a change
We are all a part of God's great big................
And the ...., you know
Love is all we need

We are the ...., we are the children
We are the ones who make a .... day
So let's start giving
There's a .... we're making
We're .... our own ....
It's true we'll make a .... day
Just you and me

Send them your ....
So they'll know that someone cares
And their lives will be .... and ....
As God has shown us by turning .... to bread
So we all must lend a helping hand

We are the world, we are the children
We are the ones who make a brighter day
So let's start ....
There's a choice we're making
We're saving our own lives
It's true we'll make a better day
.... you and me

When you're down and out
There seems no hope at all
But if you just............... there's no way we can fall
Let us realize that a change can only come
When we stand together as one

We are the world, we are the children
We are the ones who make a brighter day
So let's start giving
There's a choice we're making
We're saving our own lives
It's true we'll make a better ....
Just you and me

> USA for Africa

HOUSES IN THE USA

The USA is a very big country with many towns, villages and cities. With its large urban concentrations and extensive areas devoid of habitation America is a country of great geographical contrasts. For this reason there are also many different types of buildings. Two main residential categories exist in America: *apartments* and *houses*. Apartments or flats are on a single level or floor and are usually rental units in condominiums with multiple units and shared common spaces. Houses, by contrast, have more levels and can be large and luxurious. There are generally two or three rooms on each floor depending on how big the house is. A hall, kitchen, dining room, living room and one bathroom are usually located downstairs; the bedrooms, study and a second bathroom are found upstairs. Most houses have an attic and a large garage. They may have a backyard and a front yard which serve as additional areas where the inhabitants can relax or enjoy eating out in the open. Traditionally, houses are occupied by their owners and families tend to keep their property for long periods of time.

Several styles of American house architecture characterize each state. There are houses built in the *Craftsman* style, the *Country* style and the very popular *Colonial* style. The latter were influenced by colonialists of the 18th century. In Western and Southwestern states the Ranch style is very common. In the 1950s and 1960s the *Modern* style was also very popular. Of course, there are other examples of house styles throughout the United States and sometimes all the aforementioned styles can be found in the same area.

The *Craftsman* is one of the most common and popular styles in the United States.

Modern style by the architect Frank Lloyd Wright.

American cities are characterized by the presence of skyscrapers. This word was used for the first time in Chicago, where the first skyscraper, the *Home Insurance Building*, was built in 1884. This unique building had ten floors! Today most modern American skyscrapers are designed for offices. These extremely tall buildings often have more than one hundred floors. In Chicago, for example, there is the famous "*Loop*", one of the three downtown areas with a concentration of very tall and modern skyscrapers.

San Francisco and its Victorian houses called the *Painted Ladies*.

The *Loop* in Chicago.

Home Insurance Building.

Skyscrapers in New York

ACTIVITIES

1 Read the text "Houses in the USA" and Answer the following questions.

1. What types of houses are there in the USA?
2. Where are the apartments?
3. What are the differences between American houses and apartments?
4. What rooms can you find in the upstairs part of a house? And in the downstairs part?
5. Do houses have gardens?
6. What do people do there?
7. Why do Americans have the *Colonial* style?
8. What is the *Home Insurance Building*?
9. Where is it?
10. What are the *Painted Ladies*?
11. What is the *Loop*?
12. Are there any skyscrapers in your town?

ESERCIZI ON LINE www.medusaeditrice.it

2 Say if the following sentences are True (T) or False (F). Correct the false ones.

a. Americans live in houses, apartments and skyscrapers.	T	F
b. Apartments have just one level.	T	F
c. Houses in the USA don't have gardens.	T	F
d. American houses have many rooms and a garage.	T	F
e. There aren't different styles of houses in the USA.	T	F
f. Skyscrapers are very tall buildings.	T	F

3 *Craftsman style* homes belong to the *Arts and Crafts movement*. Find some information on this subject and write it below.

4 Here are some pictures of houses. Which one is your favourite house style? Choose and tick, then imagine your dream house and draw it.

☐ Ranch style

☐ Colonial style

☐ The Southern style.

☐ Cottage or Bungalow Style

☐ Mediterranean style

☐ Apartment.

☐ European style.

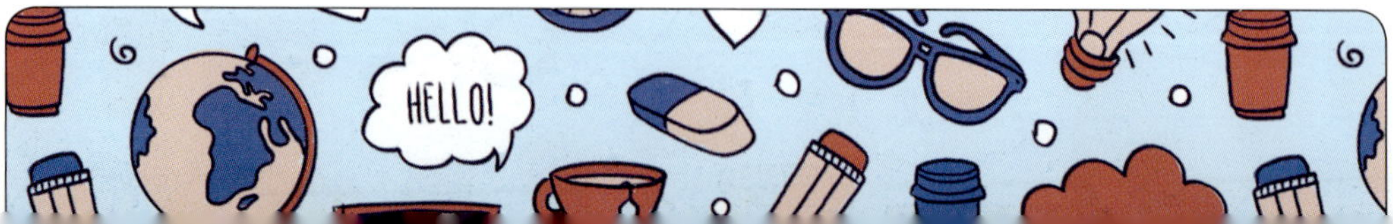

RISORSE ON-LINE
www.medusaeditrice.it

AMERICAN TRANSPORT

In the USA the public *transportation system* provides services for travelers. Everyday people use buses, trains and subways to cross American towns. There are also airplanes and coaches for long distances.

In the cities yellow taxis are on every corner! Although lots of Americans can easily drive on the wide highways, many prefer to travel by train and subway because they are the fastest means of transport.

The oldest and most famous underground railway or subway in the USA is the *New York City Subway*. Since it opened, in 1904, thousands of people have used it to reach their destination. There are 468 stations that join four New York boroughs and 27 lines each with a different colour, number and letter of the alphabet to help identify them.

The New York City Subway is opened 24 hours a day, 7 days a week! *Times Square-42nd Street* is a large New York City Subway station that is very crowded everyday of the year!

Using the subway is the cheapest way to travel, another way is to take one of the many coaches that connect America from one state to another. Many young people love travelling this way! While visiting American cities it is possible to see people skateboarding or riding bikes to go to work, that's because there are cycle paths in the towns and bikes can usually be taken on public transport. All around the States there are airports that are used by people from all over the world for tourism or business travel.

This is a photo of the newest subway station in NYC. The 2nd Ave Subway. It opened for the first time on New Year's Eve 2017.

John F. Kennedy International Airport and *La Guardia Airport* are New York's airports, they are the busiest in the USA and where millions of passengers transit each year, day and night! The *Newark International Airport* that is a little further from the city than the other two airports, is in Newark, New Jersey. As it is less crowded it is often chosen by tourists. In Washington D.C., there is the *Washington Dulles International* and the *Ronald Reagan Washington National*. One of the most famous USA airlines is *American Airways* but many others operate in the USA too.

DID YOU KNOW?

- In San Francisco, there are *Cable cars* that go up and down the rails along the streets of the steep hills of this American town. They are a historic symbol recognized around the world and are a good means of transportation.

- There are big buses and ferry tours that provide services for tourists. It's an easy way to visit the city.

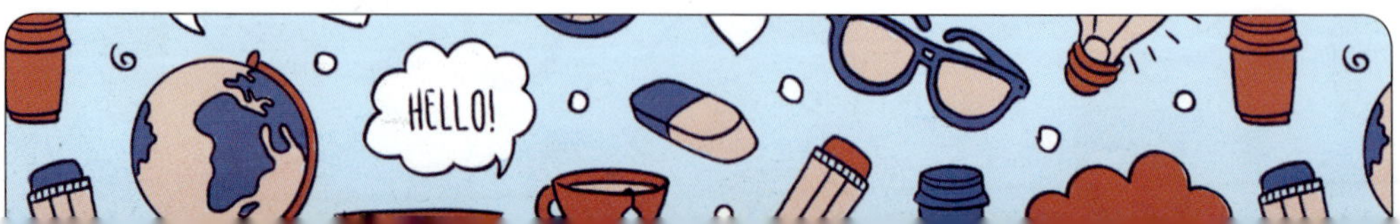

ACTIVITIES

1 Read the text and answer the following questions.

1. What are the main means of transport in the USA?
2. How do Americans prefer to travel? Why?
3. What is the subway?
4. Where is the *Times Square-42nd Street* Station?
5. When was the New York City Subway opened?
6. Why do many young people take coaches?
7. Where do coaches go?
8. What colour are American taxis?
9. How many airports are there in New York and Washington?
10. Which is the most famous USA airline?

2 Speaking and writing.

You are planning your one-week journey to New York and Washington. Look at the pictures below; choose your means of transport for visiting the towns. Write simple notes and then speak about it.

Subway train

Ferry

Bus

Train

Taxi

Coach

Bike

Plane

READING COMPREHENSION

British Music

1. Read the text and complete the exercises below.

British music is present all over the world. It is rich in stars that were and are the idols of young people. *The Beatles*, the *Rolling Stones* and *Genesis* are among the most popular stars of British music of the past. Their songs are still well-known today.

Some contemporary British singers who are popular international stars are *Elton John, Sting, One Direction, Robbie Williams, Kate Tunstall* and *Coldplay* whose songs are listened to by people worldwide. Many teenagers love *One Direction*, a band that became very popular with the song "*What Makes You Beautiful*" in 2011. The band has four members, Niall Horan, Liam Payne, Harry Styles and Louis Tomlinson.

The Beatles

The Beatles are the most influential rock band of the UK. They're a British icon. They come from Liverpool in England and their songs are very popular. Some of their songs are particularly well loved such as *Yesterday, Yellow Submarine, Hey Jude, Let It Be, All You Need Is Love* and many more. The Beatles were a symbol of the 60s and greatly influenced English and world pop music. The group was made up of four people, *John Lennon*, rhythm guitar and vocals, *Paul McCartney*, bass guitar and vocals, *George Harrison*, lead guitar and vocals and *Ringo Starr*, drums and vocals. In 1970, when their manager *Brian Epstein* died, the group started to have problems. They decided to split up and continued playing and singing separately. In 1980 John Lennon was assassinated by a madman in New York. One of his most famous songs is *Imagine*.

Another member of the group, George Harrison, died of cancer in 2001. Paul McCartney and Ringo Starr are still active to this day.

One thing is for sure *The Beatles'* melodies and their gentle songs will be forever popular.

EXERCISES

1 True (T) or False (F)? Correct the false sentences.

a. A lot of British singers are idols for young people.	T	F
b. *Coldplay*'s songs are popular.	T	F
c. *One Direction* is a band of five people.	T	F
d. *The Beatles* are Scottish.	T	F
e. *John Lennon* was a drummer.	T	F
f. *The Beatles* split up in 1980.	T	F
g. *George Harrison* is still in activity.	T	F
h. *Let It Be* is a popular song.	T	F

2 Read the text "British music" and answer the following questions.

1. Who were the most popular British music stars of the 60s?
2. When did One Direction become well-known?
3. Where do The Beatles come from?
4. What did they start?
5. Who were the members of The Beatles?
6. What musical instruments did they play?
7. Why did The Beatles separate?
8. What happened in 1980?
9. Who assassinated John Lennon?
10. What is John Lennon's most popular song?
11. What kind of music do you like?
12. Who is your musical idol?

WRITING A SUMMARY

Write a summary about "British food" and give the following information:

- what British people have for breakfast;
- what the typical English breakfast consists of;
- why the typical English breakfast isn't as common as in the past;
- what they have for lunch;
- what they have for dinner;
- what British people have for Sunday lunch.

WRITING A LETTER

1. Write a letter to a pen-friend and talk about your school day.

- Thank your friend for the last letter you received.
- What you want to speak about in this letter.
- What time school starts.
- What subjects you have had today.
- What time school finishes.
- Where you have lunch.
- If there are clubs after school.

BUILDING UP A DIALOGUE

2. Write a dialogue between a Scottish boy who is called Logan and you following these instructions.

You: Chiedi a Logan se gli piace ascoltare musica.

Logan: Risponde di sì.

You: Chiedi qual è il tipo di musica preferito.

Logan: Risponde che preferisce la musica pop, ma gli piace anche la musica rock.

You: Chiedi chi è il suo cantante preferito.

Logan: Risponde che è Alan Walker. Ama la canzone *Faded*.

You: Chiedi con quale frequenza ascolta la musica.

Logan: Risponde che lo fa ogni giorno.

You: Chiedi se è mai stato a un concerto di Alan Walker.

Logan: Risponde che è andato al *Wind Music Awards* 2016 a Verona lo scorso giugno per ascoltarlo cantare. È stata un'esperienza fantastica!

You: Chiedi quanti giorni è rimasto a Verona.

Logan: Risponde soltanto due giorni perché era impegnato per la scuola.

OPEN - DIALOGUE

3. Complete the following dialogue.

A ____________________________?

B I like football very much.

A ____________________________?

B My favourite football team is Arsenal. And yours?

A ____________________________.

B I see.

A ____________________________ ?

B Yes, I can play very well.

A ____________________________?

B I play football twice a week, on Tuesdays and Saturdays.

A ____________________________?

B Last year I won a competition with my football team. Have you ever played football?

A ____________________________.

B Fantastic! Why don't we play football next Sunday?

A Yes, it's ____________________.

________________________?

B We can play on a pitch near my school.

A ____________________________?

B Let's meet in front of my house at 5 p.m..

A ____________________________

B __________on Saturday. Bye!

LISTENING ACTIVITY

Listen to "Yellow Submarine" a song by the Beatles and complete the text with the following words:

Link: https://youtu.be/krIus0i9xn8

many more	was born	sea of green
told us	full speed	sky of blue
Everyone of us	begins	

Yellow Submarine

In the town where I ____________
Lived a man who sailed to sea
And he _________ of his life
In the land of submarines
So we sailed up to the sun
Till we found the _____________
And we lived beneath the waves
In our yellow submarine
We all live in a yellow submarine
Yellow submarine, yellow submarine
We all live in a yellow submarine
Yellow submarine, yellow submarine
And our friends are all on board
__________ of them live next door
And the band _______ to play
We all live in a yellow submarine
Yellow submarine, yellow submarine

We all live in a yellow submarine
Yellow submarine, yellow submarine
{Full speed ahead, Mr. Boatswain
[pronounced bo'sun], full speed ahead!
Full speed it is, Sgt.!
Cut the cable, drop the cable!
Aye, sir, aye!
Captain, captain!...
{Full speed ahead, Mr. Boatswain
[pronounced bo'sun], full speed ahead!
______________ it is, Sgt.!
Cut the cable, drop the cable!
Aye, sir, aye!
Captain, captain! [pronounced cap'n, cap'n]}
As we live a life of ease (A life of ease)
____________________ (Everyone of us)
has all we need (Has all we need)
_____________ (Sky of blue) and sea of green (Sea of green)
In our yellow (In our yellow) submarine
(Submarine, ha, ha)
We all live in a yellow submarine
Yellow submarine, yellow submarine
We all live in a yellow submarine
Yellow submarine, yellow submarine
We all live in a yellow submarine
Yellow submarine, yellow submarine
We all live in a yellow submarine
Yellow submarine, yellow submarine.

TRINITY GRADE 4

CEFR level A2.2

Total exam time: 10 minutes.

Conversation

Examiner:

- Good morning.
- What's your name?
- What's your surname?
- What are you wearing?
- Do you like shopping?
- What are your favourite clothes?
- How often do you go shopping?
- Where do you go? Who do you go shopping with?
- Do your parents ever shop on the internet?
- What do they usually buy?
- When are you going to go shopping next?
- What are you going to buy?

Look at the picture!

Examiner:

- How many shops are there?
- What are they?
- What are these people doing?
- What is the job of the woman in the clothes shop?
- How many people are using the escalator?
- Who is going out from the shoe shop?
- What else can you describe?
- Ask me what I bought last time I went shopping?

You: What did you buy last time you went shopping?

Examiner: OK. Thanks a lot. Bye

You: Thanks. Goodbye.

CHAPTER 08

MEN AND WOMEN AROUND THE WORLD

DIALOGUE

A great example

Max: Yesterday our teacher told us about important men and women from all around the world. It was a very exciting lesson.

David: I think it is interesting to know about the work of men and women involved in solving the problems of society.

Max: I appreciate those who devote their life to other people, to the weak and the poor, above all.

David: Last month, I read a book about *Mother Teresa of Calcutta*'s life. She was a great woman because she devoted her life to the homeless, the hungry, the poor and the disabled. She was canonized by Pope Francis on the 4th September in Saint Peter's Square, in Rome.

Max: I know. Now she is named Saint Teresa of Calcutta and in 1979 she received the Nobel Peace Prize because she worked to win over poverty and misery which are a menace to world peace.

David: A few days ago I saw a documentary on TV about *Nelson Mandela*. He was a great statesman who spent a lot of years in prison. He fought for freedom and equality between blacks and whites.

Max: I think both Saint Teresa and Nelson Mandela can be considered two great teachers and be taken as a model.

David: I agree. They set a great example by their teaching.

EXERCISE

1 Answer the following questions.

1. What did Max's teacher talk about?
2. Who does Max appreciate?
3. What did David read last month?
4. Why was *Mother Teresa* a great woman?
5. When was she canonized?
6. When did she receive the Nobel Peace Prize?
7. Why did she receive it?
8. Who was *Nelson Mandela*?

NELSON MANDELA

«A winner is a dreamer who never gives up.»

Fact file
Name: Nelson Mandela.
Date of birth: 18th July 1918.
Place of birth: Mvezo, South Africa.
Date of death: 5th December 2013.

Place of death: Johannesburg, South Africa but he was buried in the family cemetery of Qunu, a village where he grew up.

Who he was: a great statesman who fought for freedom and equality between blacks and whites.

Education: after he attended schools for blacks, he studied Law at university.

Important facts from his youth: 1944 – member of the *African National Congress* political party and beginning of the struggle against the apartheid regime of South Africa for a multi-racial democracy.

Work: lawyer/statesman.

Important events:
- 1964: sentenced to life in prison for his struggle against apartheid;
- 1990: after 27 years, he came out of jail;
- 1993: winner of the Nobel Peace Prize;
- 1994: president of South Africa thanks to the first democratic election;
- 1999: withdraws from politics, active in the struggle against HIV and campaigns to secure South Africa's right to host the 2010 football World Cup.

Nelson Mandela International Day: 18th July.

ACTIVITIES

1 Match the words.

a. Statesman	1. Libertà
b. Law	2. Lotta
c. Struggle	3. Uguaglianza
d. Freedom	4. Pace
e. Equality	5. Prigione
f. Jail	6. Legge
g. Democratic	7. Statista
h. Peace	8. Democratico

2 True (T) or False (F).
Correct the false sentences.

a. He is buried in the village of Qunu.	T	F
b. Nelson Mandela was Asian.	T	F
c. He died in Africa.	T	F
d. Nelson Mandela was a lawyer.	T	F
e. He was a member of the *African National Congress* political party.	T	F
f. He was active in the struggle against the war.	T	F
g. Mandela stayed in prison for 27 years.	T	F
h. He won the Nobel Prize for Literature.	T	F
i. Nelson Mandela campaigned against HIV.	T	F
j. The 2010 football World Cup took place in South Africa.	T	F

3 WRITING

Write about Nelson Mandela following the points of the fact file.

Nelson Mandela was born in Mvezo in South Africa on...

4 SPEAKING

Follow the points of the fact file and talk about some aspects of Nelson Mandela's life:

a. birth;
b. death;
c. statesman;
d. struggle;
e. president.

DID YOU KNOW?

The word apartheid means separation. It was a policy of racial segregation that was implemented in South Africa from 1948 to 1994.

MARTIN LUTHER KING

«I have a dream that my four little children will one day live in a nation where they will not be judged by the color of their skin but by the content of their character.»

Fact file

Name: Martin Luther King.

Date of birth: 15th January 1929.

Place of birth: Atlanta, State of Georgia, USA.

Date of death: 4th April 1968.

Place of death: Memphis, Tennessee, USA. He's buried in Martin Luther King Jr. National Historic Site in Atlanta.

Who he was: leader of the non-violent struggle for civil rights from 1957 to 1968.

Education: he studied Sociology, Philosophy and Theology.

Important facts from his youth: leader of the bus protest in Montgomery where Rosa Parks, an African-American, was against discriminated on the bus by whites. After her arrest a movement started to abolish the racial segregation laws.

Work: a clergyman, pastor of the Baptist Church.

Important events:

- He went to prison 20 times.
- 1963 - March in Washington DC and famous speech "*I Have A Dream*" in front of 250,000 people.
- 1964 - winner of the Nobel Peace Prize.
- 1968 - assassination in Memphis.
- He was shot by James Earl Ray, a man who escaped from the *Missouri State Penitentiary*, while he was standing on the balcony of the Lorraine Motel.

Martin Luther King Day: the third Monday in January.

ACTIVITIES

1 Match the words.

a. Leader
b. Civil rights
c. Protest
d. Racial segregation laws
e. Pastor
f. March
g. Speech
h. Abolish

1. Abolire
2. Protesta
3. Pastore
4. Discorso
5. Marcia
6. Leggi di segregazione razziale
7. Capo
8. Diritti civili

2 True (T) or False (F). Correct the false sentences.

a. Martin Luther King was American. T F
b. He died in Washington DC. T F
c. Martin Luther King was a lawyer. T F
d. He was leader of the non-violent civil rights movement. T F
e. He struggled against racial discrimination. T F
f. M. L. King was imprisoned 20 times. T F
g. He won the Nobel Peace Prize. T F
h. Martin Luther King was Catholic. T F
i. His killer was James Earl Ray. T F
j. M. L. King Day is celebrated in January. T F

3 WRITING

Write a text about Martin Luther King following the points of the fact file.

Martin Luther King was born in Atlanta in the State of Georgia in the USA...

4 SPEAKING

Follow the points of the fact file and talk about some aspects of Martin Luther King's life:

a. birth;
b. death;
c. pastor;
d. struggle;
e. leader.

MAHATMA GANDHI

«My life is my message.»

Fact file

Name: Mohandas Karamchand Gandhi.

Date of birth: 2nd October 1869.

Place of birth: Porbander, Western India.

Date of death: 30th January 1948.

Place of death: Delhi, India. He is buried at Raj Ghat, a memorial on the banks of the river Yamuna in Delhi on Ring Road known as Mahatma Gandhi Road.

Who he was: leader of the non-violent movement, the resistance without weapons and civil disobedience in order to obtain political and social rights; nicknamed *Mahatma, Great Soul.*

Education: he studied Law in London.

Important facts from his youth: at 13 he married a 14-year-old girl;

- 1907/1915: he lived in South Africa.

Work: a lawyer, a philosopher and a politician.

Important events:

- 1915: returns to India and protests peacefully against heavy British taxes and discrimination; for this he went to prison many times.
- 1921: leader of the *National Congress* and campaigns to help the poor and promote women's rights in India.
- 1930: non-violent protest against the British Salt Tax.
- Period of World War II: intensified the struggle for Indian independence.
- 1948: on 30th January, assassination in Delhi by a Hindu fanatic nationalist.

International Day of Non-Violence: 2nd October.

DID YOU KNOW?

His philosophy is called *Satyagraha* which means "adherence to truth". It's the opposite of oppression without using weapons but using civil disobedience. In Sanskrit, the Indian language, satya means truth and ahimsa means non-violence.

ACTIVITIES

1 Match the words.

a. Mahatma	**1.** Tasse pesanti
b. Civil disobedience	**2.** Resistenza
c. Weapons	**3.** Discriminazione
d. Heavy taxes	**4.** Diritti sociali e politici
e. Political and social rights	**5.** Movimento non violento
f. Non-violent movement	**6.** Armi
g. Discrimination	**7.** Grande Anima
h. Resistance	**8.** Disobbedienza civile

2 True (T) or False (F). Correct the false sentences.

a. Gandhi was Indian. F T
b. He died in Bombay, India. F T
c. Gandhi was nicknamed *Mahatma*, "Great Soul". F T
d. He was leader of the passive resistance. F T
e. He struggled against racial discrimination. F T
f. Gandhi was never imprisoned. F T
g. He struggled for Indian independence. F T
h. Gandhi won the Nobel Peace Prize. F T
i. He was a philosopher. F T
j. His philosophy was Sanskrit. F T

3 WRITING

Write about Mahatma Gandhi following the points of the fact file.

Mahatma Gandhi was born in Pobander in Western India...

4 SPEAKING

Follow the points of the fact file and talk about some aspects of Mahatma Gandhi's life:

a. birth;
b. death;
c. leader;
d. protests;
e. struggle.

JOHN FITZGERALD KENNEDY

«Mankind must put an end to war, or war will put an end to mankind.»

Fact file

Name: John Fitzgerald Kennedy.

Date of birth: 27th May 1917.

Place of birth: Brookline Town, Massachusetts.

Date of death: 22nd November 1963.

Place of death: Dallas, Texas. He is buried in *Arlington National Cemetery* in Virginia.

Who he was: statesman/the youngest and the first Catholic President of the USA.

Education: degree in Economics at America's famous *Harvard University*.

Important facts from his youth: volunteer in World War II.

Work: politician.

Important events:

- 1946: member of the *House of Representatives*.
- 1952: member of the *Senate*.
- 1960: President of the USA.
- Modernization of the USA thanks to a new program called "*A New Frontier*", improvement of politics, social welfare, campaigns for racial equality with Martin Luther King, foreign policy based on pacific relationships to end the "*Cold War*" with the Soviet Union.
- 1963: assassination in Dallas. He was shot by Lee Harvey Oswald, an ex-USA marine.

DID YOU KNOW?

One side of the fifty-cent coin shows the profile of J.F. Kennedy.

ACTIVITIES

1 Match the words.

a. Volunteer	**1.** Benessere
b. Racial equality	**2.** Guerra Fredda
c. Cold War	**3.** Politica estera
d. Foreign policy	**4.** Politico
e. Politician	**5.** Rapporti
f. Modernization	**6.** Volontario
g. Relationships	**7.** Uguaglianza razziale
h. Welfare	**8.** Ammodernamento

2 True (T) or False (F). Correct the false sentences.

a. Kennedy was African.	T	F
b. He died in New York.	T	F
c. Kennedy was the first Catholic President of the USA .	T	F
d. He was active in the struggle for world peace.	T	F
e. He was active in the struggle against racial discrimination.	T	F
f. Kennedy didn't know Martin Luther King.	T	F
g. He was a volunteer in World War II.	T	F
h. Kennedy won the Nobel Peace Prize.	T	F
i. His killer was an ex-soldier.	T	F
j. Kennedy's profile is on the one dollar American bank note.	T	F

3 WRITING

Write about John F. Kennedy following the points of the fact file.

John F. Kennedy was born in Brookline Town, Massachusetts…

4 SPEAKING

Follow the points of the fact file and talk about some aspects of John F. Kennedy's life:

a. birth;
b. death;
c. president;
d. campaigns;
e. struggle for peace in the world.

MALALA

«I don't mind if I have to sit on the floor at school. All I want is education. And I'm afraid of no one.»

Fact file

Name: Malala Yousafzai. Her first name Malala means *grief-stricken*. She was given this name in memory of Malalai of Maiwand, a famous Pushtun poet and warrior woman from Southern Pakistan.

Date of birth: 12th July 1997.

Place of birth: Mingora, in the Swat District of Pakistan.

Place where she grew up: Swat Valley.

Her family: Two younger brothers Khushal and Atal. Her father Ziauddin Yousafzai is a poet, the owner of a school and an educational activist. Her mother is Tor Pekai.

Who she is: A Pakistani activist for the right to female education.

The Taliban banned girls from attending school and this explains why she is known mainly for her wish to promote education for girls in the Swat Valley.

Malala received the Nobel Peace Prize in 2014 (at the age of 17) for her struggle against the suppression of children and for the right of all children to education. She is the youngest woman to receive the Nobel Peace Prize and the only Pakistani winner of this Prize.

Important facts: When she was 11, Malala wrote a blog under a pseudonym. In the blog she wrote about her life under Taliban occupation, the attempts of the Taliban to take control of the valley and of her efforts to promote education for girls in the Swat Valley.

On 9th October 2012, while Malala was getting on her school bus, a gunman tried to kill her: he asked for her by name, he pointed a pistol at her and fired three shots.

She remained unconscious and in a critical condition for several days after the attack.
In July 2013 she spoke at the headquarters of the United Nations in New York, during the Assembly of Youth. She spoke, above all, about the female condition in her country and about the importance of education for women and young people. She said that "*One child, one teacher, one book and one pen can change the world*".

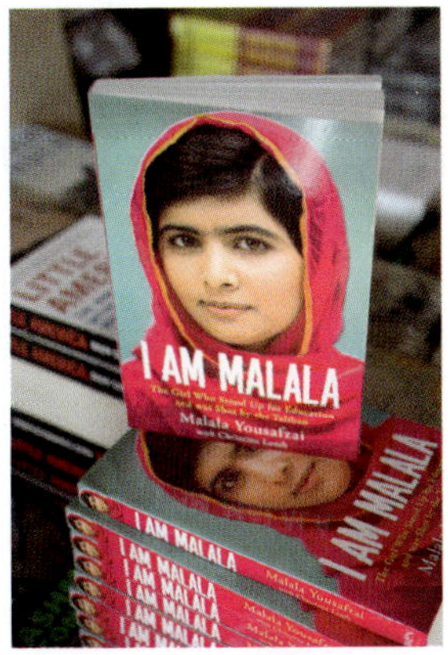

I am Malala
This book is an autobiography of Malala Yousafzai, the Pakistani girl who spoke at the Assembly of the United Nations about the female condition in her country and about the importance of education for women and young people.

ACTIVITIES

1 Match the words.

a. Grief-stricken	1. Sparo
b. Younger	2. Repressione
c. Owner	3. Promuovere
d. Activist	4. Uomo armato
e. Ban	5. Privo di sensi
f. Promote	6. Più giovane
g. Suppression	7. Colpito dal dolore
h. Gunman	8. Proprietario
i. Shot	9. Attivista
j. Unconscious	10. Proibire

ESERCIZI ON LINE www.medusaeditrice.it

2 True (T) or False (F). Correct the false sentences.

a. Malala is Pakistani.	T	F
b. She is 20 years old.	T	F
c. Her name means "*Grief stricken*"	T	F
d. She received the Nobel Prize for Literature.	T	F
e. Malala wrote a blog at the age of 15.	T	F
f. The Taliban tried to kill her.	T	F
g. In Pakistan girls are banned from attending school.	T	F
h. She spoke at the Assembly of The United Nations.	T	F
i. She spoke about female education in Pakistan.	T	F
j. She believes that education can change the world.	T	F

3 Writing.
Write a text about Malala Yousafzai following the points of the fact file.
Malala Yousafzai was born in...

4 Speaking
Follow the points of the fact file and talk about some aspects of Malala Yousafzai's life:
a. birth;
b. family;
c. Nobel Prize;
d. taliban attack;
e. speech at the United Nations.

MOTHER TERESA OF CALCUTTA

Fact file

Name: Anjezë Gonxhe Bojaxhiu, known as Saint Teresa of Calcutta. Anjezë is Agnes in English and Gonxhe means *'rosebud'*.

Date of birth: 26th August 1910.
Place of birth: Skopje, in Macedonia.
Date of death: 5th September 1997.
Place of death: Calcutta, India.

Places where she lived: She lived in Macedonia for 18 years. At the age of 18, she left home and moved to Ireland where she joined the Sisters of Loreto at Loreto Abbey in Rathfarnham; there she learned English.

In 1929 she moved to India, where she spent most of her life.
Her family lived in Skopje until 1934, when they moved to Tirana in Albania.

Who she was: She was the youngest of the five children of Nikollë and Dranafile Bojaxhiu. Her father was involved in the politics of the Albanian community in Macedonia. He died when she was eight years old.

Important events:

- 1929: she began her novitiate in Darjeeling, in India. She learnt *Bengali** and taught at St. Teresa's School.
- 1931: On 24th May she took her first religious vows as a nun. At that time she chose to be named *Teresa* after Thérèse de Lisieux, the patron saint of missionaries.
- 1937: On the 14th May she took her solemn vows. At that time, she taught at the Loreto convent school in Entally, eastern Calcutta.
- 1943: The Bengal famine brought misery and death to Calcutta. Teresa realized there was too much poverty in Calcutta and that she was to leave the convent and help the poor.
- 1944: Teresa was appointed headmistress of the school where she served as a teacher for almost twenty years.
- 1948: Teresa began her missionary work with the poor. She replaced her traditional Loreto nun's habit with a white cotton *sari* with a blue border. She adopted Indian citizenship, received basic medical training in the *Holy Family Hospital* and then ventured out into the slums.

- 1949: A group of young women joined Teresa in her effort and laid the foundations of a new religious community helping the *"poorest among the poor"*.
- 1950: On the 7th October Teresa received permission from the Holy See to start her own order. The mission of the order was to care for the hungry, the naked, the homeless, the disabled, the poor, the refugees, the blind and the lepers. It began as a small congregation with 13 members in Calcutta and then became the Missionaries of Charity.
- 1979: Mother Teresa received the Nobel Peace Prize.
- 1997: When Mother Teresa died the congregation of the Missionaries of Charity had grown to more than 4,000 sisters.
- 2003: On the 19th October Pope John Paul II beatified her in Saint Peter's Square in Vatican City.
- 2016: On the 4th September Pope Francis canonized her in Saint Peter's Square in Vatican City.

Mother Teresa Day: 5th September.

**Bengali* is a language spoken in Bangladesh and in India.

ACTIVITIES

ESERCIZI ON LINE www.medusaeditrice.it

1 Match the words.

a. Rosebud	1. Abito monacale
b. Novitiate	2. Avventurarsi
c. Nun	3. Carestia
d. Solemn vows	4. Gettare le basi
e. Headmistress	5. Santa Sede
f. Famine	6. Beatificare
g. Nun's habit	7. Canonizzare
h. Venture out	8. Bocciolo di rosa
i. Adopt the citizenship	9. Noviziato
j. Lay the foundations	10. Suora
k. Holy See	11. Voti solenni
l. Beatify	12. Direttrice di scuola
m. Canonize	13. Adottare la cittadinanza

2 WRITING

Write about Santa Teresa of Calcutta following the points of the fact file.

Anjezë Gonxhe Bojaxhiu was born in...

3 SPEAKING

Follow the points of the fact file and talk about some aspects of Saint Teresa's life:

a. birth and death; **b.** places where she lived; **c.** important events in her life; **d.** the task of her own order; **e.** beatification and canonization.

EXERCISES

The President-elect of the Italian Republic, Luigi Einaudi swears before the Parliament in a plenary session.

1 **Read the text.**

Leonilde "Nilde" Iotti

Leonilde "Nilde" Iotti, a great Italian politician, was born on 10th April 1920 in Reggio Emilia and died on 4th December 1999 in Rome.

She was the first woman in the history of Republican Italy to hold the office of the President of the *Chamber of Deputies* for three legislatures from 1979 to 1992.

She studied Literature and graduated at the "Cattolica" University in Milan.

She was a teacher for some time but preferred to leave teaching to enter politics.

She was very young when she joined the Communist Party. After the 8th September 1943, she took part in the *Resistance*. She joined the Women Defence Group, an antifascist group of the Communist Party.

She became the President of the "*Union of Italian Women*" in Reggio Emilia.

In 1946, the Communist party chose her as a candidate and she was elected to the *Constituent Assembly* of the Italian Republic which had the task to write the Constitution.

The *Constituent Assembly* worked from the 25th June 1946 to 31st January 1948.

Constitution of the Italian Republic:

- 22nd December 1947 – the Constituent Assembly approved the Constitution.
- 27th December 1947 – Enrico De Nicola, the provisional Head of the State promulgated the Constitution.
- 27th December 1947 – the Constitution was published in the Official Gazette.
- 1st January 1948 – the Constitution came into force.
- It is the fundamental law of the Italian Republic and consists of 139 articles.

Curiosity

21 women were elected to the Constituent Assembly in 1946 and 39 women were elected to the Chamber of Deputies of the first Italian Republican Parliament on 18th April 1948.

2 Match the words.

a. Politician	1. Legislatura
b. Hold	2. Insegnamento
c. Office	3. Promuovere
d. Chamber of Deputies	4. Entrare in politica
e. Legislature	5. Prendere parte
f. Teaching	6. Aderire
g. Enter politics	7. Assemblea costituente
h. Join	8. Capo di stato provvisorio
i. Take part	9. Entrare in vigore
j. Candidate	10. Rendere esecutivo
k. Constituent Assembly	11. Politico
l. Provisional Head of State	12. Ricoprire
m. Come into force	13. Carica
n. Promulgate	14. Camera dei Deputati

3 True (T) or False (F). Correct the false sentences.

a. Nilde Iotti was an Italian politician. T F
b. She was born in 1929. T F
c. She was a teacher for some time. T F
d. She joined the Communist Party. T F
e. She was provisional Head of the State. T F
f. The Constitution was promulgated in 1948. T F

4 WRITING

Write about Nilde Iotti following the points of the fact file.

Nilde Iotti was born in…

5 SPEAKING

Follow the points of the fact file and talk about some aspects of Nilde Iotti's life:

a. birth;
b. education;
c. work;
d. important facts as a politician;
e. constitution.

WRITING A SUMMARY

1. Read the text "Nilde Iotti" again and write a summary using the answers of the questionnaire.

WRITING A LETTER

2. Write a letter to a pen-friend, talk about your hero. Use these tips:

- thank your friend for the last letter you received;
- what you want to speak about in this letter;
- who your hero is;
- what field he works in;
- what he/she looks like;
- what you like about him/her;
- if you have ever seen him/her close up.

BUILDING UP A DIALOGUE

3. Write a phone conversation between Brian and you.

- Call Brian and ask how he is.
- He answers he's ill. Then ask him if he's called a doctor to visit him.
- Brian answers yes and you ask what the doctor has said and what he has prescribed.
- He answers. Suggest he has a rest and watch television tonight because an important football match is on.
- He accepts your suggestion.
- Finally say goodbye to each other.

OPEN - DIALOGUE

4. Complete the following dialogue between John and Max.

A ______________________?
B Fine, thanks. And you, Max?
A ______________________.
B Why aren't you happy?
A ____________ about school.
B I see. Why?
A I always __________ bad marks.
B Don't you __________ enough?
A Oh, yes. ______________________ but I don't like History and __________.
B What are you going to do after lower Secondary school?
A I ______________________
B So you'll __________ Latin and above all Maths.
A Yes, I ______________, John!

LISTENING ACTIVITY

Listen to "Imagine", a song by John Lennon and complete the text with the following words:

Link: https://youtu.be/DVg2EJvvlF8

heaven	below	living	there's
die	people	may	join
hunger	sharing		

Imagine

Imagine there's no ....
It's easy if you try
No hell .... us
Above us only sky
Imagine all the people
.... for today...
Imagine .... no countries
It isn't hard to do
Nothing to kill or .... for
And no religion too
Imagine all the ....
Living life in peace...
You .... say I'm a dreamer
But I'm not the only one
I hope someday you'll .... us
And the world will be as one
Imagine no possessions
I wonder if you can
No need for greed or ....
A brotherhood of man

Imagine all the people
.... all the world...
You may say I'm a dreamer
But I'm not the only one
I hope someday you'll join us
And the world will live as one

TRINITY GRADE 4

CEFR level A2.2

Total exam time: 10 minutes.

Conversation

Examiner:

- Good morning.
- What's your name?
- How are you?
- What are your hobbies?
- Do you like sport?
- What sports can you play?
- Do you watch sport programs on TV? When?
- Who is your favourite sports star?
- How often do you have Physical Education at school?
- Did you play in any school sport competition last year?
- Are you going to start any new hobbies or sports in the future?
- What is the most popular sport in Italy?

Look at this picture!

Examiner:

- What are these boys and girls doing?
- How many boys are there?
- What colours are the players' T-shirts?
- Is there a referee?
- What is he doing?
- How many windows and doors are there?
- Are the windows big or small?
- What else can you see?
- Ask me if I watched the last Olympic Games.

You: Did you watch the last Olympic Games?

Examiner: OK. Thanks a lot. Bye

You: Thanks. Goodbye.

CHAPTER 09

LITERATURE

DIALOGUE

I study Literature

Tom: This morning we had a very interesting lesson at school about English literature. I prefer studying Literature to Maths.

Luisa: What did you study?

Tom: We studied William Shakespeare: his life and works.

Luisa: What is your favourite play by Shakespeare?

Tom: I prefer his tragedies. In particular I like *Hamlet* very much.

Luisa: I prefer his comedies. *The Tempest* is my favourite work. It was the last play written by Shakespeare.

Tom: Anyway, I think Shakespeare was a great playwright and his plays are all interesting and important.

Luisa: An equally important Italian playwright Eduardo de Filippo translated *The Tempest* into Neapolitan.

Tom: Yes, I know! I tried to read it but Neapolitan is really difficult to understand.

Luisa: It's true! But I think this is really exciting: two great works by two great writers.

EXERCISE

1 Answer the following questions.

1. What did Tom study at school, this morning?
2. What does Tom prefer to study?
3. What is Tom's favourite Shakespeare play?
4. Which play does Luisa prefer?
5. What does she say about *The Tempest*?
6. What did Eduardo de Filippo translate?
7. What is your favourite play by Shakespeare?
8. What Shakespearian tragedies do you know?

GEOFFREY CHAUCER

Name: Geoffrey Chaucer.

Date and place of birth: 1340, London.

Date and place of death: 25th October 1400, London.

Who he was: Chaucer is considered the father of English literature and the greatest English poet of the *Middle Age*.

The most important facts of his life: At 19 he took part in the *Hundred Years' War* which England fought against France. The war was started by *King Edward III* in order to defend his French territories.
Chaucer lived in the service of three kings: *Edward III*, *Richard II* and *Henry IV*.
He sat in Parliament as the representative of Kent. He visited Italy where he probably met *Petrarch* and *Boccaccio*.
He was the first poet to be buried in Poets' Corner in Westminster Abbey.

Works: Chaucer's best work in Middle English was "*The Canterbury Tales*", a collection of tales which were a true mirror of England. He turned for inspiration to the people he had met in his life. He probably borrowed the idea for his masterpiece from Boccaccio's *Decameron*. Chaucer thought that the traditional pilgrimage to Canterbury, which took place every year, could be the social event to bring various people together. He imagined that 29 pilgrims meet on an April day in the Tabard Inn, at Southwark, in London. They intend going on a pilgrimage to the shrine of St. Thomas Becket in Canterbury.
The host of the Inn suggests that each pilgrim should tell two stories on their way to Canterbury and two on their way back.
The pilgrims belong to all the social classes of the time: one group of pilgrims includes the feudal world, another group is associated with religious life and another group includes townspeople.

ACTIVITIES

1 Match the words.

a. Middle Age	**1.** Deputato
b. Against	**2.** Essere seppellito
c. To defend	**3.** Prendere a prestito
d. Territory	**4.** Pellegrinaggio
e. In the service	**5.** Tomba
f. Representative	**6.** Cittadini
g. To be buried	**7.** Medio Evo
h. Borrow	**8.** Contro
i. Pilgrimage	**9.** Difendere
j. Shrine	**10.** Territorio
k. Townspeople	**11.** Al servizio

From The Prologue of The Canterbury Tales. (Lines 19/42)

Read the text and translate it into Italian.

It happened in that season that one day
In Southwark[1], at *The Tabard*[2], as I lay
Ready to go on pilgrimage and start
For Canterbury, most devout at heart,
At night there came into that hostelry
Some nine and twenty in a company
Of sundry folk happening then to fall
In fellowship[3], and they were pilgrims all
That towards Canterbury meant to ride.
The rooms and stables of the inn were wide;
They made us easy[4], all was of the best.
And shortly, when the sun had gone to rest,
By speaking to them all upon the trip
I soon was one of them in fellowship
And promised to rise early and take the way
To Canterbury, as you heard me say.
But none the less, while I have time and space,
Before my story takes a further pace,
It seems a reasonable thing to say
What their condition was, the full array[5]
Of each of them, as it appeared to me,
According to profession and degree,
And what apparel[6] they were riding in;
And at a *Knight* I therefore will begin.

GLOSSARY

1. **Southwark:** quartiere londinese.
2. **Tabard**: locanda famosa del quartiere.
3. **Happening...fellowship**: a cui era capitato di trovarsi in compagnia.
4. **They...easy**: ci sistemarono bene.
5. **Array**: abbigliamento.
6. **Apparel**: vesti.

ACTIVITIES

ESERCIZI ON LINE www.medusaeditrice.it

2 True (T) or False (F). Correct the false sentences.

a. Chaucer was French. T F
b. He was considered a great poet. T F
c. He took part in the war against France. T F
d. Chaucer sat in Parliament. T F
e. He was buried in Westminster Abbey. T F
f. The *Canterbury Tales* is in Old English. T F
g. He borrowed the idea from Dante. T F
h. The pilgrims met in the Tabard Inn. T F
i. Each pilgrim should tell two stories. T F
j. The pilgrims belong to all the social classes of the time. T F

3 WRITING

Write in your exercise book about Geoffrey Chaucer following the points of the fact file.

Geoffrey Chaucer was born in ______________________________

His best work was ______________________________

RISORSE ON-LINE
www.medusaeditrice.it

WILLIAM SHAKESPEARE

Name: William Shakespeare.

Date and place of birth: 23rd April 1564, Stratford upon Avon.

Date and place of death: 23rd April 1616, Stratford upon Avon.

Who he was: Shakespeare is considered the greatest playwright of the reigns of both *Elizabeth I* and *James I*.

His family: William was the third of eight children. His father John was a glover. His mother Mary Arden was of a good country family.

Education: He was educated at *Stratford Grammar School*, where he probably learnt Latin and Greek.

The most important facts of his life: At 18 he married Anne Hathaway. She was about 24. They had three children: Susan and the twins Hamnet and Judith. Some time after their birth, Shakespeare left his family and moved to London where he did many jobs. In 1595 he joined the Lord Chamberlain's Men, one of the most important companies of actors. The company also performed at Court. Very soon he became a famous dramatist and a shareholder in the *Globe Theatre*.

He also became a rich man and in 1597 he bought *New Place*, the biggest and finest house in Stratford.

ACTIVITY

1 WRITING

Write in your exercise book about William Shakespeare following the points of the fact file.

William Shakespeare was born in ____

____

on____________________________

____

His works consist of ______________

____

In 1611 he retired to New Place where he died in 1616. He was buried in the Holy Trinity Church in Stratford.

Works: Shakespeare's works consist of poetry, comedies, tragedies and historical plays.

Poetry: *Venus and Adonis* 1592/93, *The Rape of Lucrece* 1593/94.

Comedies: *The Taming of the Shrew* 1588/93, *A Midsummer Night's Dream* 1593/96, *The Merchant of Venice* 1594/97, *The Merry Wives of Windsor* 1597/1601, *The Tempest* 1611.

Tragedies: *Romeo and Juliet* 1592/95, *Hamlet, Prince of Denmark* 1600/1601, *Othello, the Moor of Venice* 1602/1611, *King Lear* 1605/1606, *Macbeth* 1605/1608.

Historical Plays: *Henry VI* 1588/1592, *Richard III* 1591/1594, *Edward III* 1592/1595, *Richard II* 1594/1595, *Henry IV* 1596/1597.

READING

Permanent playhouses in London

Towards the end of the 16th century several permanent theatres were built in London.

The first playhouse, *The Theatre,* was built in 1576 and the plays produced between 1576 and 1642, when the Puritan Parliament ordered the closure of the theatres, represent Elizabethan Theatre.

Elizabethan theatre was the most important cultural aspect of the English Renaissance. It offered very popular entertainment and was within every social class's reach.

Before the construction of theatres, companies performed in public places, in the courtyards of the inns. In 1574, when the Puritans banished public performances, permanent playhouses were built outside the city walls. The most famous playhouses were: *The Theatre* (1576), *The Curtain* (1577), *The Rose* (1587), *The Swan* (1595) and *The Globe* (1599).

The Elizabethan Theatre

A modern reconstruction of the Globe, named Shakespeare's Globe, in London.

The architecture of permanent playhouses

The theatres were round or octagonal in shape and were 12 metres high. They had a diameter of 25 metres and a rectangular stage.

The stage was partially covered by a thatched roof supported by two pillars and projected into a central area.

Around the stage, there were three tiers of galleries; at the back there was the actors' dressing room.

During performances spectators talked, ate, drank and commented in a loud voice. The *groundlings* paid a penny to enter the *pit*, a standing room around the stage; the spectators who paid two pence sat in the *galleries* and only the city merchants and the nobility paid six pence to sit in the *covered galleries.*

The stage was divided into an *apron stage,* projected towards the spectators; an *inner stage* where the *indoor scenes* were performed and the *upper stage* where musicians or spectators were seated. This area could also be used to perform scenes on two levels as for example the famous balcony scene in *Romeo and Juliet.*

The Tempest

The Tempest is a comedy written between 1610 and 1611. It is William Shakespeare's last masterpiece.

Prospero and his daughter Miranda have been living for 12 years on an island with two servants, the airy spirit Ariel and the monster Caliban.

Prospero was the Duke of Milan and had been deposed by his brother Antonio twelve years before.

He became a magician and by using his magical arts he created a tempest in the middle of the sea. The ship was carrying Alonso, the King of Naples, his son Ferdinand, his brother Sebastian, his old councilor Gonzalo and Antonio, the current false Duke of Milan, were all caught in the tempest. Prospero created the storm using his magical arts in order to bring his enemies to the same place.

After the ship had landed on the island Prospero separated Alonso's son, Prince Ferdinand, from the others. Alonso thought Prince Ferdinand had died in the storm. On the other side of the island Ferdinand met Miranda and they both fell in love. Ferdinand thought he was the only survivor of the storm and tried to get Prospero's approval of his love for Miranda.

Prospero approved of the love between Ferdinand and Miranda and decided to forgive all his enemies and to reveal his identity. Alonso quickly asked for Prospero's pardon.

Thanks to Ariel's magic the ship was returned to its original condition and Prospero decides to give up his magic arts and return to Milan as the rightful Duke.

DID YOU KNOW?

- The *Globe Theatre* was built in 1599 by Lord Chamberlain's Men.
- It was destroyed by fire in 1613.
- The *Globe* was rebuilt on the same site in 1614.
- Shakespeare became a shareholder of the *Globe Theatre.*
- In 1997 a modern reconstruction of the Globe was opened.
- It was named *Shakespeare's Globe* and was opened 230 m. (750 feet) from the site of the original theatre.

- Eduardo De Filippo (Naples 1900, Rome 1984), an Italian playwright, film director, actor, dramatist and poet, translated *The Tempest* into XVII century Neapolitan. The Tempest was the last play written by W. Shakespeare.
He chose this play because of the affinities in dealing with themes such as magic, dreams, love and family.

THE TEMPEST

From Act I - Scene II
The island. Before Prospero's cell.
Enter Prospero and Miranda
Miranda.
If by your art, my dearest father, you have
Put the wild waters in this roar, allay them.
The sky, it seems, would pour down stinking pitch,
But that the sea, mounting to the welkin's cheek,
Dashes the fire out. O, I have suffered
With those that I saw suffer: a brave vessel,
Who had, no doubt, some noble creature in her,
Dash'd all to pieces. O, the cry did knock
Against my very heart. Poor souls, they perish'd.
Had I been any god of power, I would
Have sunk the sea within the earth or ere
It should the good ship so have swallow'd and The fraughting souls within her.

Prospero.
Be collected:
No more amazement: tell your piteous heart
There's no harm done.

Miranda.
O, woe the day!

Prospero.
No harm.
I have done nothing but in care of thee,
Of thee, my dear one, thee, my daughter, who
Art ignorant of what thou art, nought knowing
Of whence I am, nor that I am more better
Than Prospero, master of a full poor cell,
And thy no greater father.

Miranda.
More to know
Did never meddle with my thoughts.

LA TEMPESTA

ATTO I – SCENA II.
L'isola. Davanti alla grotta di Prospero.
Entrano Prospero e Miranda.
Miranda.
Se con la vostra Arte, mio carissimo padre, avete gettato le acque selvagge in questo fragore, ora calmatele. Sembra che il cielo voglia rovesciare fetida pece ma il mare montando fino alle guance delle nubi spegne il fuoco.
Oh, come ho sofferto con quelli che vidi soffrire!
Una splendida nave (che certo aveva dentro nobili creature) tutta a pezzi.
Ah, come quel gridare mi ha battuto sul cuore.
Povere anime, tutte perdute. Se avessi avuto il potere di un dio avrei sprofondato il mare nella terra prima che s'ingoiasse il bel veliero con il suo carico di umani.

Prospero.
Calma. Non aver più paura. Di' al tuo cuore pietoso che non è stato fatto nessun male.

Miranda.
Oh, giorno di dolore!

Prospero.
Nessun male.
Nulla ho fatto se non per il tuo bene, per te, unica mia, per te, mia figlia, che non conosci chi sei, né di dove io venga, né che sono molto più di Prospero, padrone di una poverissima grotta e tuo non meno misero padre.

Miranda.
Non ho mai pensato a conoscere di più.

CHARLES DICKENS

Life

Year of birth: 1812.

Place of birth: Portsmouth, on the southern coast of England.

Year of death: 1870.

Place of death: London, he was buried in the Poets' Corner in Westminster Abbey.

Family: married Catherine Hogarth in 1835, they had ten children. In 1855 he separated from his wife.

The Author

He was the second child of eight. He didn't have an easy and happy childhood. His father was imprisoned for debts and, although he was only a child, he was sent to work in a factory for many years. Dickens didn't receive a complete education because of his family's financial problems but he loved reading. He began to study at nighttime when, at the age of fifteen, he found a job as office boy at a lawyer's. He was a writer of Victorian England and tried to involve his readers in the disturbing social reality of the time.

Personality: determined and sensitive, his attention was mainly on the gap between poor and rich people.

Influences: Fielding, Smollett, Miguel de Cervantes. The historical events of his time influenced his life, his works, and his critical thinking. Besides his own sad childhood experience, his many travels also inspired his novels.

Artist: brilliant carrier as a Parliamentary journalist, great popularity as novelist. He became a reporter of Parliamentary debates in the House of Commons and wrote for the newspaper *Mirror of Parliament*. As a Parliamentary journalist he supported any law that helped solve poor people's problems. He fought hard against the *Poor Law*, a law that forced homeless poor people to live in *workhouses* where women and men lived separately meaning that families couldn't stay together. Workhouses were dirty, squalid places to live in.

Travels: France, Germany, Italy and the USA.

Works

Dickens wrote about his time and children are often the most important characters in his novels. Through them the author describes the criminal life of London during the *Victorian Age* and the child abuse that was the normal custom of the time. However, at the beginning of his career Dickens also wrote some humoristic novels such as *Sketches by Boz* (1836) and *The Pickwick Papers* (1836-37) that were loved by a large number of readers. Among his works, some of his popular novels include: *Oliver Twist* (1837-1838), *A Christmas Carol* (1843), *David Copperfield* (1849-50), *Hard Times* (1854).

Oliver Twist and *David Copperfield* are considered by many literary critics as Dickens's masterpieces. These novels are partly autobiographical because some of the events narrated in the stories are closely related to the author's own life.

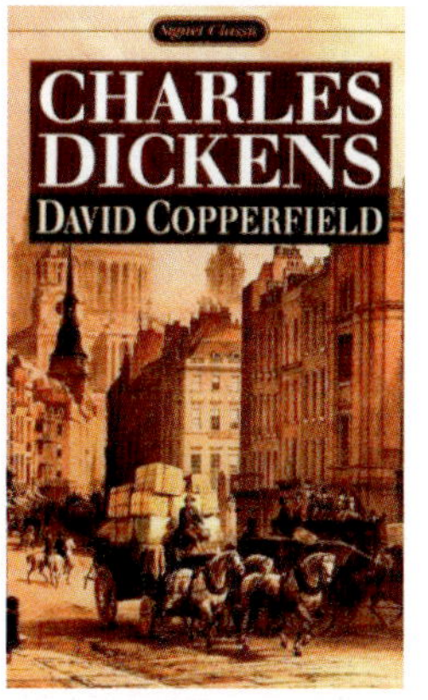

ACTIVITIES

1 Match each word with its Italian meaning.

a. Novelist	**1.** Abitudine
b. Childhood	**2.** Personaggi
c. Imprisoned	**3.** Sensibile
d. Sensitive	**4.** Infanzia
e. Characters	**5.** Imprigionato
f. Custom	**6.** Romanziere

ESERCIZI ON LINE www.medusaeditrice.it

2 True or false? Correct the false sentences.

a. Charles Dickens was born in London T F
b. He was an only child. T F
c. He died in Edinburgh. T F
d. Dickens was a journalist. T F
e. He lived and wrote a great number of his novels during the reign of Queen Victoria. T F
f. He was sensitive. T F
g. Dickens didn't support the problems of poor people. T F
h. Dickens went to work in factories for many years T F
i. He didn't travel a lot. T F
j. *Oliver Twist* is autobiographical. T F

3 Read and answer the following questions.

1. When was Charles Dickens born? Where?
2. When did he die?
3. Where was he buried?
4. What is the name of Dickens's wife?
5. Was he happy during his childhood?
6. Why did Dickens go to work in factories?
7. At what age did he start to work as an office boy?
8. What and who influenced Charles Dickens's works?
9. Where did Dickens travel?
10. What are his most popular novels?
11. What did Dickens describe in his novels?
12. What was the *Poor Law*?
13. What were the Victorian workhouses like?

READING

Read the text and complete the activities.

The Victorian society

Queen Victoria's reign was the longest in the history of England; she came to the throne in 1837 and died in 1901. She was the queen of strict moral and religious views.

Her reign was a period of extraordinary industrial development, imperial expansion and political and social reforms. The merits of these achievements partly belonged to the queen who never overruled Parliament and was a good mediator of its political activities. During, Victoria's reign, Britain became a world economic leader thanks to the important successes, supported by the queen, gained through trade with its colonies and to important inventions such as the steam locomotive.

However, the Victorian Age was also a contradictory historical period. There were social reforms and progress but also great poverty, injustice and social discontent. Many people left the countryside and went to live in the cities where families hoped to find a job in the new factories but the rapid expansion of cities had many negative effects.

People were angry about the conditions in which many families lived. All around London magnificent buildings took shape but there were overcrowded houses for the poor and the working-class. They dwelled in very bad areas, called *slums*, where disease and crime increased day by day and where infant mortality was very high because of the devastating effects of widespread cholera epidemics.

In trying to find solutions to the consequences of this incredible urban environment, the Queen and Parliament gradually started to give the working class population more services such as running water, lighting, hospitals and schools. There were police stations and more police forces to keep cities under control too.

> Children at the workhouses

DID YOU KNOW?

- Queen Victoria made Buckingham Palace the official royal residence of the British monarch in 1837.
- During the Victorian Age, the novel became the most popular form of literature.
- In the 18th century people borrowed books from *circulating libraries* and reading was their favourite hobby.
- In 1829 the Prime Minister Robert Peel established the Metropolitan Police. That's why the policemen were first known as "*Peelers*" and then as "*Bobbies*" after the popular nickname for Robert.

ACTVITIES

1 Translate each word into Italian.

a. Strict . . . .
b. Development . . . .
c. Achievements . . . .
d. Overruled . . . .
e. Countryside . . . .
f. Factories . . . .
g. Overcrowded . . . .
h. Environment . . . .
i. Slums . . . .
j. Workhouses . . . .

2 Read the text and answer the following questions.

1. Was Queen Victoria's reign long?
2. When did Victoria come to the throne?
3. Was her reign characterized by great social reforms?
4. What was the most important invention during Victoria's reign?
5. Why did Britain become a world economic leader?
6. Why did people leave the countryside?
7. Were there magnificent buildings in London?
8. What were the *slums?*
9. What was the childhood working class children like in the Victorian Age?
10. Why were people angry?
11. What solutions did the Queen and Parliament find?
12. What did Robert Peel do in 1829?

3 SPEAKING

In his novels Charles Dickens talks about children who, although they are alone and suffer, try to better their lives. He wrote «*The most important thing in life is to stop saying "I wish" and start saying "I will". Consider nothing impossible, then treat possibilities as probabilities.*»
What do you think about this quote? Write simple sentences in your exercise book and speak about them with your friends.

4 Speak about Charles Dickens. Look at the spidergram.

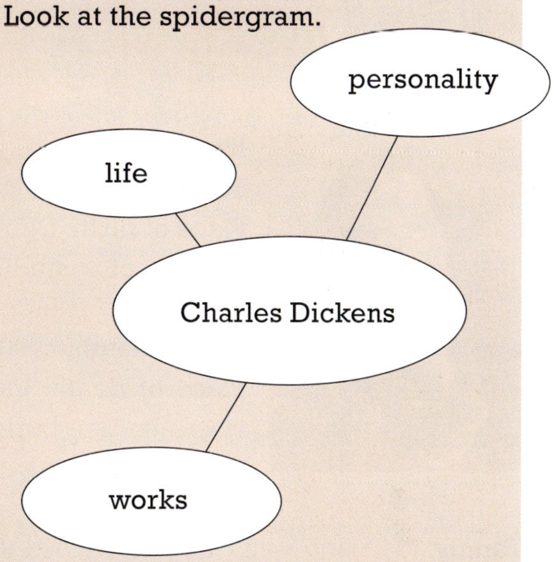

RISORSE ON-LINE
www.medusaeditrice.it

4th LESSON

OSCAR WILDE

Life

Year of birth: 1854.
Place of birth: Dublin.
Place of studies: Dublin and Oxford.
Year of death: 1900.
Place of death: Paris where he was buried. His tomb is in the same cemetery as Charles Baudelaire.
Family: marriage with Constance Lloyd and two children, Cyril and Vyvyan Holland.
Scandal and prison: Arrested in 1895 and imprisoned in Reading jail for two years for his homosexual relationship with Alfred Douglas, an English writer and translator, the son of the Marquess of Queensbury. Homosexuality was a crime in his time.

The Author

The Oxford influence: The reading of *The Renaissance* by Walter Pater, father of the Aesthetic Movement, greatly influenced Wilde. His teacher at university, the historian and writer John Ruskin, was also an important influence.
Personality: brilliant talker, affected dandy, aesthete, ambitious and extravagant wit.
Arts: a writer, a poet, a playwright, an essayist, a spokesman for the school of «art for art's sake».
Travels: Italy where among other cities he also visited Naples, the USA and France.

Works

Among his works the most popular are:

- *The Picture of Dorian Gray,* a novel (1890);
- *The Importance of Being Earnest,* a comedy (1895);
- *The Canterville Ghost,* a short story (1887);
- *The Happy Prince and the other stories* (among them there's *The Selfish Giant*), a collection of tales (1888);
- *The Ballad of Reading Gaol, a poetic work* (1898), written in Reading prison (England);
- *De Profundis*, an autobiographical letter (1897), written in prison.

A popular quote

"Keep love in your heart. A life without it is like a sunless garden when the flowers are dead."

DID YOU KNOW?

Dandy was a person who loved wearing very elegant clothes and had extravagant habits.
Wilde was a dandy. In fact when he walked in the street he used to carry flowers and loved to wear bright clothes.

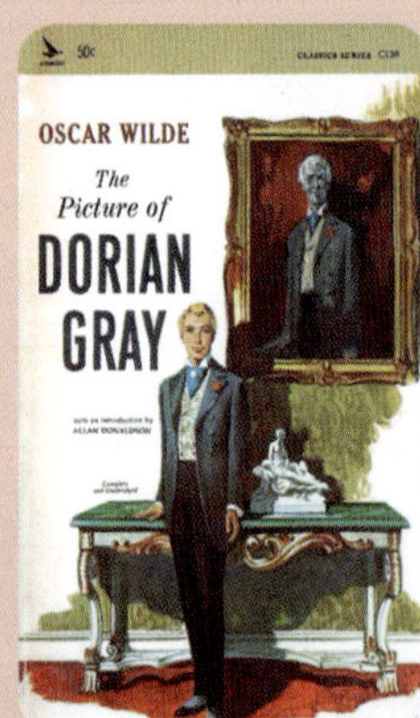

ACTIVITIES

1 Match each word with its Italian meaning.

a.	fairy tale	1.	oratore
b.	scandal	2.	portavoce
c.	historian	3.	ricercato
d.	talker	4.	storico
e.	dandy	5.	damerino
f.	aesthete	6.	saggista
g.	sunless	7.	esteta
h.	essayist	8.	senza sole
i.	spokesman	9.	scandalo
j.	affected	10.	amore
k.	sake	11.	racconto fantastico

4 Speak about Oscar Wilde. Look at the spidergram.

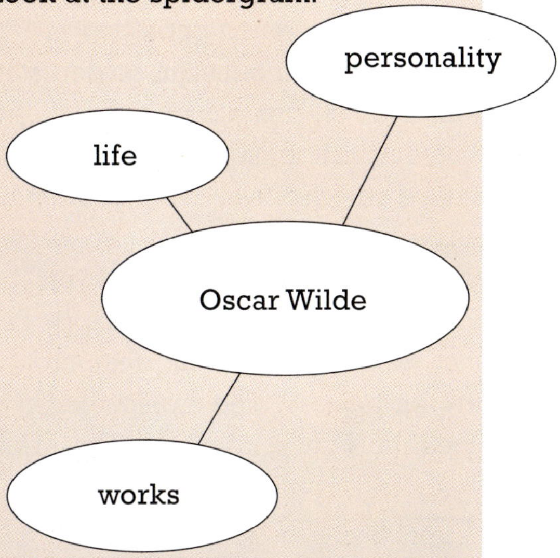

2 True or false? Correct the false sentences.

a. Oscar Wilde was born in London. T F
b. He died in Dublin. T F
c. Alfred Douglas was a writer and a translator. T F
d. Wilde was influenced by Ruskin. T F
e. He was an extravagant wit. T F
f. Wilde was in prison for two years. T F
g. He didn't travel much. T F
h. *The Importance of Being Earnest* is a sonnet. T F
i. *The Canterville Ghost* is a comedy. T F
j. Wilde wrote some works in prison. T F

3 Read the text and answer the following questions.

1. When was Oscar Wilde born?
2. Where was Oscar Wilde from?
3. Where is his tomb?
4. Who was Wilde's wife?
5. How many children did they have?
6. Why did Wilde go to jail?
7. Who influenced Oscar Wilde?
8. What was he like?
9. What was he a spokesman of?
10. Where did he travel to?
11. Which works did he write in prison?
12. What's his most popular novel?

READING

Read the text and complete the activity.

The Happy Prince

"*The Happy Prince*" is a short story written by Oscar Wilde and published in 1888. The story is about a beautiful golden statue that stands in the middle of a small town. The statue, which is on a column, is of a Happy Prince who has two sapphires for his eyes and a ruby on his sword.

One day a little swallow stops to rest between the feet of the statue of the Happy Prince. In that exact moment a big tear drop falls on the bird's head. The swallow looks up and sees the Prince is crying. The Prince tells the small bird he is sad because he can see some poor people who live in the town: a boy, a writer and a girl. The small boy is ill and his mother hasn't got any money for a doctor. The writer is cold and he hasn't got any money for wood for a fire and the girl is crying because she has lost the matches she was selling in the mud which meant nobody wanted to buy them anymore. The swallow listens to the Prince. Then he asks the bird to take the precious stones from his sword and his eyes to the boy's mother, to the writer and to the girl as he can't leave the column. But the swallow is in a hurry to fly to Egypt where it's hot, unlike the little town where it is Autumn. Finally the bird helps the Prince and takes the precious stones to the chosen poor people. The Prince is now blind as he hasn't got any eyes and the swallow can't leave him alone.The Prince then asks the bird to take the gold from his body leaf by leaf and to give it to all the poor people of the town. When the swallow comes back to the Prince it's cold. He kisses the Prince and dies. This sad event breaks the Prince's heart in two. The following morning the Mayor of the town looks at the statue without the precious stones and golden leaves and decides to melt it in a furnace. The only part of the Prince that doesn't melt is his heart. The workers throw it in a dustbin which contains the dead body of the swallow. Soon after an Angel of God flies down to Earth to find the Happy Prince's heart and the little swallow and carries them up to Paradise.

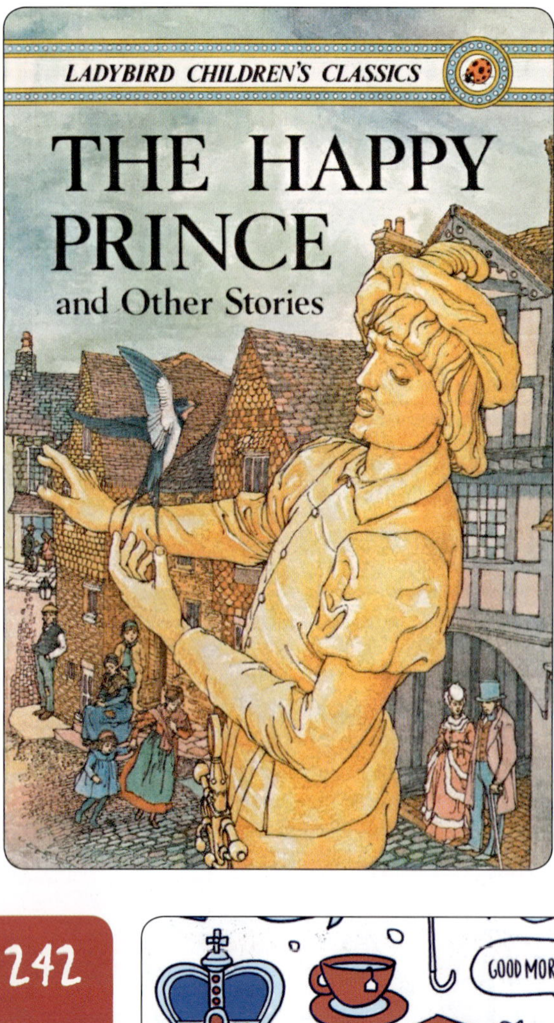

Draw eight sequences of the story in your exercise book. Then write a sentence under each sequence.

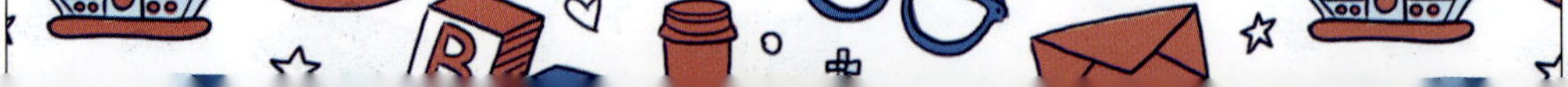

JOSEPH RUDYARD KIPLING

Name: Joseph Rudyard Kipling

Date and place of birth: 30th December 1865, Bombay.

Date and place of death: 18th January 1936, London.

Who he was: Kipling was an English journalist, novelist, poet and short-story writer.

His family: His parents were English, they met in 1863 at Rudyard Lake in Rudyard, Staffordshire, England. They married and moved to India in 1865. They were fascinated by the beauty of the Rudyard Lake area so they called their first child Rudyard.

Education: Rudyard attended Primary school in Southsea, in England. He did not continue his studies and did not go to university because his teachers thought he did not have the academic ability to get into Oxford University on a scholarship.

Important facts of his life: Kipling lived in India till the age of six, when he went to Southsea in England, together with his little sister Trix, to attend Primary school. In England they lived with the Holloway family which was the most unhappiest period of his life. His parents did not have the money to finance his studies, so he went to work in Lahore, in Pakistan.

When he died in 1936, he was cremated and his ashes are kept, in Westminster Abbey, London

George Orwell called him a prophet of British imperialism.

Rudyard Kipling received the Nobel Prize for Literature in 1907.

Works: Kipling is famous for his writings *The Jungle Book, The second Jungle Book, Kim* and *Captains Courageous.*

ACTIVITIES

1 Write the base form of the following verbs and their meaning in Italian.

a. Called ....

b. Died ....

c. Had ....

d. Kept ....

e. Lived ....

f. Married ....

g. Met ....

h. Moved ....

i. Thought ....

j. Was born ....

k. Went ....

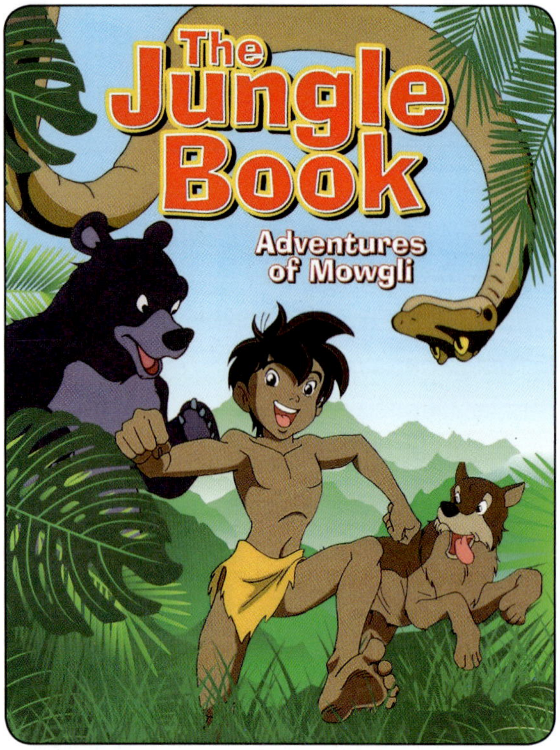

READING

The Jungle Book

The Jungle Book is Kipling's most well-known writing. It was published in 1894 and its sequel *The Second Jungle Book* was published a year later in Vermont.

Mowgli is a man-cub. He arrives at the mountain top home of the wolves.

He is taken in by Mother and Father Wolf and he grows up with the wolf pack led by Akela, the wolf leader who wants to look after him. The bear Baloo and the panther Bagheera also look after Mowgli. He learns the law of the jungle and grows up happily with the wolves. He lives in the jungle for ten years, but when Akela becomes older and weaker, Shere Khan tries to catch and eat the man-cub. So Mowgli realizes that it is time to move on and he leaves the mountain-top.

The Jungle Book is a collection of stories that uses animals to teach moral lessons.

Baloo, the old brown bear, teaches Mowgli the language of the jungle.

Bagheera, the panther warns Mowgli to stay away from the Monkeys because they are foolish and have and lawless.

When Mowgli is kidnapped by the Monkeys, he asks *Chil*, a big bird, to notify Baloo and Bagheera.

Baloo asks *Kaa*, a ten-metre-long snake for help.

DID YOU KNOW?

- The Jungle Book is a collection of stories written by Rudyard Kipling when he lived in Vermont.
- The stories were published in newspaper and magazines between 1893 and 1894.
- Some of the pictures in the original publications were drawn by Kipling's father.
- His collection of stories is now included in innumerable anthologies around the world.
- The Disney version of the Jungle Book became one of the most popular children's films of all time.
- Rudyard Kipling received the Nobel Prize for Literature in 1907.

ANIMAL GLOSSARY

WOLVES

In *The Jungle Book* Akela and Raksha are Indian wolves from the same pack.
Akela is a lone wolf and a symbol of wisdom. Wolves are very social animals living and travelling in packs. Packs include up to 8 or 9 wolves.

BEARS

In *The Jungle Book* Baloo is a sloth bear. Sloth bears are found in India and prefer drier forests and areas of exposed rock.

PANTHERS

In *The Jungle Book* Bagheera is a black panther.
Black panthers are the same species as leopards which are known for their lighter brown or golden fur with dark spots.

TIGERS

In *The Jungle Book* Shere Khan is a Bengal tiger. Bengal tigers are mainly found in India. They are known for their bold orange and black stripes and underbellies of light fur.

SNAKES

In *The Jungle Book* Kaa is a Burmese Python, a snake typically found in Southern China, in Indonesia and in India. Burmese pythons have a brown box pattern on their skin and are usually grey and white. They are quite large and 15 to 18 feet in length.

ACTIVITIES

2 **Say if the following sentences are TRUE (T) or FALSE (F). Correct the false ones.**

a. Rudyard Kipling was born in London. T F
b. His parents were English. T F
c. They married in London. T F
d. Rudyard went to England, at the age of six. T F
e. In England he lived with Holloway family. T F
f. Rudyard did not continue his studies. T F
g. His teachers thought he could go to University. T F
h. He went to work in Pakistan. T F
i. He was also a journalist. T F
j. His ashes are kept in Westminster Abbey. T F

3 **Answer the following questions.**

1. When and where was Kipling born?
2. Where did his parents meet?
3. Where did they move to after the marriage?
4. Why did they call their first child *Rudyard*?
5. What are Kipling's most famous writings?
6. Where did Rudyard attend primary school?
7. Why did he not go to University?
8. Where did he go to work?
9. Where are his ashes kept?
10. What did George Orwell call him?

6th LESSON

GEORGE ORWELL

Life
Year of birth: 1903.
Place of birth: Motihari, India from a family with Scottish origins.
Place of studies: St. Cyprian College Eastbourne in Sussex and Eton College.
Year of death: 1950.
Place of death: London.

Family: marriage with Eileen O'Shaughnessy who died in 1945 and then with Sonia Bronwell in 1949; he adopted a child called Richard Horatio Blair.

Military life: service in the Imperial Indian police for five years in Burma and resignation for a reaction against the politics of the Empire; participation in the Spanish Civil War on the side of the anarchists against Francis Franco's dictatorship. He was wounded in the war. He was a sergeant in the Home Guard during World War II.

Work: Primary school teacher, journalist and novelist.

The Author
Influences: Aldous Huxley, a British writer, was his teacher.
Personality: clear and direct, rebel wit against every form of discrimination and man's domination over other men.
Artist: his real name was Eric Arthur Blair who wrote with the pseudonym of George Orwell, journalist, essayist, writer.
Travels: France, Spain, Morocco, Germany, Austria.

Works
Among his works the most famous are:
- *Animal Farm* (1944), a political fable;
- *1984* (1948), a novel.

A popular quote
«All animals are equal but some animals are more equal than others.»

DID YOU KNOW?

Nineteen Eighty-four, George Orwell's novel, speaks about life in a totalitarian state. Each citizen's actions and thoughts are controlled by a television called *Big Brother* who is the leader of the only political party.
This novel inspired the current TV reality show *Big Brother* where a group of people live together in a house and have their daily life recorded by television cameras. Their life in the house is broadcast to a large audience. It's a very successful TV programme.

ACTIVITIES

1 Match each word with its Italian meaning.

a. anarchist	1. fiaba
b. sergeant	2. anarchico
c. wounded	3. dominio
d. domination	4. ferito
e. pseudonym	5. sergente
f. fable	6. pseudonimo

2 True or false?
Correct the false sentences.

a. George Orwell was born in India. T F
b. He died in London. T F
c. His real name was Eric Arthur Blair. T F
d. Orwell was influenced by Aldous Huxley. T F
e. He didn't support the anarchists against Franco. T F
f. He was an extravagant wit. T F
g. He didn't travel a lot. T F
h. Animal farm is a comedy. T F

3 SPEAKING
Speak about George Orwell. Look at the spidergram.

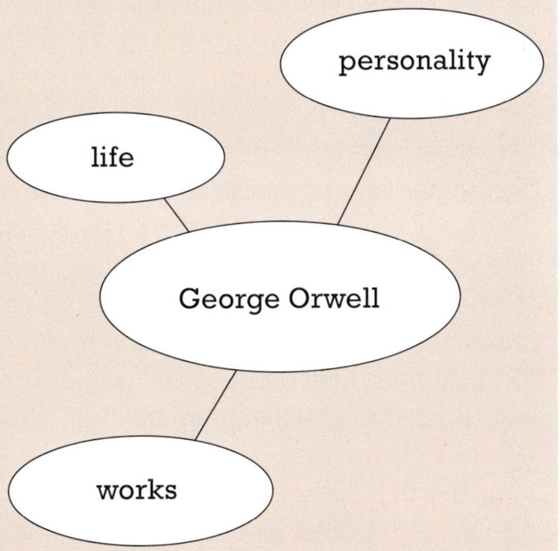

4 Questions
Read the text and answer the following questions.

1. When was George Orwell born?
2. Where was he from?
3. Where did he study?
4. Who was Orwell's wife?
5. How many children did he have?
6. How long did he serve in the Imperial Indian police?
7. Why did Orwell resign from it?
8. What was Orwell like?
9. What was his real name?
10. Where did he travel?
11. Which works did he write?
12. What's his most famous novel?

READING

Read the text and complete the activity.

Animal farm

Animal farm is a political fable written by George Orwell and published in 1945. It's an allegory of the Russian Revolution and of its consequences and is a denunciation of every form of totalitarianism.

It tells the story of a group of farm animals who, tired of the tyranny of the farmer Mr Jones, decide to rebel against him. It is their struggle against the man who dominates and exploits them every day. The revolution led by the pigs breaks out one night when Mr Jones forgets to feed them because he's drunk. The animals leave their enclosures in order to find food. At this point the farmers get angry and fight against the animals until the latter throw the men out of the farm. Soon after the pigs become the ruling class of the farm and their leader, a pig himself, is Napoleon. But over time they establish a dictatorship that is worse than the farmer's domination and exploitation. The Pigs are selfish and astute and become similar to the men in their behaviour: they start walking on two legs, drink whisky, wear clothes and sleep in comfortable beds. They have become totally corrupt and the commandment "all animals are equal but some animals are more equal than others" perfectly expresses this corruption. Finally the pigs and men form an alliance. At night they get drunk, play cards and quarrel over their games. The other animals spy the scene from a window and can no longer distinguish the animals from the men.

1. **Draw six sequences of the story in your exercise book. Then write a sentence under each sequence.**
2. **Colour the following picture.**

LYMAN FRANK BAUM

Name: Lyman Frank Baum (known by the pen name L. Frank Baum).

Date and place of birth: 15th May 1856, in Chittenango, New York, USA.

Date and place of death: 6th May 1919, in Hollywood, Los Angeles, California, USA.

Who he was: F. Baum was an American author, newspaper editor, actor, screenwriter and film producer. He is known for his children's books, particularly for his most famous work *The Wonderful Wizard of Oz.*

His family: Lyman Frank was the seventh of nine children. His father Benjamin Ward Baum, a rich business man and his mother Cynthia Stanton were of German origin.

Education: As a child he was educated at home by a tutor. When he was 12 his parents wanted him to attend the Peekskill Military Academy but he remained there for only two years. He was allowed to return home after he was struck by a heart attack.

Important facts of his life: He lived for about 20 years in the large house of his parents, *Rose Lawn,* located in Mattydale, New York. He liked Rose Lawn very much. He loved the *printed paper* and *writing* so his father bought him a small printing press. Henry Clay Baum, his younger brother helped him in the production of *The Rose Lawn Home Journal.* At 17, he began to produce a second amateur journal, *The Stamp Collector.*

He had an interest for the theatre and performed in plays many times under the stage names of Louis F. Baum and George Brooks.

In 1880 he became a theatre director and began to write plays and set up a company to act with.

In 1882 he married Maud Gage. They had four sons.

Works: Baum's works include: *The Maid of Arran, The Wizard of Oz, The Woggle-Bug, The Wonderful Wizard of Oz.*

A famous quote: *«True courage is in facing danger when you are afraid...»*

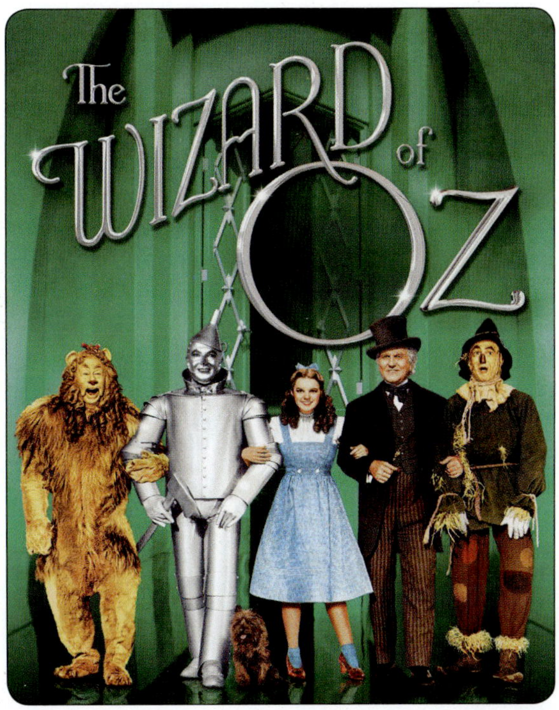

ACTIVITIES

1 Match the words.

a. Amateur	1. Regista teatrale
b. Businessman	2. Sceneggiatore
c. Children's books	3. Pressa tipografica
d. Film producer	4. Dilettante
e. Newspaper editor	5. Uomo d'affari
f. Pen name	6. Insegnante privato
g. Printing press	7. Libri per bambini
h. Screenwriter	8. Produttore cinematografico
i. Theatre director	9. Pseudonimo
j. Tutor	10. Direttore di giornale

ESERCIZI ON LINE www.medusaeditrice.it

2 Say if the following sentences are True (T) or False (F). Correct the false ones.

a. L.F. Baum was an English writer. T F
b. He was an only child. T F
c. His parents were of German origin. T F
d. He attended the Military Academy. T F
e. He lived in *Rose Lawn* for 30 years. T F
f. His father bought him a printing press. T F
g. He produced three amateur journals. T F
h. He performed under the stage name of Louis F. Baum. T F
i. He was a theatre director. T F
j. He had four daughters. T F

3 Answer the following questions.

1. When and where was L.F. Baum born?
2. Who was he?
3. Where was he educated?
4. How many years did he live in *Rose Lawn*?
5. Where was *Rose Lawn* located?
6. What did he love very much?
7. What did he do at 17?
8. What were his stage names?
9. What did he do in 1880?
10. How many children did he have?

4 WRITING

Write about L. F. Baum following the points of the fact file.

Lyman Frank Baum was born in ________
____
___
He was ______________________
________ and his parents were ________
He is known for ________________
____

READING

The Wonderful Wizard of Oz

You're Off to See the Wizard

The Wonderful Wizard of Oz You'll find he is a whiz of a Wiz If ever a Wiz there was. If ever, oh ever a Wiz there was The Wizard of Oz Is one because Because, because, because, because, because Because of the wonderful things he does

Dorothy was an orphan girl who lived with her uncle and aunt in Kansas. One day, a cyclone sucked up the farmhouse and transported it to the magical Land of Oz. Dorothy and Toto were inside the house. The land of Oz was very beautiful but Dorothy and Toto wanted to go back to Kansas.

In the land of Oz they met four witches. One of them told Dorothy that the only person who could help them go back home was the wizard of Oz.

So they followed the *Yellow Brick Road* that would take them to the Wizard. Along the way they met many unusual characters, a Scarecrow, a Tin Woodman, and a Cowardly Lion. Together they went on a quest to see theWizard of Oz but when they arrived at the *Emerald City,* the Wizard told them that before he could grant them their wishes they must first kill the Wicked Witch of the West.

They overcame many challenges but when they returned to the Great Oz, they accidentally found out that he was not a wizard after all.

He was actually a man from Omaha. He had flown to OZ in a hot air balloon and had become trapped in the magical land a long time before. He promised Dorothy that he would make a hot air balloon for them to cross the desert and return to Kansas.

Dorothy didn't succeed to get into the balloon and the man flew away by himself. A guard of the City of Emerald suggested to Dorothy that she asks the Good Witch of the South for help. Dorothy and her friends travel to the Land of the South. Their last journey ends happily: Dorothy and Toto return home.

DID YOU KNOW?

- Map of the Land of Oz is a fictional universe created by L.F. Baum, where the book series of Oz take place
- Land of Oz or simply Oz, is a nickname used in English speaking countries to refer to Australia. The use derives from the assonance in the English pronunciation between 'Oz' and 'aus' (tralia).
- In 1990 John Ritter, one of the greatest American actors, comedians and dubbers, made a TV film about Frank Baum's life: The Dreamer of Oz: The L. Frank Baum Story.
- L.F. Baum wrote thirteen novel sequels, nine fantasy novels, and a host of other works. He attempted many times to bring his works to the stage and screen.

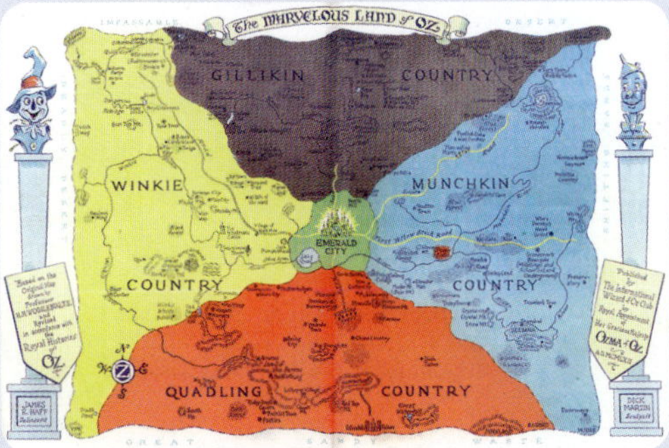

ACTIVITIES

1 Answer the following questions.

1. Where did Dorothy live?
2. Where were Dorothy and Toto when a cyclone sucked up the farmhouse?
3. How many witches were there in the Land of Oz?
4. What could the Wizard of Oz do?
5. Who did Dorothy and Toto meet along the Yellow Brick Road?
6. What happened when they arrived in the Emerald City?
7. Who was the Wizard really?
8. Did Dorothy succeed in getting into the hot air balloon?
9. What did the guard suggest that Dorothy does?
10. Did Dorothy and Toto return home?

2 Read the text and summarize it.

From *The Wonderful Wizard of Oz* by Baum, Lyman Frank.

Chapter I – *The Cyclone.*

Dorothy lived in the midst of the great Kansas prairies, with Uncle Henry, who was a farmer, and Aunt Em, who was the farmer's wife. Their house was small, for the lumber to build it had to be carried by wagon many miles. There were four walls, a floor and a roof, which made one room; and this room contained a rusty looking cook stove, a cupboard for the dishes, a table, three or four chairs, and the beds. Uncle Henry and Aunt Em had a big bed in one corner, and Dorothy a little bed in another corner. There was no garret at all, and no cellar-except a small hole dug in the ground, called a cyclone cellar, where the family could go in case one of those great whirlwinds arose, mighty enough to crush any building in its path. It was reached by a trap door in the middle of the floor, from which a ladder led down into the small, dark hole. When Dorothy stood in the doorway and looked around, she could see nothing but the great gray prairie on every side. Not a tree nor a house broke the broad sweep of flat country that reached to the edge of the sky in all directions. The sun had baked the plowed land into a gray mass, with little cracks running through it. Even the grass was not green, for the sun had burned the tops of the long blades until they were the same gray color to be seen everywhere. Once the house had been painted, but the sun blistered the paint and the rains washed it away, and now the house was as dull and gray as everything else. When Aunt Em came there to live she was a young, pretty wife. The sun and wind had changed her, too. They had taken the sparkle from her eyes and left them a sober gray; they had taken the red from her cheeks and lips, and they were gray also. She was thin and gaunt, and never smiled now.

LISTENING ACTIVITY

Listen to "Over the Rainbow" sung by Judy Garland and complete the text with the following words:

Link: https://youtu.be/PSZxmZmBfnU

rainbow	dream	clouds
	chimney tops	
fly	lemon drops	

Somewhere over the RAINBOW way up high
There's a land that I heard of once in a lullaby
Somewhere over the rainbow skies are blue
And the dreams that you dare to ____________ really do come true

Someday I'll wish upon a star
And wake up where the ____________ are far
Behind me
Where troubles melt like ________________
Away above the _______________________
That's where you'll find me

Somewhere over the rainbow bluebirds fly
Birds FLY over the rainbow.
Why then, oh, why can't I?

If happy little bluebirds fly
Beyond the rainbow.
Why, oh, why can't I?

ERNEST MILLER HEMINGWAY

Life

Year of birth: 1899.
Place of birth: Oak Park, a suburb of Chicago, Illinois.
Year of death: 1961.
Place of death: He committed suicide and was buried in Sun Valley Idaho, USA.
Place of study: Oak Park and River Forest High school.
Family: Hemingway was married four times. His wives were Hadley Richardson(1921), Pauline Pfeiffer (1927), Martha Gellhorn (1940) and Mary Welsh (1946).

The Author

His father was a doctor and his mother a singer. Hemingway spent his childhood as a very active boy, he liked hunting, fishing, boxing and playing rugby. However, as a child, he loved reading and writing too.
He began to work as a reporter in 1917 and in the following years as a novelist.
He had a very adventurous life full of important cultural experiences. He traveled in Europe and met famous writers such as James Joyce. He also had a great passion for safaris and often to Africa.
In 1936, during the Spanish Civil War, he worked as a foreign correspondent for an American news agency. He continued this activity during the Second World War.
At the end of the war Hemingway moved to Cuba and continued writing famous novels and dedicating his free time to another of his passions, fishing.
He committed suicide, just like his father.
Personality: adventurous, active, passionate. Towards the end of his life Hemingway suffered from acute depression.
Influences: modernist writers and artists. His trips abroad also inspired his novels.
Artist: his great love for writing made him a very eclectic artist and a brilliant writer who was appreciated throughout the world.
Travels: He travelled a lot, traveling in Italy, France, Spain, Africa and Cuba. He considered the latter his second home.

Works

Hemingway produced most of his work between the mid-1920s and the mid-1950s and many of them are considered classics of American literature. He won the Nobel Prize for Literature in 1954. He also gained the Pulitzer Price with *The Old Man and the Sea* in 1953. His works include:

- *In Our Time* (1924);
- *The Sun Also Rises* (1926) published as *Fiesta* in Britain;
- *The Green Hills of Africa* (1935);
- A *Farewell to Arms* (1929);
- *For Whom the Bell Tolls* (1940).

A famous quote

«*Every day is a new day.*»

ACTIVITIES

1 Match each word with its Italian meaning.

a. Suburb	1. Corrispondente
b. Suicide	2. Avventuroso
c. Hunting	3. Patria
d. Fishing	4. Eclettico
e. Boxing	5. Passionale
f. Correspondent	6. Caccia
g. Adventurous	7. Pugilato
h. Passionate	8. Suicidio
i. Eclectic	9. Periferia
j. Homeland	10. Pesca

2 Read and answer the following questions.

1. When was Ernest Hemingway born?
2. Where was Ernest Hemingway from?
3. How did he die?
4. Whom did Hemingway work for in 1936?
5. Who influenced Hemingway's works?
6. Where did he travel?
7. What were his great passions?
8. What are his most popular novels?
9. Did he move to Cuba? When?
10. When did he win the Nobel Prize for Literature?

ESERCIZI ON LINE www.medusaeditrice.it

3 True or false? Correct the false sentences.

a. Ernest Hemingway was British. T F
b. He was born in 1899. T F
c. His father was a lawyer. T F
d. He was married four times. T F
e. Hemingway travelled a lot. T F
f. Hemingway was a famous journalist and novelist. T F
g. He was a war reporter. T F
h. He worked as a foreign correspondent. T F
i. Hemingway hated fishing. T F
j. He didn't win the Nobel Prize for Literature. T F

4 Speak about Ernest Hemingway. Look at the spidergram.

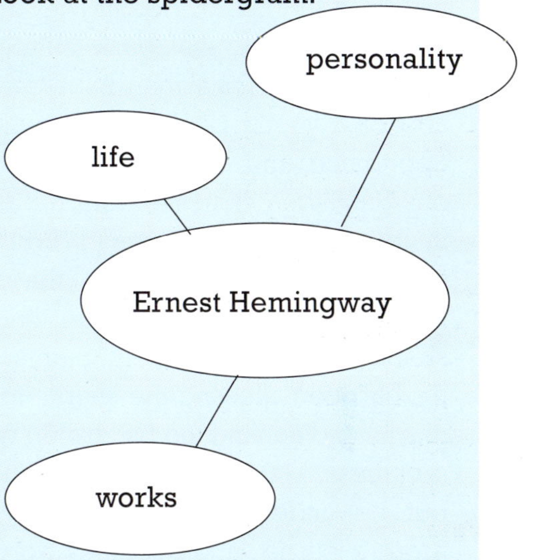

READING
The Old Man and the Sea.

The story
The most popular short novel that contains the main themes of Hemingway's work is *The old Man and the Sea.* It is the story of an old Cuban fisherman named Santiago and of a young boy, Manolin, who is his apprentice and takes care of him. One day Santiago catches an enormous marlin in the middle of the ocean. While he is sailing home with the fish the marlin's blood leaves a trail in the water that attracts sharks. Fighting with them, Santiago loses his harpoon allowing the sharks to eat the marlin and leaving the fisherman with only a carcass. Manolin isn't with the old man, but he understands the tragedy of his friend's journey and becomes worried.

From *The Old Man and the Sea*, Chapter I
The Old Man and the Sea
He was an old man who fished alone in a skiff in the Gulf Stream and he had gone eighty-four days now without taking a fish. In the first forty days a boy had been with him. But after forty days without a fish the boy's parents had told him that the old man was now definitely and finally *salao*, which is the worst form of unlucky, and the boy had gone at their orders in another boat which caught three good fish the first week. It made the boy sad to see the old man come in each day with his skiff empty and he always went down to help him carry either the coiled lines or the gaff and harpoon and the sail that was furled around the mast. The sail was patched with flour sacks and, furled, it looked like the flag of permanent defeat.
The old man was thin and gaunt with deep wrinkles in the back of his neck. The brown blotches of the benevolent skin cancer the sun brings from its reflection on the tropic sea were on his cheeks. The blotches ran well down the sides of his face and his hands had the deep-creased scars from handling heavy fish on the cords. But none of these scars were fresh. They were as old as erosions in a fishless desert.
Everything about him was old except his eyes and they were the same color as the sea and were cheerful and undefeated.
«Santiago», the boy said to him as they climbed the bank from where the skiff was hauled up. «I could go with you again. We've made some money.»
The old man had taught the boy to fish and the boy loved him.
«No», the old man said. «You're with a lucky boat. Stay with them».
«Why not?» the old man said. «Between fishermen.»

DID YOU KNOW?

- *Hemingway's* novels inspired famous films such as *The Old Man and the Sea and For Whom the Bells Tolls.*
- Hemingway had many nicknames; the most popular was "Papa". In fact the latest film, about Hemingway's life, is called *Papa Hemingway in Cuba.*

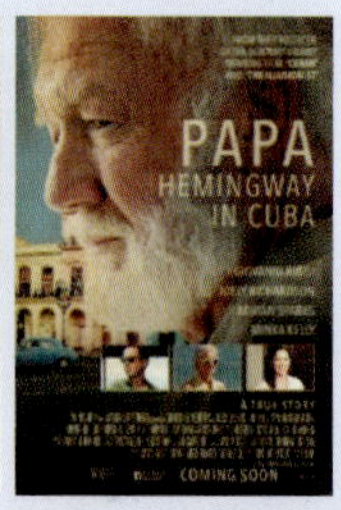

ACTIVITIES

1 Read the text and Answer the following questions.

1. Where did the old man go fishing?
2. What's the name of the boy who stayed with the old man for 40 days?
3. Why did the boy leave the man?
4. Was the boy sad when the old man came back from fishing? Why?
5. What did the boy do every time?
6. What was the old man like?
7. Were his eyes sad?
8. Did the old man encourage the boy to stay with another boat?
9. Who forced the boy to leave the old man?
10. Was the boy close to the old man?

2 Imagine the old man on his boat when he is fishing the giant marlin in the middle of the ocean. Try and Draw the scene and write simple sentences.

3 Do you know of any other stories in literature that has features in common with *The Old Man and the Sea*? Write the name of the story and a short summary below.

9th LESSON

JACK LONDON

Life

Year of birth: 1876.

Place of birth: San Francisco.

Place of study: Oakland and Berkeley.

Year of death: 1916.

Place of death: he committed suicide in Glen Ellen, California.

Family: first marriage with Elizabeth "Bessie" Maddern who bore him two daughters, Joan and Becky. They divorced in 1904 and his second marriage was with Charmian Kittredge.

Childhood and youth: Jack was poor and lived as a tramp, he grew up in the streets where he hung out with thieves and smugglers. When he was young he did many jobs: he worked as a sealer then as a war correspondent and he even went to Canada as an adventurer taking part in the gold rush. He also went to prison because he was a member of the protest march of unemployed people.

The Author

Jack London was the pseudonym of John Griffith Chaney London.

The influence of Zola and Darwin: he was a realist and was inspired by Darwin's scientific theories and Zola's naturalism. His main themes were the struggle for survival and the transition from civilization to the primitive state.

Personality: rebel, progressive and sensitive. He had alcohol problems.

Artist: he loved reading and was an avid consumer of books. When he was an adult he became an essayist, a journalist, a short stories writer and a novelist.

Works

Among his work for children the most popular are:

- *The Call of the Wild*, a novel (1903);
- *The Sea Wolf* (1904), a novel;
- *White Fang*, a novel (1906).

A famous quote

«*The proper function of man is to live, not to exist. I shall not waste my days in trying to prolong them. I shall use my time.*»

ACTIVITIES

1 Match each word with its Italian meaning.

a. youth	1. avventuriero
b. tramp	2. cacciatore di foche
c. hang out with	3. contrabbandiere
d. thief	4. corsa all'oro
e. smuggler	5. disoccupato
f. sealer	6. frequentare
g. adventurer	7. giovinezza
h. gold rush	8. ladro
i. unemployed	9. lotta
j. struggle	10. passaggio
k. survival	11. sopravvivenza
l. transition	12. vagabondo

2 True, false or you don't know? Correct the false sentences.

a. Jack London was born in Washington DC.	T	F	DK
b. He died in New York.	T	F	DK
c. His first wife was Elizabeth "Bessie" Maddern.	T	F	DK
d. London was influenced by Darwin and Zola.	T	F	DK
e. He was a rebel.	T	F	DK
f. Jack London went to prison.	T	F	DK
g. He travelled a lot.	T	F	DK
h. He went to Canada.	T	F	DK
i. *The Call of the Wild* is a novel.	T	F	DK
j. London wrote some works in prison.	T	F	DK

3 Read the text and answer.

1. Where did Jack London study?
2. What was his nationality?
3. When did he divorce Elizabeth "Bessie" Maddern?
4. What was London's real name?
5. How many children did he have?
6. Why did London go to jail?
7. Who influenced Jack London?
8. What was he like?
9. What did he love in his life?
10. What are his most popular novels for children?

4 Speak about Jack London. Look at the spidergram.

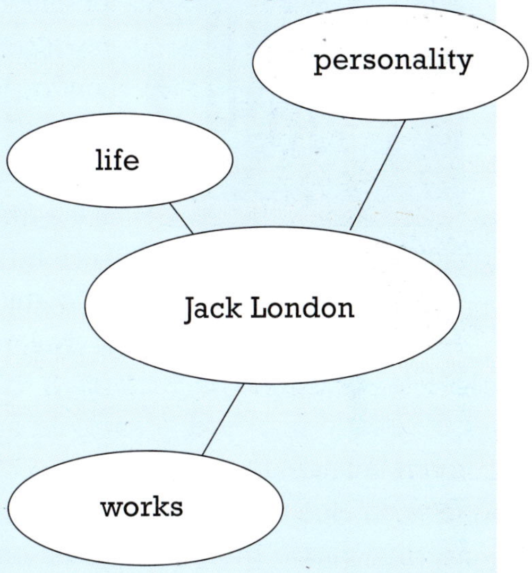

READING
White Fang (1906)

"*White Fang*" is a popular novel for children in which Jack London tells the story of a wolf. The setting is in the freezing North of Canada, where life is hard and dangerous for both people and animals. Everybody struggles for survival, as does White Fang who is busy in a continual struggle to find food, a struggle in which many animals die.

One day the wolf meets some men of the North – first a group of Indians and then some White Men – and learns to live with them as a dog.

Read the text "The She-Wolf" from "White Fang" and then complete the following activities.

One of the saddest aspects of this story is to discover that some men are cruel to their dogs. But fortunately there are some men that are kind with them.

The two men slept side by side. The fire burned down and the circle of eyes got nearer.

In the morning, Henry was first to wake up. It was still dark. Bill got ready to move on while Henry made breakfast.

«How many dogs did you say we had?» Bill asked suddenly.

«Six,» Henry told him.

«Well, there are five now. Fatty ran away in the night.»

After breakfast, they started their journey again. Daylight came at nine o'clock, and in the middle of the day the sky to the south turned red. But the colour did not stay long. By three o' clock, the arctic night was back across the silent land again.

The cries of the wolves got nearer with the darkness. The two men made camp and ate their meal. Bill went to give the dogs their food. Suddenly, there was the cry of an animal in pain. Something moved across the snow into the darkness. Bill was standing with the dogs, half a fish in one hand and a big stick in the other.

«It got half the fish,» he said. «But I hit it.»

In the morning, when Henry woke up, Bill was with the dogs.

«Frog's gone,» Bill said. «And he was our strongest dog.»

That day was the same as the other days. The men moved across the cold, white world without speaking. The dogs pulled the sled with the dead man on it. That night, Bill tied the dogs to a tree. Then the two men sat by their fire.

A sound made them turn round. A wolf moved slowly across the snow to the dogs. One Ear tried to pull away from the tree to get to the wolf.

«It's a she-wolf, Bill!» Henry said. «I see how it works now. She gets a dog to follow her, then the other wolves jump on it and eat it. That's what happened to Frog and Fatty.»

A noise came from the fire and the she-wolf ran back into the darkness.

(from adaptation by John Escott, *White Fang*, Dominoes, Oxford)

ACTIVITIES

1 True, false or you don't know?

a. It was afternoon when Henry got up. T F DK
b. Bill made breakfast. T F DK
c. There were five dogs now. T F DK
d. When they finished their breakfast Bill and Henry started their journey. T F DK
e. Bill wore a red jacket and brown trousers. T F DK
f. At 3 p.m. it was dark. T F DK
g. The two men went to sleep at 9 p.m. T F DK
h. Their weakest dog had run away. T F DK
i. Bill left the dogs in the snow. T F DK
j. The she-wolf ran back into the darkness. T F DK

2 Answer the following questions.

1. Who slept side by side?
2. When did daylight come?
3. What did Bill and Henry do in the camp?
4. What did Bill give the dogs?
5. How many dogs ran away?
6. What were their names?
7. What did the dogs pull?
8. Where did Bill tie the dogs?
9 Who moved across the snow towards the dogs?
10. Was the wolf male or female?
11. Have you got a dog? What's its name?
12. Do you like dogs?

3 Complete with information from the text.

Place ....

Characters ....

Time ....

MARK TWAIN

Life

Year of birth: 1835.

Place of birth: Florida, Missouri, USA.

Studies: he left school aged 12.

Real name: Samuel Langhorne Clemens.

Year of death: 1910.

Place of death: Redding, Connecticut, USA.

Family: married Olivia Langdon, they had three daughters.

Childhood and youth: In 1835 his family went to live in Hannibal a town on the Mississippi River, in Missouri. Samuel grew up experiencing extraordinary things and having wonderful adventures on the river. In 1853, after his father's death, he travelled to Nevada and California and over the following years worked as a steamboat pilot on the Mississippi River.

The Author

Mark Twain was the pseudonym of Samuel Langhorne Clemens.

Personality: humorist, realist.

Artist: he is one of the greatest American authors, famous for his wit. He worked as a journalist for the *Morning Call* in San Francisco, California and in 1865 he wrote his first short story *The Celebrated Jumping Frog of Calaveras Country* that was a great success. He is considered a *regionalist writer*, many readers appreciated his literary style and the themes of his books because they were so closely related to the society of the time. He was also a unique children's novelist.

Works

Among his works the most popular are:

- *Roughing it* (1872);
- *The Adventures of Tom Sawyer* (1876);
- *The Prince and the Pauper* (1882);
- *Life on the Mississippi* (1883);
- *The Adventures of Huckleberry Finn* (1884).

A famous quote

«*Work* consists of whatever a body is obliged to do. *Play* consists of whatever a body is not obliged to do.»

DID YOU KNOW?

Today millions of Americans live on the Mississippi river and steamboats still navigate its waters. There are also special steamboats for tourists.

ACTIVITIES

1 Match each word with its Italian meaning.

a. Wonderful	**1.** intelligente
b. Steamboat	**2.** stile letterario
c. Pilot	**3.** umorista
d. Pseudonym	**4.** singolare
e. Humorist	**5.** pilota
f. Realist	**6.** barca a vapore
g. Readers	**7.** meraviglioso
h. Literary style	**8.** umorista
i. Clever	**9.** lettori
j. Singular	**10.** pseudonimo
l. Wit	**11.** realista

2 Read and answer the following questions.

1. Where was Mark Twain born?
2. What was his nationality?
3. Who was Olivia Langdon?
4. What was Twain's real name?
5. How many children did he have?
6. Where did he travel?
7. What influenced Mark Twain's works?
8. How is he considered?
9. When did he write his first short story?
10. What are his most popular novels?

3 True or false? Correct the false sentences.

a. Mark Twain was born in Florida.	T	F
b. He died in New York.	T	F
c. In 1835 he went to live in Hannibal.	T	F
d. He was married.	T	F
e. He had three daughters and one son.	T	F
f. He worked as a steamboat pilot on the Mississippi River	T	F
g. Twain is considered a regionalist writer.	T	F
h. He worked as a journalist in Nevada.	T	F
i. In 1865 he became famous writing a short story.	T	F
j. Twain wrote humorous short stories.	T	F

4 Speak about Mark Twain. Look at the spidergram.

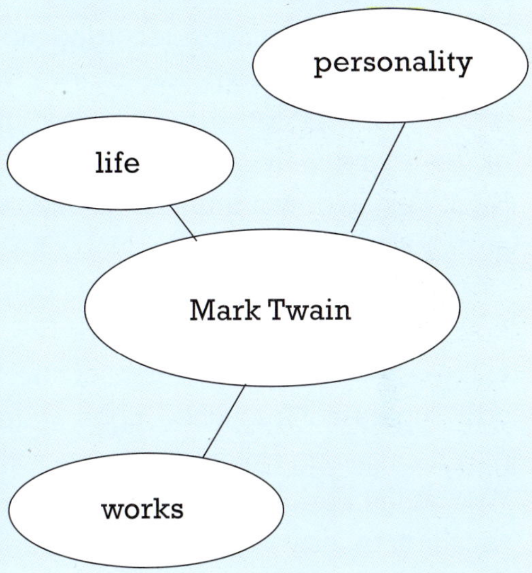

READING

1) Read the text and then complete the following activities .

The adventures of Tom Sawyer

Preface

Most of the adventures recorded in this book really occurred; one or two were experiences of my own, the rest those of boys who were schoolmates of mine. Huck Finn is drawn from life; Tom Sawyer also, but not from an individual – he is a combination of the characteristics of three boys whom I knew, and therefore belongs to the composite order of architecture. The odd superstitions touched upon were all prevalent among children and slaves in the West at the period of this story – that is to say, thirty or forty years ago.

Chapter II

Saturday morning was come, and all the summer world was bright and fresh, and brimming with life. There was a song in every heart; and if the heart was young, the music issued at the lips. There was cheer in every face and a spring in every step. The locust-trees were in bloom and the fragrance of the blossoms filled the air. Cardiff Hill, beyond the village and above it, was green with vegetation and it lay just far enough away to seem a Delectable Land, dreamy, reposeful, and inviting[...]

[...] Tom appeared on the side-walk with a bucket of whitewash and a long-handled brush. He surveyed the fence, and all gladness left him and a deep melancholy settled down upon his spirit. Thirty yards of board fence nine feet high. Life to him seemed hollow, and existence but a burden.Sighing, he dipped his brush and passed it along the topmost plank; repeated the operation; did it again; compared the insignificant whitewashed streak with the far-reaching continent of unwhitewashed fence, and sat down on a tree-box discouraged [...] He began to think of the fun he had planned for this day, and his sorrows multiplied. Soon the free boys would come tripping along on all sorts of delicious expeditions, and they would make a world of fun of him for having to work [...]the very thought of it burnt him like fire. He got out his worldly wealth and examined it. [...] bits of toys, marbles, and trash; enough to buy an exchange of work, maybe, but not half enough to buy so much as half an hour of pure freedom[...]he returned his straitened means to his pocket, and gave up the idea of trying to buy the boys. At this dark and hopeless moment, an inspiration burst upon him! Nothing

less than a great, magnificent inspiration. He took up his brush and went tranquilly to work. Ben Rogers hove in sight presently; the very boy, of all boys, whose ridicule he had been dreading. Ben's gait was the hop, skip, and jump[...]He was eating an apple and giving a long, melodious whoop, at intervals, followed by a deep-toned ding dong dong, ding dong dong, for he was personating a steamboat. Ben ranged up alongside of him. Tom's mouth watered for the apple, but he stuck to his work.
Ben said «*Hello, old chap, you got to work*».
Tom wheeled suddenly and said «*it's you, Ben! I warn't noticing.*»
«*I'm going in a-swimming, I am. Don't you wish you could? But of course you'd druthers work, wouldn't you?*» [...]
Tom contemplated the boy a bit, and said «*What do you call work? [...]Well, maybe it is, and maybe it ain't*[1]»
«*Oh come, now, you don't mean to let on that you like it?*»
«*Like it? Well, I don't see why I oughtn't to like it. Does a boy get a chance to whitewash a fence every day?*»
Ben watching every move and getting more and more interested, more and more absorbed. Presently he said, «*Tom, let me whitewash a little.*»
«*No, no, [...] Ben. You see, Aunt Polly's awful particular about this fence[...] right here on the street, you know... but if it was the back fence I wouldn't mind and she wouldn't. Yes, she's awful particular about this fence; it's got to be done very careful; I reckon there ain't one boy in a thousand, maybe two thousand, that can do it the way it's got to be done.*» [...]

«*I'll be just as careful. Now lemme*[2]*try. Only just a little. I'd let you, if you was me, Tom.*»
[...] «*I'll give you the core of my apple.*»
«*Well, here. No, Ben, [...] I'm afeard*[3]*.*»
«*I'll give you all of it!*»
Tom gave up the brush with reluctance in his face, but alacrity in his heart. And while the late steamer *Big Missouri* worked and sweated in the sun, the retired artist sat on a barrel in the shade close by, dangled his legs, munched his apple, and planned the slaughter of more innocents.He had had a nice, good, idle time all the while, plenty of company, and the fence had three coats of whitewash on it! If he hadn't run out of whitewash he would have bankrupted every boy in the village. Tom said to himself that it was not such a hollow world, after all. He had discovered a great law of human action, without knowing it, namely, that in order to make a man or a boy covet a thing, it is only necessary to make the thing difficult to attain.

[1] ain't: isn't; [2] lemme: let me; [3] afeard: afraid.

ACTIVITIES

1 Read the text and answer the following questions.

1. What day is it?
2. How did Tom feel?
3. Who asked Tom to work?
4. What was Tom doing when his friend arrived?
5. What is Tom's friend's name?
6. What was Tom's friend eating?
7. Where was he going?
8. What did he ask Tom? Why?
9. Did Tom accept?
10. What did Ben give Tom?
11. What did Tom do while Ben was painting the fence?
12. What did Tom say to himself?

2 Colour the picture and write some simple sentences about the story.

EXAM TRAINER

READING COMPREHENSION

The Canterville Ghost

The Canterville ghost is a popular short story written by Oscar Wilde and published in 1887.

The story is set in England in the nineteenth century and is about an American family that moves into the haunted castle of Canterville.

The Otis family is made up of six people: Harim Otis, an American politician and his wife Lucretia and their four children, Washington, their eldest son, Virginia, their sixteen-year-old daughter and the naughty twins called Stars and Stripes. In the dungeons of their castle lives the ghost of Simon de Canterville, a 16th century nobleman.

He's forced to live forever until an ancient prophecy is fulfilled: "a sinner will save himself if a good young person weeps for him". But the Otis family doesn't believe in ghosts.

Every night the ghost of Sir Simon tries to frighten the family. They hear clanking chains and observe reappearing bloodstains on the floor near the sitting room fireplace where the ghost killed his wife, Lady Eleanor of Canterville. Mrs Umney, the housekeeper, tells them that the stain is evidence of the ghost and can't be removed. One day Virginia, who is the only person interested in Sir Simon's life, meets the ghost and decides to help him. Sir Simon realizes that Virginia is a sensitive girl. He decides to tell her the story of his crime and and that he hasn't slept for three hundred years. Now he says that he wants desperately to rest in peace and tells Virginia about the ancient prophecy. Sir Simon says it may come true if she weeps and prays for him and if she takes him to the Angel of Death and implores mercy upon him. Finally Virginia agrees to carry out his wishes. She disappears with the ghost and reappears at midnight telling her family that Sir Simon has passed on to the next world and has left the castle forever.

QUESTIONS

1. What kind of story is *The Canterville ghost*?
2. Where does the story take place?
3. When does the story happen?
4. Who was Sir Simon de Canterville?
5. How many children have the Otises got?
6. What do the Otis family see on the floor in the sitting room?
7. Why can't the bloodstains be removed?
8. Do the Otises fear the ghost?
9. Who is interested in Sir Simon's life?
10. For how many years has Sir Simon been unable to sleep in peace?
11. Does the Canterville ghost leave the castle forever?
12. Do you like this story? Why? Why not?

LISTENING ACTIVITY

Bob Dylan, a popular American singer, won the Nobel Prize for Literature on 13th October 2016. According to the Swedish Academy his songs are poetry. Here is one of the most popular and best songs of this great singer.

Link: http://bit.ly/1RsafZk

Listen to "Blowin' in the Wind" a song written by Bob Dylan in 1962 and complete the text with the following words:

seas	exist	washed	free	see
roads	fly	look up	ears	deaths

Blowin' in the Wind

How many ....must a man walk down
Before you call him a man?
How many .... must a white dove sail
Before she sleeps in the sand?
Yes, and how many times must the cannon balls ....
Before they're forever banned?
The answer, my friend, is blowin' in the wind
The answer is blowin' in the wind
Yes, and how many years can a mountain ....
Before it's ....to the sea?
Yes, and how many years can some people exist
Before they're allowed to be ....?
Yes, and how many times can a man turn his head
And pretend that he just doesn't ....?
The answer, my friend, is blowin' in the wind
The answer is blowin' in the wind
Yes, and how many times must a man ....
Before he can see the sky?
Yes, and how many ....must one man have
Before he can hear people cry?
Yes, and how many ....will it take 'till he knows
That too many people have died?
The answer, my friend, is blowin' in the wind
The answer is blowin' in the wind

WRITING A SUMMARY

1. Read the fact file about Oscar Wilde on page 240 and write a summary. Give the following information:

- who was Oscar Wilde;
- where and when was he born;
- where he studied;
- talk about his marriage and children;
- why he went to prison;
- what his personality was like;
- who influenced him;
- what type of artist he was;
- which are his best works;
- when and where did he die.

WRITING A LETTER

2. You're staying in London for three weeks to improve your English. Write a letter to your family. Tell them:

- something about London: monuments, weather and people;
- what you do in the morning, in the afternoon and in the evening;
- something about the school you're attending;
- what you think of this experience.

BUILDING UP A DIALOGUE

3. Write the conversation between Charles and Patty following the instructions.

Charles: chiede perché è stata negli USA un anno fa.

Patty: risponde per un viaggio con la scuola.

Charles: chiede per quanto tempo è rimasta lì.

Patty: risponde per dieci giorni.

Charles: chiede quali città ha visitato.

Patty: risponde Washington, New York e Philadelphia.

Charles: chiede se ha visto la Campana della Libertà a Philadelphia.

Patty: risponde di sì ed è stato molto interessante.

Charles: chiede che ne pensa di questa esperienza

Patty: è stata fantastica e tornerebbe di nuovo negli USA

COMPLETE A DIALOGUE

4. Complete the dialogue between a shop assistant and a customer in a clothes shop.

A 1 ______________________!

B Good morning!

A 2 ______________________?

B Yes, please!
3 ______________________?

A Yes, of course. The changing rooms are over there.

B 4 ________ a lot .

A You're welcome. 5 ________________?

B It doesn't fit very well. It's too large.
6 ______________________?

A Oh, yes. 7 ________________. How is it?

B 8 ______________________

A Oh, well.

B 9 ______________________?

A It's 10 ________________ !

TRINITY GRADE 4

CEFR level A2.2
Total exam time: 10 minutes.

Conversation
Examiner:
- Good morning!
- What's your name?
- How did you come here?
- Have you got a mobile phone?
- When did you buy it?
- What's your phone number?
- How often do you eat fast food? Where?
- What did you have for breakfast this morning?
- What food do you love having on your birthday?
- What are you going to do on your next birthday?
- What time does your family have breakfast on Sundays?
- What do you usually do with your family at the weekend?

Look at this picture!
Examiner:
- How many people can you see in this picture?
- Where are they?
- What are the girls doing?
- What do they look like?
- Can you describe the room?
- What is on the table?
- What colour is the fridge?
- Are there any flowers?
- Where is the dog?
- What is on the floor?
- Ask me if I went to a restaurant last Sunday.

You: Did you go to a restaurant last Sunday?
Examiner: OK. Thanks a lot. Bye
You: Thanks. Goodbye.

CHAPTER 10

THE ENGLISH-SPEAKING COUNTRIES

A MAP OF THE COMMONWEALTH

1. Look at the map and put the following words in the correct box.

Australia British Isles Canada India New Zealand South Africa USA

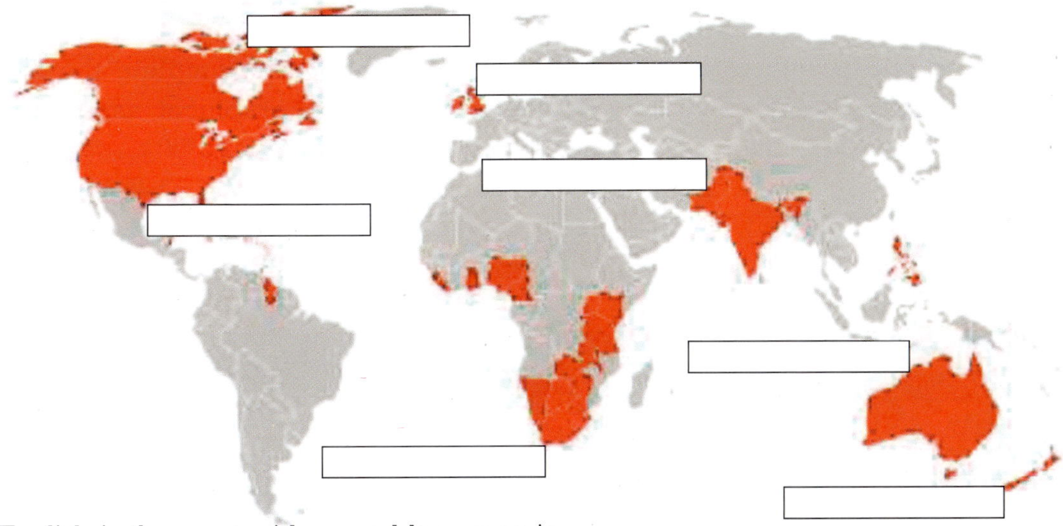

English is the most widespread language in the world even if the most spoken is Mandarin Chinese. English is spoken all over the world with different accents and is the language of the European Union, the United Nations, technology, music, business, the internet and cinema.

The diffusion of this language has a historical reason: Britain had a powerful and world-wide empire. In fact in the 19th century the British Empire covered a quarter of the world. As the British Empire came to an end the USA affirmed its influence and many immigrants moved there from all over the world in order to look for a job and a better future. English is the official language not only of Great Britain and the USA but also Australia, Canada, India, New Zealand and South Africa.

EXERCISES

2 Answer the following questions.

a. Why is English the most widespread language in the world?

b. Which is the most spoken language in the world?

3 Match each country with its continent.

a. Australia	**1.** Africa
b. Canada	**2.** America
c. India	**3.** Asia
d. New Zealand	**4.** Europe
e. South Africa	**5.** Oceania
f. The British Isles	
g. USA	

1st LESSON

WELCOME TO CANADA

COUNTRY

***Canada* in North America.**

The word Canada means *village* and is of Iroquoian origin, *kanata*. The Iroquoians were indigenous people who lived along the shores of the St. Lawrence River from about the 14th to the late 16th century. This word was also used by Jacques Cartier, a French explorer in 1535 to refer to the area where the city of Quebec is now located. Canada was both a British and a French colony. After the Seven Years' War between the British and the French it was ruled by Britain from 1713. On 1st July 1867 Canada became independent.

Look at the map and complete the fact file about the geographical aspects of Canada.

- **Fact file**
- **1. Geographical aspects:**

a. the highest mountain: ________________

b. the longest river: ______________________

c. the largest lake: ______________________, the second largest lake in the world. Canada is the land of Great Lakes.

d. there are rainforests in the south, cold bare tundra and evergreen forests in the north.

• **2. Capital city:** ______________________

• **3. Other important cities:** ______________ ______________________, ______________

• **4. Form of government:** a Federal State with a Constitutional Monarchy. The Head of State is Queen Elizabeth II but the Prime Minister governs the country. It is a country of the British Commonwealth.

5. Population: about 35 million.

6. Climate: continental in the internal area, temperate in the South-West and cold in the North.

7. Currency: Canadian dollar.

8. Languages: English and French.

DID YOU KNOW?

- Canada is the second largest country in the world.
- The Canadian Shield is an ancient rock that stretches from the Arctic to the Great Lakes.

Flag

Read and then colour in the Canadian flag

The name of the Canadian flag is the *Maple Leaf.* The maple leaf is red and its background is white in the centre and red on the two sides. Maple syrup is a symbol of Canada. It's made by boiling the tree sap that is collected by farmers in early spring.

The tree sap was collected and used by the Native Americans and by European settlers, too.

Niagara Falls

If you go to Canada you can tour the Niagara River by boat to see the spectacular Niagara Falls. They are actually three waterfalls, 52 m high, between Canada and the USA. The Canadian waterfalls are called the *Horseshoe Falls* and the American ones are the *American Falls* and *Bridal Veil Falls.*

The indigenous people in Canada

The first inhabitants of Canada came from Asia through the Bering land bridge about 40,000 years ago.

They were the ancestors of the Canadian Indians and of Inuit people that still live in wooden houses in Canada today.

At the beginning the Inuit people, called 'Eskimo' by the Indians, lived in igloos and wore polar bear fur clothes.

Igloos are houses made of ice.

Polar bear

About 15,000 polar bears live in Canada. The Inuit people call them Nanook.

ACTIVITIES

1 Answer the following questions.

1. Where is Canada?
2. When did Canada become independent?
3. What's the capital city?
4. Who is the Head of State?
5. How many languages do Canadians speak?
6. What is the name of the Canadian flag?
7. What colour is it?
8. When did the first inhabitants arrive in Canada?
9. Where did they come from?
10. What animal lives there?

ESERCIZI ON LINE www.medusaeditrice.it

2 True or false? Correct the false sentences.

a. Canada is a European word. T F
b. Jacques Cartier was a British explorer. T F
c. Canada was both a French and a British colony. T F
d. The war between the French and the British lasted seven years. T F
e. There are rainforests in northern Canada. T F
f. The climate is mostly continental. T F
g. Maple syrup is a Canadian symbol. T F
h. The Indians called the Inuit people 'Eskimo'. T F

2nd LESSON

RISORSE ON-LINE
www.medusaeditrice.it

WELCOME TO SOUTH AFRICA

Country

The official name is the Republic of South Africa

South Africa is the cradle of humankind. Here the first hominin fossils were discovered. The first inhabitants were the *Khoisan* and the first Europeans to arrive in South Africa were the Portuguese explorers *Bartholomew Diaz* who rounded the *Cape of Good Hope* in 1488 and then *Vasco da Gama* who got there in 1488 while he was sailing towards India. But the first to settle in the country were the Dutch sailors of the East India Company in 1652.

The inhabitants of the colony were called *Boers,* a Dutch word. The word Boer means "farmer".

At the end of the 17th century South Africa became a British colony. There were a lot of wars between the Boers and the English between the 19th and 20th centuries under Queen Victoria.

After World War II the country became a dominion of the British Commonwealth and the National Party began the racial segregation known as *apartheid.* Nelson Mandela, a great African statesman, fought against apartheid.

Look at the map and complete the fact file about the geographical aspects of South Africa.

Fact file

1. Geographical aspects:

a. the highest mountain: ______________

b. the longest river: ______________

c. the largest lake: ______________

d. there are rainforests, desert, savannah, mangroves and wetlands

2. Capital city: it has three capital cities P______________the administrative capital, B______________ the judicial capital and C________ T________ the legislative capital.

3. Other important cities: J______________, the largest city.

4. Form of government: a *Parliamentary Constitutional Republic*. It is a member of the *British Commonwealth*.

5. Population: about 55 million

6. Climate: warm and Mediterranean in the south-west, temperate in the interior and sub-tropical in the north-east.

7. Currency: the South African rand.

8. Languages: English as well as another ten languages.

Flag

Read and colour in the flag of South Africa

The *flag* of South Africa is black, green, red, blue, yellow and white. Black is the colour of the majority of people in the country, green is the symbol of large fields, yellow and white are the colours of gold and diamonds of which South Africa is rich, red is the symbol of the blood shed in wars and blue represents the colour of its oceans. This flag was adopted in 1994.

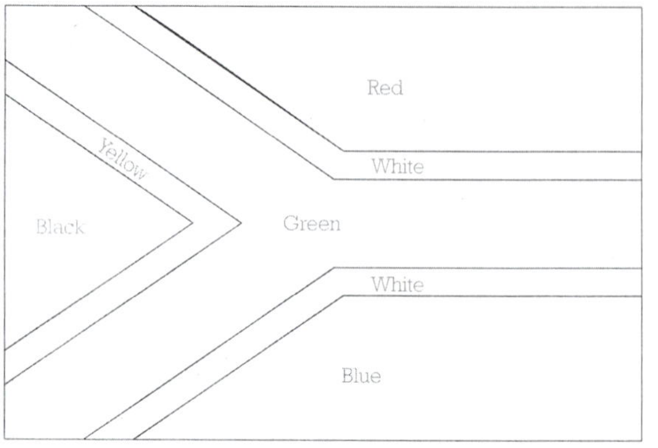

Savannah

In South Africa you can visit the largest game reserve, the *Kruger National Park* in the south-east where there are a lot of wild animals such as: elephants, giraffes, rhinos and so on.

It became the first National park in South Africa in 1926.

Write the name of the animals under each picture.

ACTIVITIES

1 True or false? Correct the false sentences.

a. South Africa is in Oceania. T F

b. Bartholomew Diaz was a British explorer. T F

c. South Africa was a British colony. T F

d. It is a Constitutional Monarchy. T F

e. There are rainforests and savannahs in South Africa. T F

f. The climate is wet. T F

g. The flag of South Africa is red, yellow, blue, white, green and black. T F

h. South Africa is part of the British Commonwealth. T F

2 Answer the following questions.

1. Who rounded the Cape of Good Hope?
2. What happened in 1652?
3. When did South Africa become a British colony?
4. What are its capitals?
5. Where is the *Kruger National Park*?
6. What is the currency of South Africa?
7. Why is South Africa the cradle of humankind?
8. Who was a great African statesman?

WELCOME TO INDIA

Country

Republic of India in South Asia

The word *India* comes from *Indus*, one of the longest rivers in Asia. One of the most ancient civilizations was born on the shores of the Indus River between 2600 and 1500 B.C..

Look at the map and complete the text with the following words:

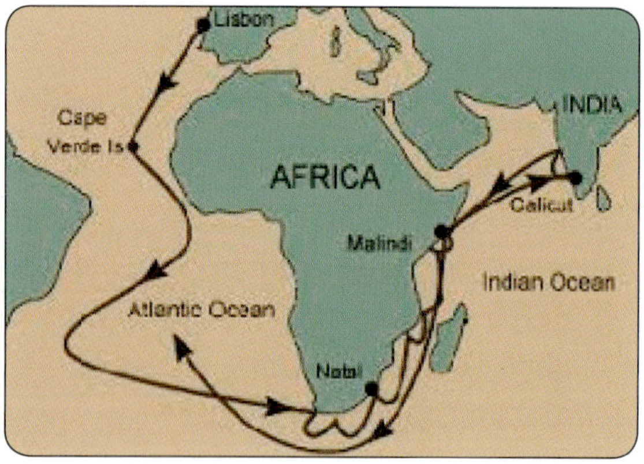

North West Africa	Calicut	Lisbon
Eastern Africa	European	Malindi
Portuguese		

Vasco da Gama was a ___________ explorer. He was the first _______ to get to India on 20th May 1498.

He left from ___________, the capital of Portugal.

The navigator sailed along the coasts of ________________ and around the Cape of Good Hope. Then he sailed along the coasts of ________________ to ___________.

Finally Vasco da Gama got to __________ in India crossing the Indian Ocean.

British rule

India was a British colony: in the 17th century it was a trading post of Britain and the British East India Trading Company dominated it in the 18th century. Under Queen Victoria India was governed by a viceroy.

In 1947 the country became independent also thanks to Gandhi who collaborated with Louis Mountbatten who was the last British viceroy.

Look at the map on page 275 and complete the fact file about the geographical aspects of India.

Fact file

1. Geographical aspects:

a. the highest mountain: ________________

b. the longest river: ____________________

c. the largest lake: _____________________

d. the Great Himalayan Range lies in the North and contain the highest mountains in the world. Here there is an area rich in tundra, a desert area in the west and a tropical area in the south-west where there are rainforests.

2. Capital city: ______________

3. Other important cities: ________________, ________________, ________________

GOOD MORNING!
HAVE A NICE DAY!

4. Form of government: a Federal Parliamentary Republic. It is a country of the British Commonwealth.

5. Population: about one billion.

6. Climate: it's a hot tropical country.

7. Currency: the rupee.

8. Languages: Hindi and English.

Flag

Read and then colour in the Indian flag.

The name of the Indian flag is *Tiranga* which means tricolour. It is deep saffron, a kind of golden yellow, white and green. A blue Ashoka Chakra, which is a wheel with 24 spokes, is in the centre. The deep saffron represents courage, the white represents peace and green is the symbol of prosperity. The wheel in the centre represents the wheel of justice and its spokes symbolize the 24 hours that compose a day and progress.
It was adopted in July 1947.

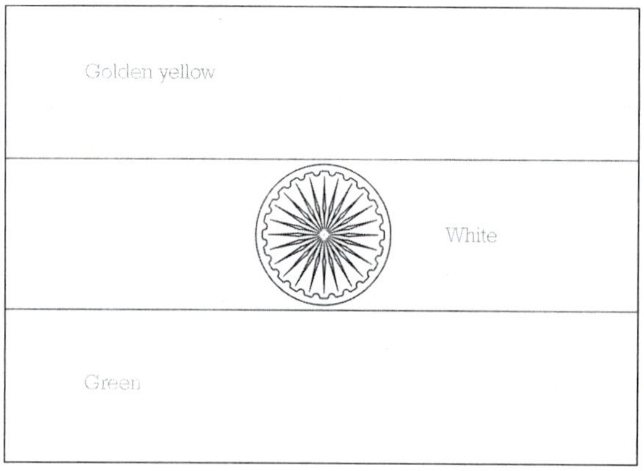

Hinduism

Hinduism is the most widespread religion in India. It dates back to pre-historic times. According to Hindus there is a universal soul or a God called Brahman. For Hindus the soul is reincarnated and can experience life in different forms, human, animal and plant.

Symbols

Read and colour the Indian symbols.

The *tiger* is the national animal of India. It's called the *Royal Bengal Tiger* and is a symbol of power and strength.

The National Flower: the *lotus*, it is the symbol of long life, honour and triumph. It's dark pink and white.
India has a national bird, too, the *peacock* and is the symbol of grace, pride and beauty.

ACTIVITY

Answer the following questions.

1. Where is India?
2. When did India become independent?
3. What's the capital city?
4. Who was the first European to arrive in India?
5. How many languages do Indians speak?
6. What is the name of the Indian flag?
7. What colour is it?
8. When was it adopted?
9. What is the most important religion?
10. Which animals are national symbols?

WELCOME TO AUSTRALIA

Country

The official name is the Commonwealth of Australia.

The word Australia is of Latin origin. It comes from *Australis* that means southern. It was discovered by a Dutch explorer in 1642, but the British captain *James Cook* was the first navigator to land on the continent in 1770. Later the British Crown sent its prisoners to the island to work on the land. They were the first white Australian settlers.

Look at Captain Cook's voyage. Follow the green route and complete the text with the following words:

Africa Atlantic Australia Britain England Indian New Zealand Pacific South America Tahiti

Captain James Cook left from .... on a ship called Endeavour. He sailed across the .... Ocean, along the coast of .... and reached....... . Then he sailed across the .... Ocean and got to the coasts of .... Finally Captain Cook landed in .... on 29th April 1770.

When he and his crew left again, they crossed the .... Ocean. Then they sailed along the coasts of western .... and went back to Great ....

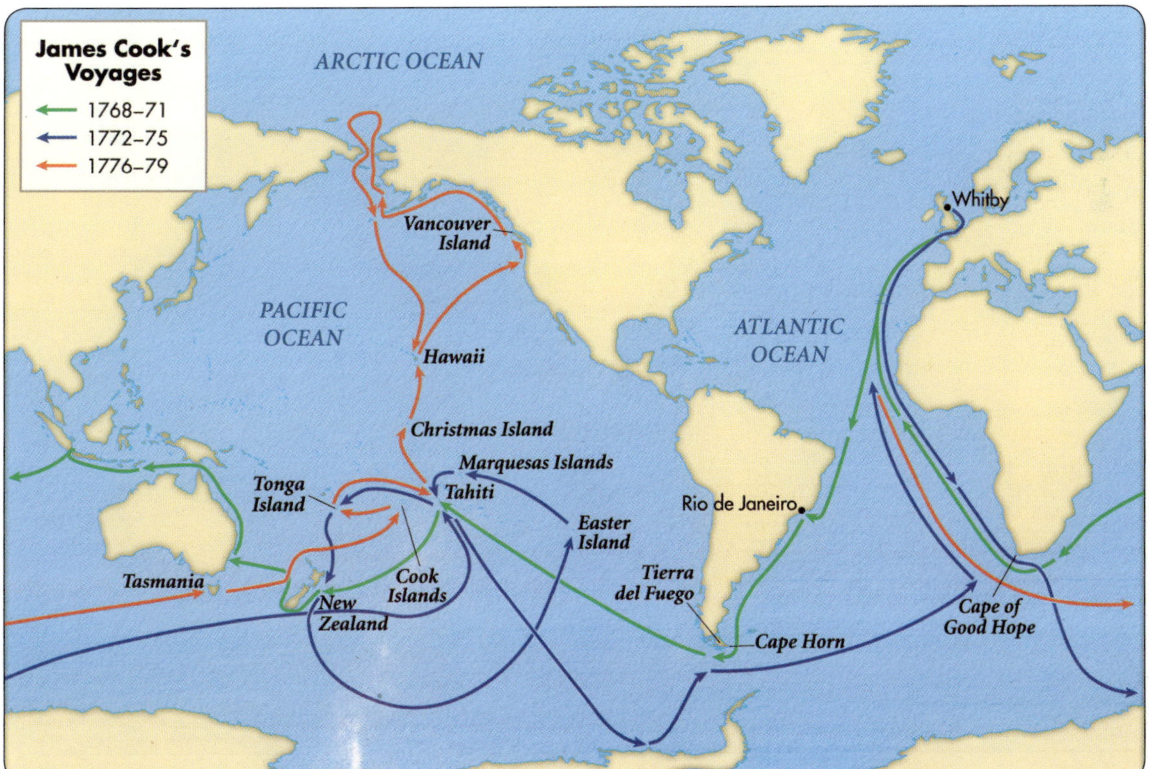

Look at the map and complete the fact file about the geographical aspects of Australia.

Fact file

1. Geographical aspects:

a. the highest mountain: ____________ in New South Wales.
Uluru is a monolith, a massive sandstone rock in central Australia, sacred to the Aborigines, the native inhabitants.

b. the longest river: ____________ in New South Wales.

c. the largest lake: ____________ in the deserts of central Australia, the largest salt lake in the world.

d. there are tropical rainforests all over the country and a desert area in the inland part.

e. the *Great Barrier Reef,* off the north-eastern coast, is the largest coral reef in the world.

2. Capital city: ____________

3. Other important cities: ____________, ____________

4. Form of government: *Constitutional Monarchy* with a *Federal Parliament.* The Head of State is Queen Elizabeth II. She is represented by a Governor-General.

5. Population: about 24 million.

6. Climate: mostly continental and temperate by the sea.

7. Currency: Australian dollar whose symbols are $ for banknotes and c for coins.

Flag

Read and colour in the Australian flag

The Australian flag has six white stars on a blue background and the Union Jack in the top left corner. There is a large white, seven-pointed star, under the Union Jack which represents the Australian states and five small, white seven pointed stars on the right that represent the Southern Cross constellation.

The Aborigines

They are the indigenous Australians that have lived in this island for probably more than 40,000 years. They moved from South East Asia.

The word *Aborigine* means "original inhabitant" and comes from Latin "ab" that means *from* and "origo" that means *beginning*.

Some peculiar animals

The kangaroo and the koala live here. The former means "*I don't know*" and the latter "*no drink*" in the language of the indigenous people.

Symbols

The *Boxing Kangaroo Flag* is a national symbol of Australia used by people during cricket, tennis and football matches and at Commonwealth and Olympic Games.

The kangaroo is dark yellow with red boxing gloves and the background is green.

The *golden wattle* is the national flower of Australia.

ACTIVITIES

1 True or false? Correct the false sentences.

a. Australia is a Latin word. T F
b. James Cook was a British explorer. T F
c. Australia was a French colony. T F
d. The Head of State is the Prime Minister. T F
e. There are rainforests in southern Australia. T F
f. The climate is temperate by the sea. T F
g. The Boxing Kangaroo Flag is a national symbol. T F
h. The Aborigines are the indigenous Australians. T F
i. Kangaroos and koalas live in Australia. T F
j. The Australian currency is the pound. T F

2 Draw and colour in the symbols of Australia in your exercise book.

WELCOME TO NEW ZEALAND

Country

The official name is New Zealand. It's in Oceania

The country was discovered by *Abel Tasman*, a Dutch explorer, in 1642. The word New Zealand comes from *Nova Zeelandia* that was used for the first time by an unknown Dutch cartographer in 1645. When the British explorer *James Cook* arrived on the island in 1769, he used the English word New Zealand.

The first inhabitants of the island came from Polynesia and arrived there between 1000 and 1300 A.D.. They were the ancestors of the *Maoris* who live in New Zealand today. It was a British colony and in 1840 the British government and the Maoris signed the *Treaty of Waitangi* thanks to which a British colony was founded in Wellington. In 1947 New Zealand became independent.

Look at the map and complete the fact file about the geographical aspects of New Zealand.

Fact file

1. **Geographical aspects:**

a. New Zealand is in the ______________ Ocean and consists of two ___________, North Island and South Island divided by the _________ strait

b. the highest mountain: ________________

c. the longest river: ________________

d. the largest lake: ________________

e. there are rainforests, geysers in the region of Rotorua, sandy beaches, active volcanoes and fjords. The landscape is spectacular

2. **Capital city:** ________________________

3. **Other important cities:** ________________

4. **Form of government**

Constitutional Monarchy with a *Parliamentary system*. The Head of State is Queen Elizabeth II. She is represented by a Governor-General. The Head of Government is the

Prime Minister. New Zealand is a member of the British Commonwealth.

5. Population: about 4 million.

6. Climate: warm.

7. Currency: the New Zealander dollar.

8. Languages: English, Maori and NZ Sign language.

Flag

Read and colour in the flag of New Zealand

The flag of New Zealand has four red stars with white borders on a blue background and the Union Jack in the top left corner. The red stars are on the right and represent the Southern Cross constellation. The Union Jack is the symbol of the British Commonwealth of which New Zealand is a member. It was adopted in 1902.

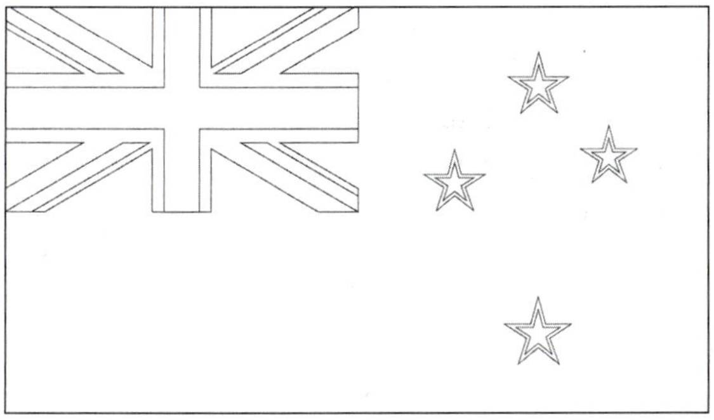

The Māoris

The *Māoris* are the indigenous inhabitants of New Zealand. They are of Polynesian origin and arrived in the country in the 2nd century A.D.. They called the new land Aotearoa which means "Land of the Long White Cloud" probably due to the presence of volcanoes. Today the majority of them live on the north island of New Zealand.

The Maoris greet each other by pressing their noses together. This is a traditional greeting called hongi.

Some peculiar animals

The kiwi, the kakapo and the tuatara live in New Zealand.

The kiwi is a bird that can not fly. It is a nocturnal animal.

The bird is a national symbol.

Kiwi is a Greek word and means "wingless".

The nickname for New Zealanders is Kiwis.

The kakapo is a parrot. It is the largest parrot in the world.

The tuatara is a reptile.
It's the oldest reptile in the world.

DID YOU KNOW?

- In New Zealand Christmas falls in the summer holidays because December is a summer month. People have picnics and go to the beach.
- Famous films such as *The Lord of the Rings*, *The Hobbit* and *The Chronicles of Narnia* were made in New Zealand.

ACTIVITIES

1 True or false? Correct the false sentences.

1. New Zealand is in Asia. T F
2. James Cook was a British merchant. T F
3. New Zealand was a Dutch colony. T F
4. The Head of State is the British Monarch. T F
5. There are rainforests in New Zealand. T F
6. The climate is temperate. T F
7. The kiwi is a national symbol. T F
8. The Maoris are the indigenous people of New Zealand. T F

2 Answer the following questions.

1. Who discovered New Zealand?
2. What happened in 1840?
3. When did New Zealand become independent?
4. Where can you find geysers?
5. What is the capital city of New Zealand?
6. Why is the Union Jack a part of the New Zealand flag?
7. How do the Maoris greet each other?
8. What animals live in New Zealand?

CHAPTER 11

NOWADAYS

EUROPE WITHOUT FRONTIERS

Background

«....We are reunited here, in this new Assembly, not as representatives of our several countries or various political parties, but as Europeans forging ahead, hand in hand, and if necessary elbow to elbow, to restore the former glories of Europe...... There is no reason for us not to succeed in achieving our goal and laying the foundation of a United Europe. A Europe whose moral design will win the respect and acknowledgement of all humanity, and whose physical strength will be such that no person will dare to disturb it as it marches peacefully towards the future.» (Winston Churchill, August 1949, at the first meeting of the Council of Europe in Strasbourg).

Winston Churchill, the British Prime Minister (1940-45 and 1951-55), proclaimed these important words during his speech at the meeting of the Council of Europe after the Second World War. He was one of the founders of the European Union and he believed that a European Union of States could ensure peace for the future of its member countries. In addition, there was the important diplomatic work of other founding fathers, among them two Italians, *Alcide De Gasperi* and *Altiero Spinelli*. The first was Prime Minister as well as Minister for Foreign Affairs from 1945 to 1953 and took part in the *Marshall Plan* whose aims were to work together, to cooperate and to overcome borders. The second spent his political life arguing that only the union of the European states could protect each one from any economic or wartime crisis. In 1984 is his ideas became the *Spinelli Plan*.

"Hard to say now.... I look forward to a United States of Europe, in which the barriers between the nations will be greatly minimised and unrestricted travel will be possible."

(*Winston Churchill*
wrote on 21st October 1942).

1st LESSON

RISORSE ON-LINE
www.medusaeditrice.it

The Current Situation

Today, people from different countries believe in a future Europe without frontiers, that is a genuine unity of nations. However, since the time that public opinion believed in ideas of cooperation up to the present day deep political and social differences have emerged. Over the past years many excellent laws have been passed by the EU which has undergone an important process of development. However lately, we seem to be going through an overwhelming negation of the values on which the European Union has been based ever since its inception. On the one hand, there are many, mostly young people, who study and work in various European nations, and learn to speak foreign languages and become part of the country where they move to. They are the perfect example of what *open frontiers* means. Then there are other nations who make different political decisions and create laws for common problems such as immigration and refuse to accept refugees or give humanitarian aid. This attitude leads to *closed frontiers*.

Brexit

On 23rd June 2016, the British people, through a referendum, expressed their will to leave the EU. It was called *Brexit*. The fact that

DID YOU KNOW?

European Parliament-Strasbourg.

- Strasbourg, Brussels and Luxembourg are the three capitals of the European Union.
- Strasbourg has important European seats like the *Council of Europe*, the *European Court of Human Rights* and the *European Parliament*.
- All EU countries share a common anthem. It is the theme of the *Ode to Joy* from the 4th movement of Beethoven's 9th Symphony. There is also *Europe Day* which is celebrated on 9th May. The European Union member states are 28.

> European Parliament- Strasbourg

Great Britain decided to keep its national currency rather than accept the Euro, has been considered a negative political choice. They believed it showed a nationalism that was in conflict with Churchill's principles concerning the EU. At the same time, Brexit is a clear expression of the will of Great Britain to close its frontiers and exclude other European nations and their problems. That is why, after the referendum, many have expressed great concern about Brexit. However many still believe in the EU and accept the presence of people from other countries in their land. Looking at the past, it is impossible to forget that the history of mankind is littered with horrible wars and the deep moral suffering that derives from them. In this respect the founders' ideas on a great union of European nations are still valid. People need to feel safe and in peace, and governments need to invest in education and innovation so that the European Union can maintain its economic competitiveness and create new jobs. This is the hope of many young people that believe in a better way of communication and cooperation.

The European Union

The EU defends important values such as *freedom, democracy* and *social justice*. But what advantages does being part of this Union of countries give to European citizens? First of all people don't have to use a passport to travel around the union, an ID card is sufficient. They can study, work and live in any EU country and can shop using the euro. They can also feel protected by laws that are based on common rules. Among the EU's aims, is the protection of the environment and this is why the EU applies strict rules that each nation must adopt.

DID YOU KNOW?

The European flag

The Council of Europe described the symbolism of the European flag as follows: "Against the blue sky of the Western world, the stars represent the peoples of Europe in a circle, a symbol of unity. Their number shall be invariably set at twelve, the symbol of completeness and perfection ... just like the twelve signs of the zodiac represent the whole universe, the twelve gold stars stand for all peoples of Europe – including those who cannot as yet take part in building up Europe in unity and peace".

(European Council, 1955).

ACTIVITY

1 Read the text and answer the following questions.

1. Who was Winston Churchill?
2. What did Churchill believe?
3. Who was Alcide De Gasperi?
4. What did the Marshall Plan consist of?
5. What did Altiero Spinelli do?
6. What happened on 23rd June 2016?
7. Do the British use the Euro?
8. What are the capitals of the EU?
9. What is the anthem of the EU?
10. How many countries are in the EU?

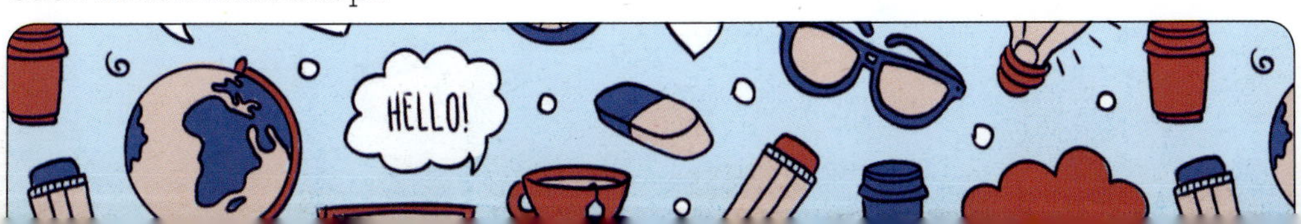

2 Write down the names of the countries that form the EU and their capitals in the grid below. Find their flags and glue them into your exercise book.

Country	Capital	Country	Capital

3 Colour only the countries of the EU.

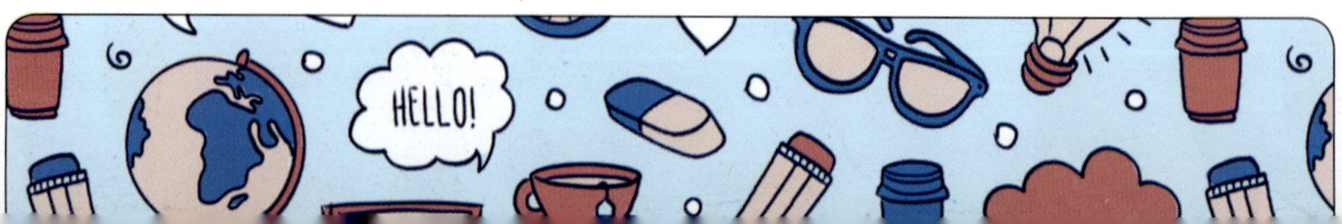

4 Colour the flag of the EU.

5 Imagine and draw a new EU flag.

Travelling and studying in Europe

Nowadays, many students travel around Europe and enjoy interesting cultural exchanges. There are *school exchanges,* which are reciprocal visits abroad by school pupils for a short period of time; *student exchanges,* which consist of students studying abroad, this experience can last up to one year. These kinds of projects take place all over Europe because there is an educational desire to teach young people how to be part of the EU, to be intimate with educational institutions and social organizations. Young teenagers from all over the world spend an enjoyable time together. Let's read about some European study programmes.

The *Erasmus Programme (European Region Action Scheme for the Mobility of University Students)* is a European Union (EU) student exchange programme established in 1987. *Erasmus+* also called *Erasmus Plus (2014/2020)* is the new programme that combines all of the EU's current schemes for education, training, youth and sport, which started in January 2014. The Erasmus Programme had previously been restricted to applicants who had completed at least one year of tertiary-level study, but it is now available to secondary school students. Students who join the Erasmus Programme

study abroad for at least 3 months or do a for a study period for at least 2 months of an academic year in another European country. The Erasmus Programme guarantees that the period spent abroad is recognised by their university when they return.

The new *Erasmus+ Programme* includes the "*Lifelong Learning Programme*" (Erasmus, Leonardo da Vinci, Comenius, Grundtvig), "*Youth in Action and five international co-operation programmes*" (Erasmus Mundus, Tempus, Alfa, Edulink and the programme for co-operation with industrialised countries).

> Students who are enjoying a cultural experience.

ACTIVITY

ESERCIZI ON LINE www.medusaeditrice.it

Say if the following sentences are True (T) or False (F) and correct the false ones.

a. School exchanges last for a long period of time. T F

b. The Erasmus Programme was established in 1987. T F

c. The Erasmus Programme is available to secondary school students. T F

d. Students who join the Erasmus Programme study at least 5 months. T F

e. Students do a study period of at least 2 months. T F

f. The period that students spend abroad is recognised by their university. T F

COMMUNICATION... HOW MANY WAYS?

Human life is almost completely controlled by computers that people have at home, in schools, in offices and even in cars! All over the world today there has been an explosion of social media and consumerism. It is something unprecedented in human history and human evolution. Different types of technological gadgets are popular possessions for both teenagers and adults. Everyone has a mobile phone or a laptop and everybody wants the latest models! Sales campaigns are everywhere and people move quickly towards new lifestyles which are common to people all over the world thanks to globalization.

New trends

Communication experts underline that today's chats and text messages are most people's favourite way of communicating. The main reason for this trend is that using social network is an easy and fast way to talk and, moreover, it eliminates every distance. However there is also a negative aspect, according to experts this kind of communication is destroying the pleasure of face to face interaction! Lots of people automatically send texts even when they are in trouble or in need of help. It would be more useful to meet friends or family in person and confront their feelings.

Nowadays many say that people don't know how to communicate with one another and that they find personal relationships very difficult. Others say that these new patterns of communication express human behavior of the modern age and the cultural changes that society is undergoing. They maintain that these changes are natural and not so wrong after all. Currently the use of mobile phones and computers is increasing amongst people of all ages but especially among teenagers.

ACTIVITY

Say if the following sentences are True (T) or False (F). Correct the false ones.

a. Today, people don't use many social networks. T F
b. Computers, smartphones and mobile phones are people's possessions. T F
c. Virtual communication is fast. T F
d. People don't send text messages unconditionally. T F
e. There isn't a new lifestyle. T F
f. Today, the use of mobile phones and computers is increasing. T F

Teenagers

To communicate with teenagers and to guide them through a rapidly changing world may not be so easy. However most parents, teachers and educators usually try to offer an understanding ear, a clear will to help them and share their everyday problems or just be part of their lifetime experiences. Firstly, it is important to consider how teenagers communicate.

According to a recent public opinion poll, teenagers' lives today are more complex than in the past. They have an incredible exposure to social media by constantly using their mobile phones, computers and online games. Researchers have shown that teenagers have a tendency to become addicted to social network sites and this is the reason why there is a decline in physical activity, the rise in sedentary lifestyles and a strong tendency of being alone and communicating in a virtual way.

Something wrong... something right!

Mobile phones are a necessity for most young people nowadays, this is how they make countless virtual friends with whom they share emotions, information and pictures, or play games. Moreover, school surveys say that students' parents have to face their children's daily high level of distraction from school because of social media.

Boys' and girls' personalities grow considerably during their teen years and it may be difficult for parents to impose rules. However there are many helpful pieces of advice which help children reach their educational goals and allows parents to guide their children during this difficult transitional phase. How teens use social media and which social media platforms they use is something that educators should be aware of. But, of course, the complexities of teens' social media usage also means that adults shouldn't generalize about what they do with technology. In fact, when used correctly, social media helps improve young people's knowledge and enriches them both culturally and educationally.

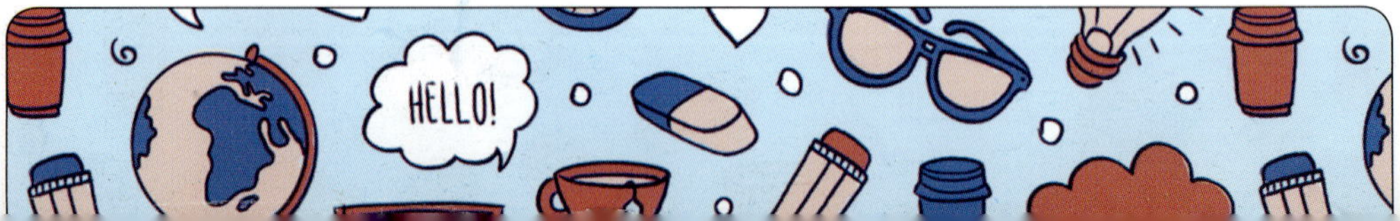

Social networking, pay attention!

Social networks have totally opened and modified the frontiers of communication. They are boxes in which are placed virtual things such as blogs, user profiles, photo galleries, text messages, music downloads and communities in which you can share interests, ideas and information. It is clear there are endless possibilities. Many teenagers believe that if they are not "present" on line, it seems nothing is happening in their lives. But everything that is on the internet is as public as speaking up in a pub, in a square or on a bus. Chatting online gives the impression of being in the company of a few friends only, but in reality you can be heard or seen by a variety of individuals. Teenagers need to pay attention and consider the negative aspects of networking. They are often fertile ground for cyber bullies who can transfer embarrassing photos and write offensive words thus creating panic disorders which can sometimes have tragic consequences.

DID YOU KNOW?

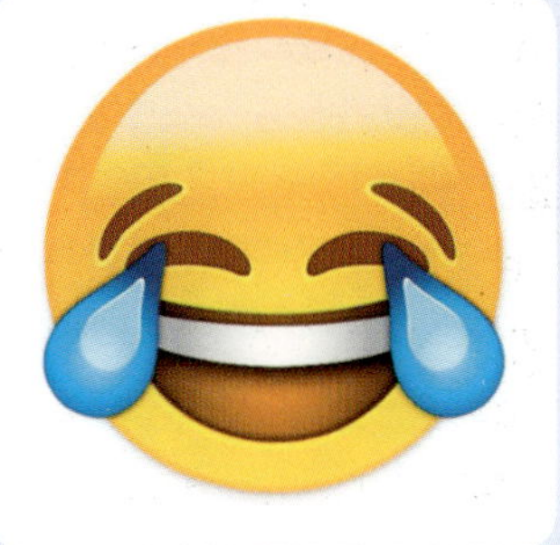

Here are some important rules to protect everybody from the negative effects of networking.

Read what the positive and negative aspects of networking are!

- communicate quickly with many people;
- post information about school and free time;
- have friends from all around the world;
- learn languages and cultures meet friends from many different countries;
- share difficulties with your friends when you feel lonely;
- use technology to enrich your learning of school subjects.
- never accept meeting up with new online friends;
- never post any personal information;
- never give your address or your mobile phone number:
- don't answer if unknown people try to contact you and talk to your parents about it;
- never post anything offensive;
- never answer embarrassing messages from cyber bullies and talk to your parents about it;
- never keep suspect messages to yourself because of your shyness;
- pay attention to SPAM;
- never spend too many hours networking and don't let it distract you from your school homework.

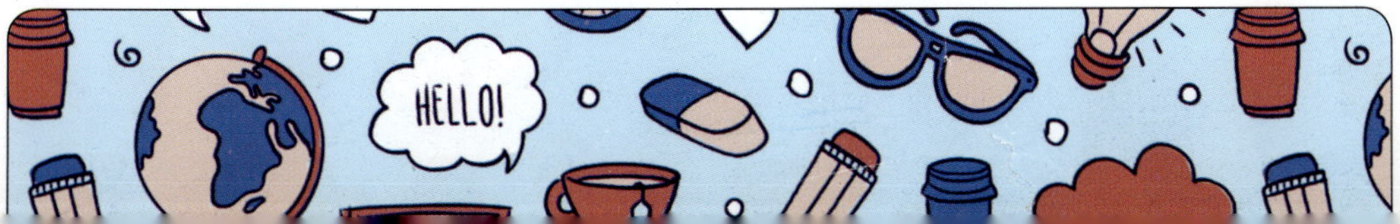

DID YOU KNOW?

- *Safer Internet Day* is organised by Insafe (SID) in February of each year to promote safer and more responsible use of online technology and mobile phones, especially among children and young people across the world.
- Reports make clear that teens are online a lot: 92% of teens say they go online daily; 24% of teens are online "almost constantly."
- Despite all the media reports that teenagers are abandoning Facebook, the site remains the most popular and most frequently used social media platform for their age group. *Snapchat* and *Instagram* are popular too.

insafe

European Commission

ACTIVITIES

1 These words are connected to the internet. What is the definition of these words?

a. Social network ....
b. Networking ....
c. Newsfeed ....
d. Blog ....
e. Link ....
f. Post ....
g. Tweet ....
h. Follower ....
i. Website ....
j. Account ....
k. Tag ....
l. Hashtag ....
m. App ....
n. Real time ....
o. Smartphone ....
p. Emoji ....

2 Find information about the "Facebook" website and write it down below.

....
....
....
....

3 Read the texts: "Teenagers" and "Social networking, pay attention!" Answer the following questions.

1. What are the favourite ways for teenagers to communicate? Why?
2. Are the teen years easy to live today?
3. Do parents and teachers help teenagers? How?
4. What do teenagers use computers or mobile phones for?
5. How have people's lives changed since social networks became popular?
6. Do teenagers spend a lot of time networking?
7. What is cyber bullying?
8. What can teenagers do if they have social media problems?

4 Write a short paragraph about social networks, mention:

- if you use them or if you don't use them what you know about them;
- which ones you use,
- when you use networking sites,
- who you talk with,
- what else you do on line;
- if you have had any problems networking.

....
....
....
....
....
....
....
....
....
....
....
....

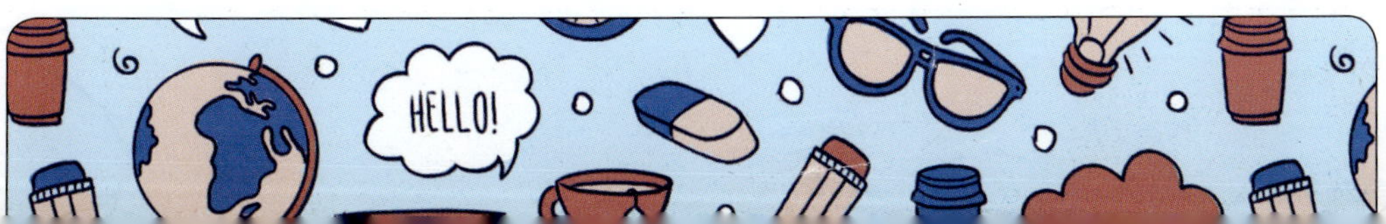

SPEAK ENGLISH?
YOU'RE WELCOME
HELLO!
SEE YOU SOON!
GOOD MORNING!
HAVE A NICE DAY!
DO YOU SPEAK ENGLISH?